NORTH WEST NATURE

EXPLORING NATURE RESERVES AND COUNTRY PARKS

with

Pauline Mellor

CONTENTS

(Map key numbers in brackets)

FRONT COVER, Main Picture: A tranquil view from Guides Farm at Grange-over-Sands, Cumbria, overlooking Morecambe Bay towards Arnside Knott, in June 1984. *Peter Cherry.* Inset: Painted Lady butterfly on bramble, *Watercolour by Pauline Mellor.*

REAR COVER: Swans at Pennington Flash, near Horrock's Hide, in November 1986. *Howard D. May.*

Mellor, Pauline
  North-west nature: exploring reserves
  and country parks. — (The Countryside
  for pleasure series.)
  1. Parks — England, Northern — Guide-books
  2. England, Northern — Description and
  travel — Guide-books. 3. Natural areas —
  England, Northern — Guide-books
  I. Title II. Series
  914.27'04858   SB484.G7

ISBN 0-947971-12-2

02665011 PO

PEREGRINE FALCONS.

2

Author's Note

MOST importantly as far as certain venues are concerned is the purchase of a tide table booklet — particularly from the safety angle — and make no mistake about this, marshes, estuaries and islands such as Hilbre can be very dangers without correct tidal information and calculations. Laver's Liverpool Tide Table booklet is available from good stationers or direct by post from The James Laver Printing Co. Ltd., Argyle Street, Liverpool L1 5BL. It contains tide predictions for the year plus the average tidal differences at a variety of places other than Liverpool. For example, at Southport always subtract 12 minutes from high-tide time. At Hilbre, always subtract 16 minutes and so on, as the list describes. Cost of this invaluable little booklet is 35p plus postage at the time of writing (1986).

My routine in December or early January each year is to underline all the highest tides (during daylight hours only) for the year ahead in the new booklet, then I transfer this information adjusted to the twelve hour clock, instead of the twenty-four hour numerals they use (plus adding the hour for British Summer Time where this applies) onto the respective dates of the new calendar. My entries for April 1986 looked like this:

23 Wed	11.12am	30.5 (ht in ft.)
24 Thu	11.54am	31.8
25 Fri	12.34pm	32.5
26 Sat	1.18pm	32.4

. . . and so on. The asterisks show at a glance the very highest tides, which indicate the possibility of a good day's 'birding' at one of the high-tide wader roosts and also allows forward planning of days out and holidays. The whole task is not as complicated as it might sound and represents maybe an hour's work one winter evening, which lasts the whole year through.

For John and Sylvia . . . with love

Copyright © Pauline Mellor & Silver Link Publishing Ltd.

First published in the United Kingdom, April 1987.

ISBN 0 947971 12 2

Maps and illustrations by Pauline Mellor.

Typeset by Keystrokes Ltd., Morecambe. Printed in the United Kingdom by Netherwood Dalton & Co. Ltd., Huddersfield, Yorkshire.

Silver Link Publishing Ltd would like to thank:
David Bellamy,
Clare Harpur, Nature Conservancy Council,
David Woodfall, Lancashire Trust for Nature Conservation.
All reserve and country park managers who have given their assistance and advice.

FOREWORD
by
DAVID BELLAMY

BRITAIN is thrice blessed. It has a diverse landscape steeped in history, both natural and people-made. It has a Government-sponsored body, the Nature Conservancy Council, together with a Royal Society for Nature Conservation and many other similar bodies which help to protect and look after this heritage of living landscapes. Britain also has, and always has had, a plethora of amateur natural historians — caring, well-informed people who are the eyes and the ears of all countryside matters to whom the official bodies can turn for expert local advice.

This book brings together these three aspects of our countryside. Pauline Mellor is the local expert who guides us on a personal tour through 28 nature reserves and parks now in the safe hands of conservation bodies, each one an integral part of the living heritage of the wonderful north-west of England.

Read it, treasure it and work with Pauline to ensure its future.

David Bellamy, Bedburn, 1986

Introduction

I well remember as a small child in the late 1950s sitting beside our 'wireless set', listening avidly to the BBC's 'Walks with Romany' series. His relaxed, informal narrative brushed lightly, yet expressively over the whole spectrum of interest associate with a countryside walk. As I recall, stoats ran across his path, birds sang and foxes were heard barking during winter courtship. Comments focussed on the day's weather and the seasons in general. Sightings of fruits and flowers led naturally into explanations of their herbal, or as the case may be, poisonous properties. Folklore, customs and even country superstitions were given an airing, as was any other chance topic or occurrence which sparked off passing comment.

Although at that time I very often did not understand all that was being said, I knew enough to realise I liked the idea of going out and about in the countryside in this aware and observant manner, and I admired and respected his wide ranging knowledge. His natural manner and ease of presentation fired my enthusiasm and I resolved, in my then childish way, to follow in his footsteps as it were, and nature-watch at every possible opportunity.

I hope my enthusiasm will become apparent in the following pages — for my book, in common with Romany's walks, is not merely a collection of favourite nature areas, but a collective description of the species, incidents, discoveries, experiences and sheer enjoyment that has increasingly coloured my leisure time to the point where it is no longer a hobby — more a way of life.

Although television now provides a splendid array of nature programmes from fantastic and far-flung places around the globe, I would like to impress on people the wealth and diversity of nature to be observed during a country walk in my own part of the world — the north west of England. Nature is freely available to anyone and everyone who watches, listens and thinks during their strolls in the countryside. The writing of this book, and my most recent visits to these places have taken place over a time-scale of 15 months beginning in the summer of 1985. Some of the memories however, are almost as old as myself . . .

A certain amount of equipment will become necessary if you find yourself getting 'hooked' on the nature-watching habit. Binoculars, either 8×30 or 7×40 strength will become a 'must' for serious bird watchers. A telescope, perhaps as a Christmas or birthday present, can be useful in certain situations, though not a necessity — unless you intend to spend all your waking hours 'sea-watching'! A camera and a small variety of lenses to record your finds can quickly develop into an obsession all by itself. Bird-song records are useful, though expensive, and your local library may have a tape and record borrowing section as well as useful field guides. Also, do not forget the library's reference section, which sometimes contains the larger and more expensive books and guides to natural history. Finally, a tiny hand lens with a magnification of ×20 and made by Swift is useful for the serious botanist and indispensable on field trips for the identification of mosses, liverworts and lichens.

Joining a local natural history society, RSPB group, or a conservation society, such as any of the county trusts for nature conservation will put you in touch with like-minded people, speed-up the learning process through lectures, field trips and guided walks and in some cases allow access to certain restricted reserves for research, photography or some specific study. In return, you help local conservation matters by being a member and lending whatever support you feel able to supply, be it active or otherwise. Importantly, membership of a local conservation society does eventually have a bearing, by sheer weight of members, on national conservation issues.

Mileages for the walks described in these pages are only mentioned where the distance, if completed, is fairly long; the rest are more or less 'go-as-you-please' and can be made as long or short as you prefer on the day — and I only walk in a direct line when shopping! I give an indication in the text as to how arduous the shorter walks are, together with a 'quick guide' paragraph at the end of each chapter, for while distances may not be long, there may be steep climbs or 'rocky' sections involved in the route. Where possible, I have given an alternative path to avoid these difficulties. Conversely, the opposite is also true for certain venues — Morecambe Bay and Hest Bank for instance, where both are quite easily covered without once leaving the car!

In order to avoid creating a complicated map-reading exercise, the maps I have produced are only loosely based on Ordnance Survey material, and detailed with sufficient data to identify the route described in the text. My advice to any reader who is planning to visit an unknown venue (particularly a hilly or coastal location), is to arm themselves beforehand with the appropriate O/S Landranger map, since unforseen circumstances at any stage of your walk may necessitate a sudden deviation from the route I have described and illustrated.

Finally, the un-named 'we' occasionally mentioned in the text refers to those persons who sometimes join me on my nature walks — my parents, their dog, or one or two close friends, all of whom are nature lovers. Some of them are also car owners and are good enough when the weather makes my motor cycling impossible, to ensure that I still get out and around our fair county. My thanks to them all.

Key references:

(P)	Car Parking
[T]	Toilet
☎	Public Telephone
🚐	Caravan Site
- - - -	Path
= = = =	Track

〰〰	Tidal Waters
🌳🌲	Woodland
〰〰	Fresh Water, Rivers
░░	Shingle
▓	Mud
⌇⌇	Wetland, Marsh
▨	Rocks
▨	Urban Areas

South Walney Nature Reserve

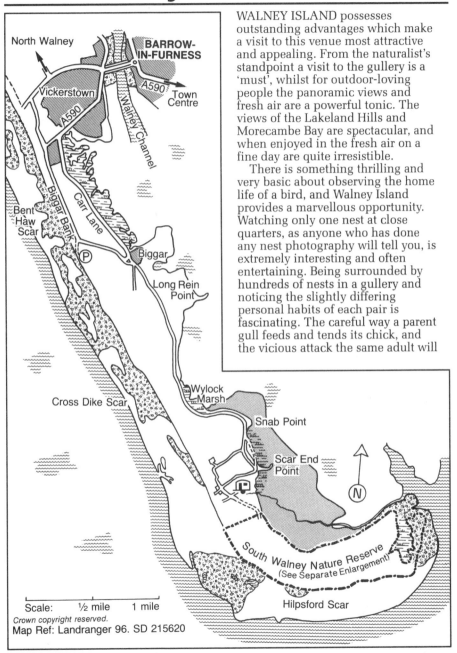

WALNEY ISLAND possesses outstanding advantages which make a visit to this venue most attractive and appealing. From the naturalist's standpoint a visit to the gullery is a 'must', whilst for outdoor-loving people the panoramic views and fresh air are a powerful tonic. The views of the Lakeland Hills and Morecambe Bay are spectacular, and when enjoyed in the fresh air on a fine day are quite irresistible.

There is something thrilling and very basic about observing the home life of a bird, and Walney Island provides a marvellous opportunity. Watching only one nest at close quarters, as anyone who has done any nest photography will tell you, is extremely interesting and often entertaining. Being surrounded by hundreds of nests in a gullery and noticing the slightly differing personal habits of each pair is fascinating. The careful way a parent gull feeds and tends its chick, and the vicious attack the same adult will

North Walney

BARROW-IN-FURNESS

Vickerstown

A590

A590

Town Centre

Walney Channel

Bent Haw Scar

Biggar Bank

Carr Lane

P

Biggar

Long Rein Point

Cross Dike Scar

Wylock Marsh

Snab Point

Scar End Point

N

South Walney Nature Reserve (See Separate Enlargement)

Hilpsford Scar

Scale: ½ mile 1 mile

Crown copyright reserved.

Map Ref: Landranger 96. SD 215620

LESSER BLACK BACKED GULLS.

make on another's chick, should it stray within reach, is a natural and integral part of life in the colony, though distasteful viewed through human eyes. However, keeping to the marked footpaths and causing as little disturbance as possible whilst passing through the gullery, will ensure you are not responsible for frightening agile chicks away from their own safe territory and into someone else's, where they will be attacked. South Walney Reserve is administered by the Cumbria Trust for Nature Conservation.

AMENITIES: There is only a small clean toilet block, with no facilities for disabled people. Unfortunately, this venue is not recommended for the handicapped: there is a rough track leading to the lighthouse which by-passes part of the reserve and a determined person only temporarily confined to a wheelchair may wish to be pushed along here, for there are good views to be had of a variety of species, although you have been warned — it is rough! Taking a packed lunch and flask of coffee is

essential; there are no shops nearby and stew or soup in a flask is a good idea for winter visits. Entry to the reserve is by permit only, obtainable at the warden's hut and costing 50p per adult and 25p for a child — please use the honesty box (which appropriately is a nesting box!) if the wardens are not around. Dogs are not allowed between April 1 and August 31. Opening times are: May — August (inclusive), 10am — 5pm. September — April (inclusive), 10am — 4pm. The reserve is closed on Mondays, with the exception of Bank Holidays.

MAP REF: SD215620. Follow the A590 from Levens Bridge, on the A6, into Barrow-in-Furness town centre. At the first traffic island turn left, and then right at the second island, after which you will cross the bridge over the docks. Turn right at the third island and then left at the fourth, which then takes you across the bridge to Walney Nature Island. At the traffic lights on the far side of the bridge turn left and follow the main road round to the right, taking

8

the fourth turning on the left into Carr Lane, sign-posted Biggar village and South Walney Nature Reserve. Continue on this narrow, minor road, past Biggar village (ignore the left turn into caravan site) keeping straight on into the road heading towards the farm. The track bends to the left and finally terminates in a small, grassy car park adjacent to the warden's house. A speed limit of 15 mph applies to the latter part of this minor track, which crosses private land, and you are requested not to cause obstruction by parking anywhere on its length.

Starting from the car park, there are three trails marked by colour-banded posts (red, green and blue), of which the red trail (when the green trail extension to the Groyne hide is tagged on) is the longest and most comprehensive — taking this path will make certain you do not miss any part of the reserve. The blue trail is shorter, and takes a slightly different route to the red, but it reaches the start of the green trail extension, enabling you to include the Groyne hide if desired. Detailed leaflets showing trails and giving reserve information are available at the warden's hut. Access to the shingle spit is not allowed two hours before (or following) high tide and is completely out of bounds from April 1 to August 31, as this spit is a very

important nesting site for terns and waders and it must not be disturbed during the breeding season.

I normally keep left after passing through the small gate, to circle the reserve (on the red trail) visiting the hides in numbered sequence from one to four. Because I usually time my visits to coincide with a high tide, this method of circling the reserve not only allows sea duck to be viewed, brought in by the water on the eastern side, but it also brings the benefits of overlooking the high-tide wader roost from number two hide. Finally, the return walk back to the car park along the western side often reveals waders 'buzzing' up and down the tide-line, looking for new feeding places on the fast uncovering shore.

The area surrounding the lighthouse is private, and avoiding wandering into this part will be appreciated by the local residents.

The noise and bustle of a gullery in full production is marvellous to observe, and later in the season when the young swell the numbers, the smell of rotting guano becomes acridly strong — and surprisingly it does give you an appetite for your sandwiches! As you walk along, the birds are for the most part unconcerned about human visitors, they have seen it all before and are quite unperturbed by binoculars and clicking, whizzing cameras. You will

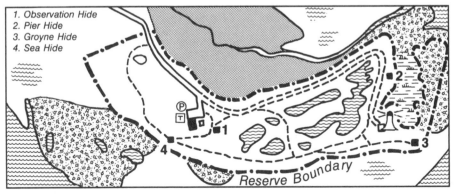

1. Observation Hide
2. Pier Hide
3. Groyne Hide
4. Sea Hide

Reserve Boundary

9

feel privileged to observe the gulls' private life so closely. The colony is rather like a group of overcrowded tenements, slightly insanitary, and with a lot of bickering and stealing of nest material from the neighbours. Yet there is also plenty of protection, for many pairs of eyes keep a look-out for danger and thus protect the whole community. Fights break out between neighbouring pairs and although they look savage, with clashing beaks and much wing-pulling, there is usually more noise and bluff than actual damage.

On the other side of the coin are the pairs of gulls quietly and tenderly preening each other adroitly with those strong and intimidating beaks, oblivious to neighbours or curious human eyes, busy building the pair-bond that will keep them together, tending their young until they are ready to fledge, the breeding season finished for another year. The tired and bedraggled parents then have a short time in the autumn in which to feed and repair damaged feathers, by much bathing and preening, before the harsh rigours of winter have to be endured.

Stroll quietly along the path and you will encounter nests in the oddest places, with perhaps the most amusing being found in the centres of discarded tyres. The gulls take readily to these human-created homes, like wrens in kettles and robins in tin-cans and of course, tyres do give distinct advantages to the young, being sheltered from strong wind, and when danger threatens they scuttle to hide in the tyre wall! I can imagine a lot of dispute occurring between the adults over these prestigious homes early in the season, before territories have been settled, although many of the Herring gulls never actually leave Walney in winter. Even in the bird world, it would seem that possession accounts for nine-tenths of the law.

The actual nest structures are composed of many objects besides grass and straw; everything is utilised it seems: string, rope, toffee papers and crisp bags, plastic bags, bits of wire, plastic, or metal bottle tops and ring-pulls from cans. Just about anything can be seen adorning a gull's nest.

Walking towards the lighthouse along the stone track, you are still only on the fringe of the gullery; as you near its centre, the nests, birds, noise and activity intensifies and some of the adults can become actively aggressive, as they anxiously attempt to drive you away from their nests by a forceful display of aggression.

If you can bear to glance up from the frenetic activity taking place all around, spare a look for the view, and what a splendid semi-circular panorama it is: from Black Combe on your left, that tall, dark conical western starting point to the lakeland hills, across Barrow's famous ship-building cranes and derricks, over Morecambe and Heysham to Ward's Stone, the highest point in the Bowland Fells, towering above sad and fated Abbeystead village and down to the hinterland marshes of Pilling and Fleetwood, before terminating on the far right at Blackpool's monument to fun and gaiety, the renowned tower, where some Walney gulls go to beg scraps from happy holiday-makers. A very clear day will show the view continuing into Wales, and occasionally the Isle of Man is visible, turning the panorama full circle — marvellous!

Ringing programmes (attaching metal and coloured plastic rings to a bird's leg — either nestling or adult) conducted by authorised and trained persons, have shown that Walney gulls travel great distances in search of food and visit many inland rubbish tips. Some Walney gulls fly as far south as Wigan several times a day to keep up with the demands of

EIDERS.

a growing family. The fact that gulls are scavengers and help to keep our countryside clean unfortunately results in a substantial number being poisoned every year, as substances which have no right to find a way onto our tips often do so with tragic results, both for the birds and ultimately our environment. A January morning a couple of years ago found 20 dead and dying gulls at Pennington Flash Country Park following their feeding at the adjacent refuse tip; a sad comment on our society which throws everything away — no matter what harm may come of it. Most of the poisoned birds were already dead, but a particularly gutsy-looking Herring Gull with, at this stage, only paralysed legs, was brought home and nursed back to fitness — much against his will I might add! More

seriously affected birds, where the paralysis had reached chest and lung level, were painlessly destroyed.

Gulls are not the only birds Walney boasts, nor is summer the only time to bird-watch: autumn especially sees a wealth of migrating species; terns and particularly waders pass by on their way south to warmer places. The reserve also plays host to nesting Oystercatcher and Little Tern, plus three other species of terns, together with Ringed Plover and the country's most southerly colony of breeding Eider Duck: the male with his pied plumage and greenish head patches can be clearly heard, crooning his 'ow-OW-ow' call amidst the screaming gulls. The female eider, in her mottled brown dress occasionally nests among the gulls and is easily missed as she sits tight, relying on her dull colours to hide her. She will allow very close approach, yet it is unfair to stretch her maternal instinct to its limit — if she does happen to leave her nest the eggs will readily be taken as an easy meal by the gulls, so please walk past and do not test her devotion by stooping to touch, or as I saw someone do recently, lift a female to photograph the nest before replacing her.

The reserve and the island in general have some unusual plants; the very poisonous Henbane (*Hyoscymus niger*) with creamy blooms interlaced with sinister purple veins, grows around the southern end of the island. Incidentally, Henbane is a member of the same group as the Tobacco Plant and our cultivated tomato! Flowering Water Crowfoot, Sea Holly, Sea Sandwort, Bugloss and the bright blue Germander Speedwell all flourish along with scattered plants of Houndstongue, its foetid scent unpleasantly reminiscent of mice . . . The tiny pea-shaped flowers of Birdsfoot (*Ornithopus perpusillus*) blossom and being so small can be easily missed. Tassel Hyacynth and Oyster Plant grow in tucked-away places while great vivid clumps of the aptly named Bloody Cranesbill adorn the roadside verges. A sand colonising moss, *Brachythecium albicans* is particularly evident on the dunes, along with odd patches of hair moss.

Winter also brings its share of interest to Walney: although I had read the literature for the reserve, which indicated that Herring Gulls are present all year, I was unprepared for the truth of this statement. A mid-January visit totally surprised me, for not only were the gulls present, but they were also mostly paired-up and vigorously defending intended nesting sites. Perhaps the biggest surprise was the fact that not a single nest remained, of the hundreds we had viewed the

previous June. Most nests had looked solid enough and I would have expected something to remain, even given the gales and bad weather which must attack this part of the coast, yet it was almost as if someone had been spring-cleaning.

During our winter visit the tide came in whilst we ate hot soup, pushing a small, yet well-mixed variety of waders extremely close to our parking spot at Biggar Bank; never have I observed Oystercatcher and Redshank so close to the car. Accompanying them were a few Sanderling, Dunlin, Ringed Plover, Turnstone and one or two Grey Plover. Cormorants and Eider Duck flew past south towards the reserve and sure enough, when we reached the southern end, our walk revealed a good number of eiders completely engrossed in nuptial activity, the drakes resplendent in immaculate breeding garb, the green head stripes looking as though they had been freshly painted. Equally smart were the pairs of Red Breasted Mergansers, some closely seen on the reserve's oyster pools, others were fishing out in the bay along with Great Crested Grebe and flotillas of Shelduck.

Walney is a satisfying, exhilarating and interesting place to visit at any time of the year.

QUICK GUIDE: Area comprises exposed duneland reserve. Described visit involves mainly level walking on stone and grass tracks. Four hides. Panoramic views. Main attraction — the gullery. BIRDS: Gulls, seaduck, waders, wildfowl, terns and migrants. FLORAL HABITAT: Duneland, fresh water pools, saltmarsh, shingle and heathland.

Humphrey Head, Allithwaite

THIS headland outcrop, resembling a beached whale, stands proud from the surrounding countryside near Grange-over-Sands in South Lakeland, pointing like some lone finger across the Bay to Morecambe town. The head rises to a height of 53 metres at the triangulation pillar, with almost vertical cliffs down the western side, sloping from its slightly domed top gently away to sea-level on the eastern shore. Its natural history and geology have strong echoes of Ingleton's twin valleys; on the one hand limestone cliffs and grassland abounds with lime-loving plants, on the other, oak woodland predominates, supporting species normally associated with a more acidic habitat. I like to feel that Humphrey Head once belonged to the Cartmel range of fells and at some time in the distant past it tried to escape south, but on reaching Morecambe Bay's notorious quick-sands, it sank down onto its haunches, forever imprisoned, and must be content with this small gesture of defiant independence . . .

AMENITIES: There are none — strictly make and take your own! Nearest toilets are in Grange-over-Sands, which also provides a choice of pubs, cafes, and shops. If picnics, walking and wildlife are your idea of enjoyment then this place is heaven. The only defined footpath is through the wood, the rest is go-as-you-please, except for a small piece of private land around the Reception Centre. Dogs are allowed. Unfortunately, this venue is unsuitable for the disabled. A word of caution: this is a dangerous place if not treated with care and respect, the cliffs are acute and crumbly — children and dogs must *not* be allowed to run or play near the

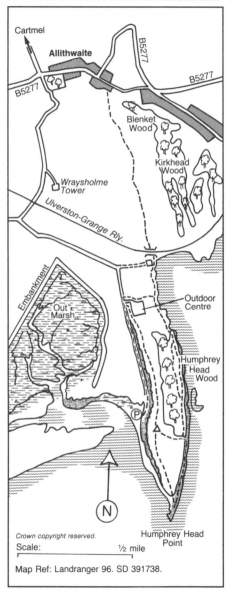

Crown copyright reserved.

Scale: ½ mile

Map Ref: Landranger 96. SD 391738.

edges, nor should rock-climbing be indulged in, unless you are properly equipped, as part of an experienced party.

13

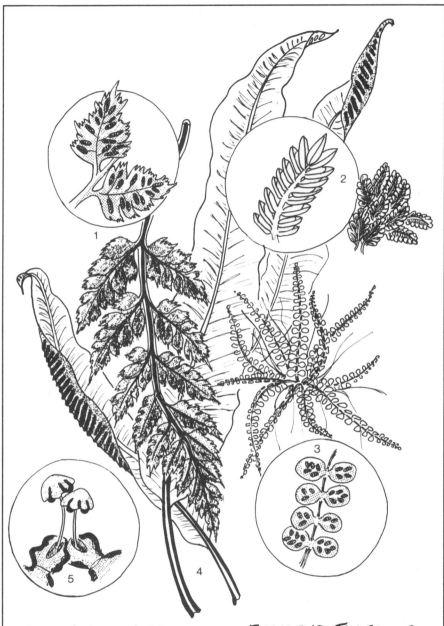

1. BLACK SPLEENWORT.   2. FISSIDENS TAXIFOLIUS.
3. MAIDENHAIR SPLEENWORT. 4. HART'S TONGUE FERN.
5. PRESSIA QUADRATUS.

MAP REF: SD 391738. Follow the B5277 from Grange towards Flookburgh, through the small village of Allithwaite, taking a left turn into narrow single track road, sign-posted Humphrey Head, just after derestriction signs at the Flookburgh end of the village. Go over railway crossing (there are no barriers) and fork left at the next junction: continue along the narrow track, passing over a cattle grid at the far end and park anywhere on the stony foreshore. The Reception Centre a little way back up the road — it is not for public use, being only concerned with private bookings for outdoor sports.

Having parked, the easiest circuit of the promontory is to walk along the firm sands to the furthest point, then climb steadily upwards to the ordnance column. Bear in mind that the tide does come in around the headland and a check on your tide tables (see Author's Note on page 3 for explanation how to use these) may be advisable before choosing this venue. There is a route straight to the top of the Head from the parking area, and wild flowers grow in profusion along the steep banking. However, I do not recommend this route; it is a dangerous path and one false step will find you back on the car park, possibly even on the roof of your car — the quick and painful way.

During a visit in late July, one of the first plants I encountered — and could hardly miss — was Great Mullein, in height just a couple of inches shorter than myself at 5ft 6in! Its large and lovely yellow petals are joined to form a flattish tube and the leaves are densely matted and felted with white hairs. In amongst the lower scrub, bright blue Harebells fluttered though they appeared less flimsy here than those found on open heaths and windy grassland. Yellow-flowering Nipplewort,

Wall Lettuce, white Enchanter's Nightshade and green Wood Sage all vie for the protection of this sheltered spot.

Two plants which had not yet flowered I recognised as Orpine, and I experienced a stab of disappointment at missing the delicate pink flowers. Hedge Woundwort, with its superb deep purple and white-flecked flowers and yellow Agrimony sprout from carpets of dark green Ivy accompanied by the positively glossy leaves and curling tendrils of Black Bryony. Close by, a patch of Black Horehound grows, unmistakeable with its evil acrid stench, as you will discover if a leaf is crushed between finger and thumb.

Tumbling from the rocks on this side of the Head is the Holy Well of St. Agnes. In the 18th and early 19th centuries the clear mineral water was bottled and sent to refresh the holiday trade at Morecambe and is claimed to have cured diseases ranging from worms to gout.

Out in the open along the cliffs, many species of plants grow at varying levels; Thrift, now past its best, being a spring flowerer. Sea Plantain, with its linear fleshy leaves, cuts down on moisture loss in this salty atmosphere, and does not easily absorb sea spray either, when the water crashes up the cliffs during rough weather. Small Scabious, with beautiful pale lilac nodding heads resembles a larger and more purple type of Thrift. A hybrid subspecies of Spiked Speedwell grows high on the ledges along here, causing excited 'twitching' among botanists due to its rarity: the wonderful shade of blue of the small neat flowering spikes does much to increase its attractiveness in my opinion. Rock Samphire grows in clusters sprouting from the cliff, the leaves exuding a spicy scented oil when crushed: an infusion of 1oz to a pint of boiling water is said to be an excellent herbal treatment for obesity — so too, I should think, is the collection of it, scrambling around these lower rocks!

At the southern end of Humphrey Head in the low grassland, the rich rosé blooms of flowering Betony is found in several spreading patches, vying with the spindly stalks and heavy heads of Crow Garlic and the creamy delicacy of Dropwort flowers. Surrounding these are chance clumps of Heather and the brilliant yellow blossoms of St. John's Wort.

A steady stroll from the point to the apex will reward you on a clear day with a splendid view across the huge expanse of Morecambe Bay; on the far left the limestone outcrop of Whitbarrow Scar at the southern end of the lakes and letting your eyes span the River Kent with its viaduct, rising at Arnside Knott, with Warton Crag a little further to the right and Newbiggin Crags and Hutton Roof sandwiched in between in the middle distance. Behind Morecambe and Lancaster rises the wild moorland terrain of the Bowland Fells.

Crickets sing endlessly on hot afternoons in July, while the dark green oak leaves, weather-beaten and dehydrated, patter in the nearly always present breeze. Very few days are becalmed on Humphrey Head, due to its exposed position, as can be seen by the severe lean of the hawthorn bushes and lack of growth on their windward side. A Green Woodpecker screams at a pair of hunting Kestrel who, by the sound of things, have a family in the wood, raucously and endlessly demanding the next meal, which may be a newly-flown woodpecker chick, unaware of the dangers awaiting outside the nest. Hence the parent birds screamed warnings that hunters are about their deadly business . . .

In the pause between the end of winter and the true start of spring, Humphrey Head presents a quite different and no less charming picture to mid-summer visits. Our last meander in early March coincided with a high tide of 30ft or so, which encouraged by a strong south-westerly wind, came right up to the car park. On our way to the summit some rather choice mosses caught my eye in the lower recesses, the attractive bright fronds resembling green fingers of *Fissidens taxifolius*. There was also a small clump of Black Spleenwort fern, tucked in between Maindenhair Spleenwort and Hart's Tongue ferns. Tiny bright green lobes with purple edges and minute green 'umbrellas' announced the presence of the liverwort *Preissia quadrata*; the dainty umbrellas are fruit capsule holders — the fruit being spores which are released into the air in a similar manner to the fungi family. Lower down still, look out for the dark tiny tree-like forms of the moss *Thamnium alopecurum* and nearby the bronzy-green colouring of that delightful moss *Ctenidium molluscum*.

From the summit on this cold March day we sat and watched as massive skeins of waders flew in from the middle of the bay, gathering on the sandy foreshore before retreating onto the higher ground of the private and inaccessible Out Marsh. Thousands of Knot, Oystercatcher, Dunlin, Redshank and some Grey and Ringed Plover streamed landwards in a sinuous procession, to alight and chatter excitedly. Several hundred Shelduck waddled onto the marsh and proceeded to display and chase neighbouring shelduck couples with much grunting and barking — a deep loud and far carrying 'ark, ark . . . ak-ak-ak'. The waders were nervous and full of energy and many will soon depart, as the spring migration north and eastwards begins in earnest as thousands of waders move en-masse to their breeding grounds inland.

As our coasts lose wintering waders, our woodlands in April and May gain summer visiting warblers which have spent the winter abroad and once again the woods will echo to the songs of Blackcap, Wood Warbler, Garden Warbler, Willow Warbler and Chiffchaff, all heralding the advent of yet another nesting season. However, this being an early March visit we had to be content with resident 'English' songsters — chortling Chaffinch, the squeeky trill of the Dunnock, the ringing tones of a male Great Tit . . . 'teechew-teechew-teechew'! . . . and the scolding 'ticking' of a Wren, while in the background Curlew called and gave their bubbling song and Lapwing swooped and displayed with 'peewit' notes over the distant farmers' fields.

The woodland floor, like the bird-life, reacts to the increasing light provided by the lengthening days; the new uncurling leaves of Arum or Lords and Ladies as it is sometimes known, burst from the earth, Bluebell shoots expand almost before the eyes, and violets, Wood Sage and Honeysuckle all show bright new growth, while Dog's Mercury and Ivy are already flowering. Even a Daisy pushes the first of its prolific blooms up to the sun.

Carpets of mosses provide brilliant verdancy in March; Hair Moss (Polytrichum commune) has dark green rosettes of leaves, while Plagiothecium undulatum is unmistakeable with long, pale minty-green fingers vying with the feathery, apple shades of Thuidium. Near to the path on a deathbed of these mosses lay the well-eaten remains of a Roe Deer, perhaps a casualty of the severe winter weather. However, its passing had provided a much-needed feast for the carnivores and scavengers and foxes had undoubtedly taken their share, with rats and crows waiting their turn at nature's table.

Some of the dead branches on the ground were hosting the black, jelly-like bags of the fungi Black Bulgar (Bulgaria inquinans) which is very similar to Witches Butter (Exidia glandulosa) though lacks the latter's tiny pimples. High in one of the aged oaks the fern common polypody had grasped a hold and makes an unusual sight in this lofty niche! As we approached the stile to leave the wood, a very live Roe Deer bounced away, drawing acid comments from a nearby Jay, followed seconds later by whistling wings and a blur of blue which marked the passage of a male Sparrowhawk — this quickly silenced all the wood's songsters. Having regained the road, we made our way back to the parking spot, to the accompaniment of singing Robin and Chaffinch — evidently the Sparrowhawk had not passed this way.

With the tide disappearing as quickly as it came, we sat in warm sunshine, magnified by the car windows, which also shielded us from the wicked wind, and enjoyed hot soup while three Pied Wagtails picked over the tide debris and waders began flying away from the marsh, back into the bay to resume their feeding.

QUICK GUIDE: Area comprises exposed limestone headland. Described visit involves level walking on firm sand, rising open grassland and gently undulating woodland paths. Summit involves a short, steep, sharp climb or a longer, more steady climb. Panoramic views. BIRDS: Waders, wildfowl, raptors and woodland species. FLORAL HABITAT: Coastal, saltmarsh and mud, limestone grassland and cliffs and mixed woodland. FAUNA: Deer and foxes.

Leighton Moss RSPB Reserve, Silverdale

SOMEHOW I doubt that this reserve requires much introduction, for anyone with even the slightest interest in nature generally and birds in particular will probably have made at least one visit. Birds being free to come and go as they please, you never know just what you are going to be privileged to see at Leighton Moss, and as with Martin Mere, this uncertainty adds greatly to the appeal of bird watching.

AMENITIES: Toilets and disabled facilities are to the rear of the main building. If you are out for the whole day it is advisable to make and take your own food, especially in winter. The Information Centre and gift shop has some very tempting items on offer; all in the best RSPB tradition. Dogs are not allowed anywhere on the reserve. Provision is made at this reserve for the disabled and wheelchairs; however some of the paths are rugged and stony in places, making chair-pushing a little difficult at times. Ramps giving access to the hides are provided and some have lower viewing slits for chairbound persons. Entry to the pay section is by permit only, available at the shop, price £2 per full day, or £1 if you come late in the day. Entry is free to RSPB members. Allen Pool and Eric Morecambe Pool hides are open to members at all times.

Opening times are as follows: Reserve open every day: (Tuesdays, 09.00-21.00 or dusk) Centre and shop January to March; Wednesday, Saturday, Sunday 10.00-17.00. April to December; Wednesday, Thursday, Saturday, Sunday and Bank Holidays, 10.00-17.00. August to Christmas also open Friday 13.00-17.00.

There are two public hides (free access) halfway along the public causeway whic bisects the reserve, and one of these has disabled facilities — lower viewing slits, movable stools and ramp access.

MAP REF: SD 480750. On leaving the car park at Warton, turn right and follow minor back road to Crag Foot and by turning right at the staggered T-junction, rejoin the other road from Warton. Continue round the sharp left-hand bend, passing over a stream outlet for the reserve, go over the busy railway crossing (with barriers) and take the next two right turns, followed by a right turn into the reserve forecourt. Parking facilities are at the front and rear of the building.

Leighton Moss is famed countrywide perhaps more than anything for its breeding Bittern and Bearded Tits, or Reedlings as they have been re-christened. Also, it is one of the few places, in Lancashire at least, to see truly wild Otters. I never have, as yet, but I live in hope! The fact that the reserve is owned by the Royal Society for the Protection of Birds, gives an immediate indication of the appeal of Leighton Moss — binoculars often become quite steamed up in the excitement of the moment! There we all sit, in hushed expectation, until someone utters the magic formula 'Bittern!' 'Osprey!' 'Hen Harrier!' or any one of half a dozen other species which will cause the hide to erupt as people and cameras burst into action — sometimes frightening the bird in question into sudden flight!

From the car park, set off to the various hides in the pay section. The paths are surrounded by 'fields' of waving Common Reed (*Phragmites australis*) interspersed with a few

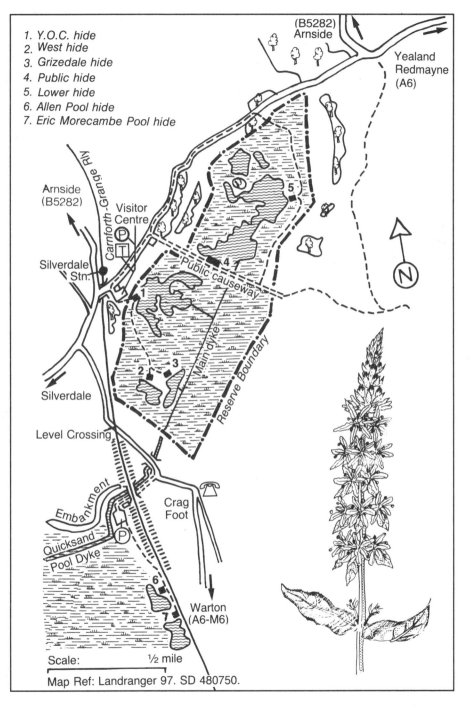

1. Y.O.C. hide
2. West hide
3. Grizedale hide
4. Public hide
5. Lower hide
6. Allen Pool hide
7. Eric Morecambe Pool hide

(B5282)
Arnside

Yealand
Redmayne
(A6)

Arnside
(B5282)

Visitor
Centre

Silverdale
Stn.

Silverdale

Level Crossing

Carnforth-Grange Rly

Public causeway

Main dyke

Reserve Boundary

N

Embankment

Quicksand
Pool Dyke

Crag
Foot

Warton
(A6-M6)

Scale: ½ mile

Map Ref: Landranger 97. SD 480750.

willows round the edges and this part, in springtime, is bathed in bird-song. Chiffchaffs warble their liquid notes, 'tsip-tsap, tsip-tsap, tsip-tsap, tsip . . .' while their near relative the Willow Warbler, also sings, his melodious cadences falling like sweet spring rain. Blackbird and Song Thrush also compete, their magnificent notes polished to perfection by constant repetition, while Reed and Sedge Warblers chatter their strident discordant songs from all quarters of the reserve, and in the not-too-distant elms a Green Woodpecker chuckles. The air is filled with bird music, but even so the king of 'song' must be the Bittern. Bitterns 'boom' from various points on the reserve and if you are fortunate enough to be ner a 'booming' Bittern, you will notice the sound is so resonant, it vibrates through the very earth, travelling up the legs to strike you deep in the chest region. Under good conditions a 'booming' Bittern can be heard up to three miles away.

One spring morning I became 'twitchily' ecstatic as an obliging Bittern flew across my vision, in flight with trailing legs, strongly reminiscent of an extra large Water Rail. Although it was flapping in a seemingly ungainly manner, it managed to cross my vision and sink without trace into the reeds before I had the chance to focus the binoculars. Ten minutes later a sharp-eyed young man spotted another bittern, standing in the reeds on the far side of the water and we all had a decent, if distant look at this one; the Bittern however, must have been experiencing that queasy feeling of 'being watched' by unseen eyes . . . for presently he sidled back into cover!

From the most westerly hide, some rather choice waders can sometimes be observed, perhaps more in autumn than at any other season: Redshank and Greenshank stride

about on red and greenish legs respectively, and both are regular visitors. Ruff and their females, reeves, however, cause much confusion; in winter plumage the male resembles his female and both sexes can at times be rather nondescript, although quite often possessing widely divergent coloured feathers. Some birds are 'brownish' in colour like Redshank, others are nearly as pale as Sanderling. Leg colour is just as variable — yellow, orange or green have been noted and even the Field Guide states that they are rather puzzling! Yet three rules of thumb do usually apply, the first being that the male is larger than the female. Both sexes appear as a plump wader with a correspondingly small head and short bill and in flight, two white oval patches are visible at the base of the tail and are sometimes joined together, but are always on the tail, not the rump. Lapwing, Common Snipe and Common Sandpiper also feed here, in among Coot, Moorhen and an occasional Heron.

Following your meander round the hides in the pay section return to the car park and leaving your vehicle where it is, turn right out of the main gates and walk up the road to the next right turn, going down the often (in winter) flooded causeway (wellingtons are sometimes necessary) to the public hides situated halfway down, on the left. A day in the Silverdale area, perhaps visiting one of the other venues I mention, can be greatly enhanced by calling in for half an hour at these freely accessible hides. The wildfowl in late winter and early spring are a great attraction for many people and fine views can be had of such species as the tiny colourful Teal, the bright and angular looking Shovelar and smart and finely elegant Pintail. You can also see the Large tri-colour Shelduck 'sailing' like galleons among the smaller dumpy brown-eyed Wigeon, together with the less common sleek Gadwall, his speckled mate showing plainly the tips of her white speculum (the coloured section of a duck's wing) which distinguishes her from the female Mallard. The cheeky red-eyed and headed Pochard provides a wonderful contrast of auburn, grey and black, and the jet and pristine white of Tufted Duck, Scaup and Goldeneye are a feast of enjoyment. Swans of all three species — the red-billed Mute and the two black and yellow-billed members, the Whooper with a longer V-shaped yellow mark and the Bewick with a more rounded

yellow patch, are all visitors to Leighton.

Those of you with permits can continue along the public causeway to the large gate, to turn left back into the reserve through a smaller gate, and wander along a wooded track, bordered by fields on the right, to the last hide, which overlooks the same water expanse as the public hides, but which also reveals an otherwise hidden area. This cannot be seen from the causeway and more wildfowl than previously suspected can often be found skulking down here; also, you are nearer to the dead trees, which is a definite bonus if

BITTERN.

GREENSHANK.

they happen to house a sleeping Osprey . . .!

On leaving the hide, keep left on the path through the woodland, exiting at a small gate onto the road with approximately a mile of comfortable tarmac walking back to your vehicle. On your return, you will pass one of the few easily reached vantage points overlooking the reserve, and from here I have watched a graceful and beautifully marked male Hen Harrier leisurely quartering the reedbeds.

Many plants on the reserve will not be seen by visitors, although quite a few do grow beside the paths, free from competition with common reed. These include common and marsh orchids, Yellow Iris or flag and the pink and elegantly tattered petals of Ragged Robin. Common Dog Violets grow in the drier positions, whereas purple Loosestrife, Marsh Marigold and Common Valerian prefer to grow in the wetter parts of the reserve. From the causeway I

have noticed the huge leaves of Water Dock in the open shallow pools and the bushes along this stretch play host to at least three species of lichen: Oak Moss (Evernia prunastri) or Mousse de Chene as the French call it, which despite the name is a lichen and not a moss. The exceedingly common lichen Hypogymnia physodes with its frilly blue-grey lobes, flourishes here along with the tangled hair-like structures of the lichen Usnea subfloridana. Reliable reports indicate that the uncommon Rigid Hornwort grows here in the ditches and ponds; also recorded are seven species of dragonfly and five types of bats. The common Pipistrelle bat can often be seen and heard hawking insects across the water in the evening anytime from May to October. Its calls, when close by, registering as a faint 'ticking', more a sensation 'felt' by your ears, than actually heard. On the other hand, tasty morsels are literally snapped-up by the bat, its mouth closing with an audible crack, followed by clearly heard crunching noises — a delightful accompaniment to your beef and pickle sandwiches!

A hide apiece overlooks the recently created Allen and Eric Morecambe Pools, and both face due west over a stretch of marsh from Ings to Jenny Brown's Point, and it shows much promise for birds and bird-watchers alike. On leaving Leighton's Information Centre, turn left out of the car park and then left again at the next two junctions, recrossing the railway and turn immediately right after the small bridge over the stream-outlet, into a rough track, running along the south bank. Park your car either at the road-end, or continue along the track, passing under the low railway bridge to fin a space in the specially provided stone-covered parking area at the rear of the farm building. Keeping the railway line on your left, walk down the edge of two fields, crossing two stiles and finally reaching the hide.

This is a morning venue for the best viewing, especially in winter when the sun is low and slanted directly into the hide after lunch-time. A visit in early September yielded a flock or 'charm' of Goldfinch feeding on thistles growing at the rear of the hide. The birds flew up at our approach, flashing red and gold, but they quickly returned when we had settled ourselves in the hide, and could be heard chattering amongst themselves all the time we were there. Out front, two Herons were striding about on long thick-kneed legs and a number of Teal were swimming in apparently aimless circles, like little toy boats. A pair of Mute Swans floated back and forth before pulling onto the bank to preen. Two Greenshank could be heard approaching across the marsh . . . 'tu-tu-tu, tu-tu-tu' . . . long

before they came into sight. One commenced feeding the second his legs touched the ground, the other obligingly settled for sleep, just as speedily, directly opposite the hide — we could see every feather.

A flock of Lapwing and a gaggle of Greylag Geese were both placidly going about their business, until a male Kestrel began hovering over the railway embankment. This caused disquiet among the geese, which started 'honking' and 'head-bobbing' in a show of restrained, yet mounting anxiety, which brought three magpies to investigate the fuss. The Kestrel made a 'stoop' into the grass and came up empty, landing in the nearby willow to consider his mis-timing, whereupon the three magpies tormented and harried him, till he could stand the cacophony no longer and he moved off somewhere quieter — leaving the magpies and geese 'crowing' victoriously. The Greenshank, uncaring and oblivious throughout, slept on . . . was this perhaps the first rest on his southbound journey? If so, how far had he travelled and for how many hours? From Scotland perhaps, or even the Arctic Circle . . ?

QUICK GUIDE: Area comprises low-lying reed-bed reserve. Described visit involves mainly level stoned-up tracks, with some tarmac walking. Six hides. Fairly sheltered. *BIRDS*: Waders, wildfowl, raptors, finches, migrants, swamp, scrub and tree warblers, plus specialities — Bittern, Bearded Tit, Marsh Harrier and Osprey. *FLORAL HABITAT*: Freshwater pools (shallow), reed-bed, scrub, deciduous woodland, wetland, heathland, salt marsh and saline pools (shallow). *FAUNA*: Otters and deer.

Eaves Wood, Silverdale

A mature and lovely woodland containing all manner of trees and shrubs, Eaves Wood is a delightful mixture of deciduous and evergreen trees, crowning a large limestone knoll. Quietly serene, the wood is owned and protected by the National Trust. Criss-crossed by many paths, it is supremely easy to become confused and lost and find yourself wandering in circles — I sometimes think that some of the trees uproot themselves periodically during the hours of darkness and change places with each other, and that this accounts for the subtle changes I feel have occurred between visits! If the thought of becoming frequently lost un-nerves you, then I strongly suggest a large scale map and compass should be used here. One pointer to direction — assuming you can find it — is the viewpoint and monument overlooking Silverdale village, the 'Pepper-Pot' as the locals call it, and you can see why! But even this, I could believe, receives a 'shake' now and again from some unseen giant hand and is then replaced in a slightly different spot . . .

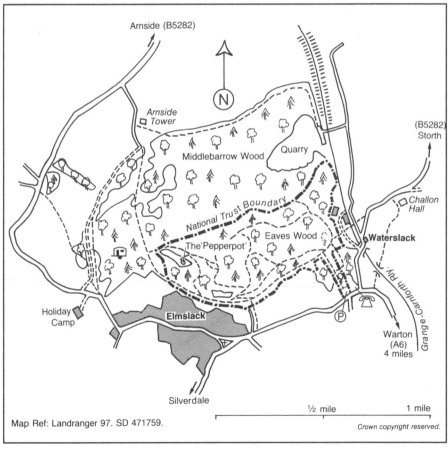

Map Ref: Landranger 97. SD 471759.

Crown copyright reserved.

AMENITIES: Toilets with level but narrow access are available in Silverdale village, on the left of the track to the left of the Community Hall; unfortunately, there are no disabled facilities. Paths are mostly good, though some near the summit cross a patch of limestone pavement where careful footwork is requied. Unfortunately, I cannot recommend this venue for the severely handicapped or wheelchairs, as gates are locked and stiles are narrow and one in particular is made from stone slabs — a tight squeeze even for walkers. Dogs are allowed. Shops can be found in the village, for food, or you can make and take your own, especially in winter.

MAP REF: SD 471759. Turn left out of the main gates at Leighton Moss Centre and then right at the T-junction opposite the golf course. Continue past Silverdale railway station and at the next junction, where the road bends right for Arnside, carry straight on and immediately past the telephone box turn right into the slightly concealed entrance to the National Trust car park.

Eaves Wood is beautiful, especially in spring, magical even. It has a quality which I am at a loss to accurately define; it is sad, although never ominous, with an impression of passive unreality, a special stillness, even when filled with spring birdsong and breezes. Even the autumn gales do not seem to be blowing as strong once you are inside. It is my all too active imagination I hear you say — yet in no other wood do I experience this unique feeling of friendly remoteness.

The flowers in spring are on view from the moment of opening the car door: waving clumps of flimsy yellow Welsh Poppy grow near the entrance, and nearby there is the brilliant blue of Wood Forget-me-Not. Exquisite swathes of wild Lily-of-the-Valley make sweetly fragrant carpets of tiny creamy bell-shaped flowers, interspersed with masses of Ramsons (Wild Garlic), wafting its redolent and, in my view, gorgeous garlic scent from heads of luminous white star-shaped blooms. Tall and healthy looking specimens of apple-green Hart's Tongue Fern protrude from many of the boulders and the tiny bluish-mauve Wood Speedwell creeps among the other plants, its pale green leaves covered underneath with splotches and bruises of purple.

Until you get your bearings, especially if alone, I suggest a circuit of the wood in a clockwise direction, keeping the perimeter wall in view on your left, until eventually you arrive back at your starting point. Wood Ants nest in several places adjacent to the path and the occupants will be encountered in hundreds of thousands, many yards from the domed nest structures which measure three to five feet across and, according to my reference book, can contain as many as 300,000 individuals. The sound of many tramping insect feet in the leaf litter has to be heard to be believed!

During one visit to Eaves I discovered a Tree Creeper collecting beakfuls of nest lining material before flying into a tight crack in the bole (trunk) of an aged Yew tree; he was unconcerned by my presence and I slowly assembled the correct lens onto the camera and waited, standing motionless for nearly half-an-hour, hoping the sun would reach the place where he was disappearing every six or seven minutes. Then, a 'huffling' noise behind, made me look, very slowly, over my shoulder and down into the bright black eyes of a Wood Mouse, who was sitting on the path a yard away returning my stare. He had a casual wash over each ear and round his muzzle, finishing with a wipe of his nose, then leaped into his hole, only to reappear moments later, a yard in front this time, perhaps to check whether I looked any less odd viewed from another angle. Very slowly, I raised the camera — and he vanished into his 'back-door', not to return — another good photographic opportunity missed. I never did photograph the Tree Creeper either, as the sun did not reach quite far enough, and a subsequent visit, when I was hoping to photograph the parent birds feeding the young, showed the nest to have been dug out, the teeth and claw marks in the soft bark strongly suggesting the culprit to be a Grey Squirrel.

On the open, heathy plateau surrounding the 'pepper-pot' Blue Moor Grass *(Selesria cerulea)* carpets the ground, its grass 'flowers' short-stalked and of a wonderful, almost bluebell shade down one side of the spike and a bright green down the other. Some of the limestone boulders poking through the moorland grass contain the pale greenish, almost waxy looking rosettes of the lichen *Squamarina crassa*. On the monument itself, the dull yellowish-brown crusts of the lichen *Caloplacca heppiana* can be found. I surprised a Roe Deer on re-entering the wood — we startled each other in fact — and he crashed away in alarm, his bobbing pale rump conspicuous, leaving me struggling to regain my composure and re-swallow my heart!

The boulders and tree stumps in the woodland are clothed with the lovely moss *Ctenidium molluscum*, with its typically inward curling leaves like huge patches of moquette, while the moss *Thidium*, with feather-like leaves, reaches its true and luxuriant proportions here in Eaves. Dog Lichen *(Peltigera canina)* can be found battling for position with *Ctendium*, its dark lobes white underneath, whilst pale 'roots' or rhizinae fasten it to the stone. When fruiting, extra lobes appear shaped like orange thumbs, growing upwards from the main structure.

Clusters of Common Dog Violets flower from every niche and cranny early in the year and the tiny attractive Spring Sedge is abundant. Warblers sing lustily, each proclaiming his little piece of Eaves Wood: Wilow Warbler, Chiffchaff, Blackcap, and Garden Warbler together the 'apple of my eye' the Wood Warbler. His far-carrying tremulous and liquid notes can be heard long before the songster is seen, and when close, is loud and resonant . . . 'piu, piu, piu . . . tip . . . tip . . . tip, tip, tip . . . schreeee . . . !' Occasionally, on the outskirts amid Rue-leaved Saxafrage and Shining Cranesbill, a Lesser Whitethroat utters snatches of his scratchy song. A male Pied Flycatcher was found singing in spring too, resplendent in black and white dress, twisting and turning, throwing his song around . . . 'see-it, see-it, see-it!' terminating in a 'whickering' trill. All these songs mingle together in a marvellous *pot-pourri* of sound, together with the more common woodland birds; Blackbird, thrushes, Robin, Wren, Dunnock, tit-mice and the short descending bubble of the male Chaffinch — this is spring in lovely Eaves Wood.

Autumn brings rich warm reds and clear golds to replace the translucent greens; one path has a large circle of old Beech trees across it, producing a halo of saffron light. The trees were planted purposefully, but how long ago and for what reason I wonder — a whim? Or was it intended to house some pagan ritual? I would not be at all surprised to encounter dancing fauns, complete with glasses of wine — or indeed Puck himself . . .

Fungi abound at this time, including russulas under the beeches

LILY of the VALLEY & WELSH POPPY.

1. HORSE CHESTNUT. 2. COMMON ALDER. 3. HOLLY. 4. SYCAMORE.
5. CRACK WILLOW. 6. SMALL-LEAVED LIME. 7. COMMON BEECH.
8. COMMON YEW. 9. SESSILE OAK. 10. SILVER BIRCH.
11. TURKEY OAK. 12. COMMON ASH. 13. SCOT'S PINE.

— increasing the feeling that elves and imps are not far away. Other fungal species noted were the Blusher, Common Earthballs, Common and Giant Puffballs and the glistening Mica Inkcap. Feeding on the latter were two large, conspicuous slugs — of a pale greyish-white colour — perhaps an evolutionary precaution to match the pale limestone? Their black faces and eye antennae, together with the bright orange 'frill' around the pale body or sole of the creature, proving a striking contrast and a much more attractive animal than the more usually seen black garden slug!

Tree species are numerous; oaks, Beech, Yew, Hazel, Ash, birches, pine, Small Leaved Lime, Guelder Rose, Spindle and Whitebeam (with unmistakeable upward facing leaves white felted below), Sycamore, larches and Spurge Laurel and there are probably one or two other species which I have missed, and may hopefully discover during my next ramble around enchanting Eaves Wood.

QUICK GUIDE: Area comprises hilly, wooded limestone outcrop. Described visit involves (at the outset) uphill main paths — minor paths are confusing and often peter out. Some stone stiles. The limestone clintfield near juncture with Middlebarrow Wood is slippery and dangerous in wet weather. Sheltered. Viewpoint and panorama. *BIRDS*: Common mixed woodland species, scrub and tree warblers, flycatchers, finches and buntings. *FLORAL HABITAT*: Mixed open woodland on limestone, heathland, limestone pavement. *FAUNA*: Deer, Wood Ants and Wood Mice.

28

Hawes Water, Silverdale

THIS is a short, pleasant descending meander through scrubby woodland, past a small lake fringed with reed, set at the heart of a triangle comprising Eaves Wood on the western side, Gait Barrows to the north and Leighton Moss in the south. The proximity of these three venues to Hawes Water results in a certain amount of 'over-spill' of some species, although it is always worth a look, for there are plants here which are not found at the neighbouring sites. Apart from the special botanical reasons for visiting Hawes, it is an agreeable walk of short duration which dovetails pleasantly with a bird-watching venue, such as Leighton Moss.

AMENITIES: There are none, strictly make and take your own. The nearest toilet facilities are at Leighton Moss, if you are visiting this reserve, otherwise public facilities are at Arnside or Silverdale. Paths are reasonable, although unfortunately not good enough for access with a wheelchair. Dogs are allowed on the public paths, but not on either of the small reserve areas through the marked gates.

STOP PRESS: As this book went to press, a change of ownership was anticipated, possibly affecting public access to this site. Prospective visitors should check in advance by contacting LTNC, The Pavilion, Cuerdon Valley Park, Bamber Bridge, Preston, Lancs, PR5 6AZ.

MAP REF: SD 475766. Turn left out of the car park at Eaves Wood and take the next left at the junction beyond the telephone box. Ignore the next two left turns, one into the garden centre, the other directly over the railway bridge, and continue for approximately a quarter of a mile until Challon Hall where a gate, (spanning the public footpath) is seen set at right-angles to the road, on the right-hand side — please do not obstruct this entrance, instead park your car on the left-hand side of the road in a small unofficial lay-by, under the trees.

Directly above your head at this parking spot a nest hole can be seen in one of the trees, facing the road — the original architect of this home, a Great Spotted Woodpecker having moved on to excavate elsewhere after just one season's use, leaving new tenants to take up possession — a pair of Starling. In contrast to the woodpeckers these birds fuss and generally make a raucous show of rearing their offspring.

On leaving your vehicle, cross the road to the gate, pass through and follow the gradually descending stone footpath; Black Bryony with its heart-shaped glossy leaves is discernible beside the path. Not quite so noticeable are its spikes of tiny yellowish-green flowers, strongly recalling the Enchanter's Nightshade, which along with Common Dog Violets, also grow beside this track. The spathes and shields of Arum, yellow Nipplewort and purple Hedge Woundwort fight for space with the prolific Dog's Mercury.

A Chiffchaff takes up residence on the hillside to the left of the path every spring and his song can still be heard, faintly carrying even on the far side of the lake! On the right, at the bottom of the slope, a tiny meadow beckons; one corner contains swarms of the buttery-golden heads of Cowslip, interspersed with the tall reddish-purple, loosely arranged flowers of Early Purple Orchid. The once-common Cowslip is sadly declining in our countryside due partly to the removal of its habitat by intensive farming and chemicals, and also, in the past, picking by the armful. However, our Bluebells seem to survive this human predation year after year without apparent diminishment, which strongly suggests that the destruction of habitat and not picking is responsible for the cowlip's disappearance. Early Purple Orchids, whilst looking lovely, have a rather noxious smell, which the flower guides liken to 'tom cats', and anyone in close contact with a healthy, virile and 'entire tom' will immediately appreciate this description!

The nearby Ground Ivy, which apart from spreading by runners looks nothing like Ivy, is a member of the *Labiatae* or two-lipped family, and most resembles a purple and smaller version of Red Dead Nettle. Its leaves, in common with many individuals of this genus, (mints, Hyssop, Wild Sage and Thyme, Balm and Marjoram) embody an aromatic scent, quite often pleasant and of culinary or medicinal value. Pliny the Elder, a scientist writing between AD 23 and AD 79, advocated growing Balm where bees were kept because they liked its delicious lemony zest and it was said to keep the swarm at home . . . Ground Ivy in contrast, is rather acrid, though not as foetid as the archangel and horehounds in the *Labiate* family.

During June, the nettles in this small meadow were found to be enveloped in Peacock Butterfly caterpillars — it was impossible to estimate the numbers of black, prickly bodies — each with a row of minute blue spots along their median lines. The increasingly uncommon Ragged Robin flutters beside bright yellow Meadow Vetchling, distinguished by its arrow-shaped leaves from its near relative Bird's Foot Trefoil. Close by, the

intensely bluish-mauve Tufted Vetch vies with Skullcap, which pushes weakly-looking stems up through the grass. As a herbal tonic for the nervous system, Skullcap is said to be unsurpassed in the treatment of complaints varying from hysteria and convulsions to the ill-effects of rabies. Patches of the pale and characteristically feathery leaves of Silverweed, crowned here and there by its sulphur yellow potentilla-type flowers is dwarfed by the pinkish umbels of Hemp Agrimony, standing tall above the rest.

Retrace your steps out of the meadow and turn right into the track once again. A little further on at the bend in the path, the attractive cream and pink flowers of Toothworth grow in April and May. It is a member of the broomrape family and like them it is also parasitic, feeding on the roots of other species, mainly favouring Hazel trees. Being a parasite, it obtains nutrients direct from its host, and needs neither leaves nor chlorophyll, which is so necessary to our 'green' plants for the manufacture of sugar, with the aid of sunlight. Its nearest ground-growing rival, the fungi family, which also lacks chlorophyll (and therefore a green colouring) mostly appear in autumn, long after the Toothwort has reproduced and died-back.

The open heath abutting the water, through the first reserve gate, holds one or two exciting surprises; the mauve-pink hue of Bird's Eye Primrose with its yellow eye in the centre of each flower, is a show-stopper! It flowers soon after its yellow cousin, the Common Primrose, has set seed. Common Primrose can be found nearby in April. The tall and deliciously scented Fragrant Orchids show themselves in June and bear no relation whatsoever to 'tom cats' unless your puss is a pampered Persian, a shampooed, talcum-

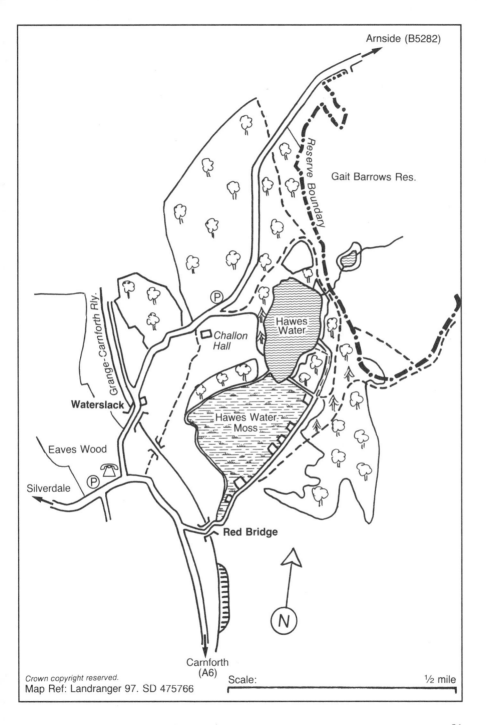

Arnside (B5282)

Gait Barrows Res.

Reserve Boundary

Hawes Water

Challon Hall

Grange-Carnforth Rly.

Waterslack

Hawes Water Moss

Eaves Wood

Silverdale

Red Bridge

N

Carnforth (A6)

Map Ref: Landranger 97. SD 475766

Scale: ½ mile

EARLY PURPLE ORCHID.

similar to those found 'next door' at Gait Barrows — and because these two reserves lie 'cheek by jowl' it is but a short flight for them between the two sites. Species seen include Brimstone, Small Pearl Bordered Fritilliary, Peacock, Red Admiral and Small Tortoiseshells accompanied by the 'skippers', 'blues', 'browns' and 'whites' which all frequent this open heath throughout the warmer months.

High overhead, Swifts and Swallows shriek and twitter, while Reed Warblers 'wheeze and chatter' discordantly from the waterside plants. One plant I had previously overlooked here is Black Bog Rush (Schoenus nigricans). In fact, it is not a rush at all, but a member of the sedge (Cyperaceae) family and is quite easily seen, once you know what to look for. The inflorescence ('flower' head) is an unusually dark blackish-brown as its latin name — nigricans — suggests.

An anxious sounding Bullfinch was giving his 'wheeb-wheeb' call in response to the Redpolls 'chuch', while the already mentioned 'clockwork' Chiffchaff was still going strong near the road! On a very early spring visit we heard what sounded suspiciously like a Hawfinch whistling and ticking loudly from the very top of a fir tree, yet keeping himself skilfully and irritatingly hidden — a very characteristic trick of the Hawfinch — before flying away, leaving behind a fleeting impression of brownish-salmon pink and a flash of white. All this lovely sound is interwoven into an ever-present backcloth of birdsong in the first half of the year.

Once back on the path, ignore the wide track leading to the waters edge and instead follow the track round past a steep rocky banking on the left, sprouting Yew trees, Hart's Tongue Fern, Wall Rue and Maidenhair Spleenwort. Cross over the stream and you enter the wooded

powdered idol, sitting smugly among his silver cups and coloured ribbons! This year I counted six spikes of Dark Red Helleborine in this area and these are likewise possessed of a heady perfume. The wind ruffled the Quaking Grass and caused quivering almost 'tinkling' notes among the Harebells, whilst the tiny white blooms of Fairy Flax and Eyebright are nearly hidden by the heathland grasses.

Not surprisingly, the butterfly species recorded for Hawes Water are part of the reserve through a second small wooden gate, where more Cowslips, Early Purple Orchids and violets flower beneath the trees. The narrow track winds round into another heathland extension adjoining the water, where a further surprise awaits in the form of Common Butterwort — first a parasite in the Toothwort, now an insectivorous plant. The flower, both in shape and colour, is strongly reminiscent of a pale coloured violet but with an unusually long spur. However, the rosette of pale green leaves, with their in-rolling margins are sticky and not in the least heart-shaped like violet leaves, and insects in various stages of decay can be seen trapped by the viscous exudate — for the plant supplements its diet with a touch of 'meat eating!'

Another member of the primrose family, Yellow Loosestrife, can be found near the waters edge and boundary fence in a very damp spot — a rather more subtle and elegant plant than its relation, the showy Dotted Loosestrife, so often seen in gardens and hiding a Wood Ants nest at the neighbouring Gait Barrows reserve.

Springtime along this path some years ago brought an unidentified fungi to my attention, growing like two pairs of mottled door knobs from a live tree bole: puzzled, I photographed them and put the slide away for twelve months. A knowledgeable acquaintance finally provided the answer — they were the young stages of the fungi Dryad's Saddle (Polyporus squamosus) and when fully grown into a mature bracket fungi, can attain a mind-boggling two feet in diameter — and perhaps would not look out of place on the back of a horse!

Although it is possible to continue past the cottages and allotments to return by a circular route, via the road, returning past the junction and telephone box near Eaves Wood. I

prefer to retrace my steps exactly the way I came, for the road is busy and dusty with frequently passing large lorries, which coming at the end of such a quiet, peaceful stroll, spoil the benefits of this tranquil little haven.

QUICK GUIDE: Area comprises low-lying reserve. Described visit involves (at the outset) slightly descending good path soon levelling out. Narrow level good tracks in reserve areas. Sheltered. BIRDS: Common mixed woodland species, swamp, scrub and tree warblers and occasional grebes. FLORAL HABITAT: Limestone cliff, base-rich meadow, heath, wetland, fresh water (deep), reed-bed, scrub and mixed woodland. FAUNA: Butterflies.

DOG VIOLET & TOOTHWORT.

Gait Barrows, Silverdale

THIS venue is a unique and extremely precious part of our heritage — as indeed all our countryside is — however, whereas certain habitats can be 'recreated', given time and effort, with a fair degree of accuracy, limestone pavement cannot, having been formed during the Ice Age. Although still being modified by water action to the present day, limestone pavement if destroyed disappears from this planet for ever. Some horrific destruction occurred at this location when quarrying took place, but thankfully it was stopped before all was lost. Even so, the scars remain as an ugly reminder of a near-tragedy. If I had to choose a favourite outing from this book of

(B5282)
Arnside

(A6)
Beetham

Car Parking for
Permit Holders
Only.

Stile

Limestone
Pavement

Carnforth
(A6)

Reserve Boundary

Alder
Carr

Meadows

Hawes
Water

Silverdale

N

Crown copyright reserved.
Map Ref: Landranger 97. SD 479776.

Scale:

½ mile

favoured sites, it would be a very difficult decision, nevertheless I have a sneaking suspicion that this gorgeous botanist's 'heaven' would finally come out at the top of the league! Perhaps I should add though, that if the thought of spending hour-upon-hour stepping from one limestone block to another in search of plants does not really fire your enthusiasm, then you would be wise to give this reserve a miss and choose one with a more varied and diverse wildlife habitat.

AMENITIES: None, strictly make and take your own. The nearest public toilets are in Arnside or Silverdale. This reserve is wardened and only accessible by permit, issued in advance and free of charge by writing to the Nature Conservancy Council, North West Regional Office, Blackwell, Bowness-on-Windermere, Cumbria LA23 3JR. Unfortunately for the handicapped, this venue is for the able-bodied only and care must be exercised even by the fit and agile; limestone pavement consists of 'clints' and 'grikes' (flat slabs of rock alternating with deep clefts and fissures) and one false step can easily result in a broken ankle or worse, and in wet weather the rock becomes slippery and extremely hazardous. Dogs are not allowed on the reserve.

MAP REF: SD 479776. From the lay-by at Hawes Water, travel a scant mile further in a northerly direction, turning right into a concealed entrance gate and track, set slightly back from the road. A board near the gate announces the reserve. If you reach the junction for Arnside (left) and Yealand Redmayne (right), you have overshot the entrance! Go through the gate and follow the stony track to a small, hidden car park on the left of the public track, marked for permit holders only.

In common with Eaves Wood, Gait Barrows is another place in which you can easily become disorientated and horribly lost. At Eaves however, certain parts can be recognised after a few attempts; here all is mystifyingly similar and in any case, the care needed to watch where you are stepping makes orientation even more difficult. A map and compass should be used, particularly if you are alone. In Eaves Wood the chances that you will meet a local walking a dog are quite high, and you can ask directions — not so here: I have chatted to people on the car park who were just leaving and also to local people strolling on the public track, but I have never yet met anyone actually on the pavement itself.

Leave the car park and turn left into the stone track and continue to the gate and stone stile — a further similarity with Eaves — and another tight fit! After the stile, turn left from the public pathway into a grassy track marked 'No Entry Without a Permit' and continue for approximately 200 yards, until the limestone blocks come into view on the right, through the thinning gaps in the trees. Find a space and step through onto the pavement. At this point let me add yet another word of caution; if it is sunny and you are depending on a favoured guide-book for flower identification, wear sunglasses — or carry a bottle of eyebright lotion! Otherwise the reflections from white rock and book pages will soon render your eyes 'gritty', sore and bloodshot, leading to an unpleasant journey home.

May, June and July are probably the best months, with the highest number of plants in flower: yellow and orange poppies head the amazing cast and can be found just inside the main entrance gate. Dotted Loosestrife grows in a large clump to the left of the information board at the car park and Wood Ants have a

35

nest near here, which the loosestrife seems to guard, as I quickly discovered whilst sitting on the ground eating sandwiches before setting off, when an army of these ants marched out of the undergrowth and started searching my belongings! I was forced into a hasty retreat to the opposite side of the car park before they carried off my rucksack and equipment!

Brilliant carpets of Biting Stonecrop are encountered before reaching the pavement, although of the specialities here I must vote the rare, Angular Solomon's Seal as the prize plant of the day, with its creamy drooping bells and bright green leaves, nestling in a 'solution cup' — a shallow circular depression in the rock. The most unexpected plant growing in another 'cup' has to be Great Reedmace (typha latifolia), more normally associated with very wet habitats. Large five-petalled Tutsan shows above the grikes, the centre of each flower containing bunches of prominent yellow stamens. Nearby, the slightly fleshy leaves and pink umbel-type flowers of Orpine protrude from a cleft, as does the acrid smelling Herb Robert and its near relative the non-scented Bloody Cranesbill, with rich magenta coloured petals. Dropwort, with celery scented leaves, delicate pink buds and creamy white flowers is rooted in many of the clefts. I was amazed to see the pitcher-shaped flowers of Common Figwort standing tall from another grike — and was irritated to find I had photographed my feet as well as the plant when the slides came back! Common figwort is more normally associated with shady, woodland habitats, yet here it is growing out in the open. Of the ferns, probably seen at their best at the tail end of the year, there is a lovely selection; Wall Rue, Hart's Tongue, Hard Shield, Rigid Buckler, Rustyback and Maidenhair Spleenwort can all be found

enjoying the warm protected grikes.

Stepping from clint to clint in criss-cross fashion, gradually make your way southwards and downwards on the various sections of pavement, surrounded by trees and shrubs, including Oak, Silver Birch, Hazel, Hornbeam, Yew, Holly, Wild Privet, Dogwood, Ash, Guelder Rose, Sycamore, Beech and Spindle. As I was about to part the leaves and step quietly onto the next section of pavement, my eyes caught movement on the opposite side of the clearing — a Fallow Deer lay relaxed, front legs tucked up, sunbathing and chewing his cud . . . I sank out of sight to swap lenses on the camera with fumbling, sweating fingers, each metallic click and grind making his ears twitch, even though he was fully 150ft away. I managed three rapid shots, each wind-on and click of the camera shutter replacing his former placid expression with growing concern. I glanced away, searching for a means to creep closer and when I looked back the pavement was empty . . . I almost felt that my imagination was working double-time again! However, the film was developed in due course and contained not blank shots, but three deer slides recalling a lovely impromptu moment with a very wild animal.

More flora flourishes in the open places off the pavements; the stony tracks, the desolate area around the building near the reserve centre and even the devastated parts which were formerly quarried, all contain an exquisite selection of flora. Species include delicate Eyebright, the magnificent and commanding spikes of Dark Red Helleborine, Scarlet Pimpernel appears like bright drops of blood spattered on the floor, while Great Mullein approaches small tree proportions. Wild Thyme creeps about in great cushions of deep green and purple, Heath Speedwell and its cousin Thyme-Leaved

FALLOW DEER.

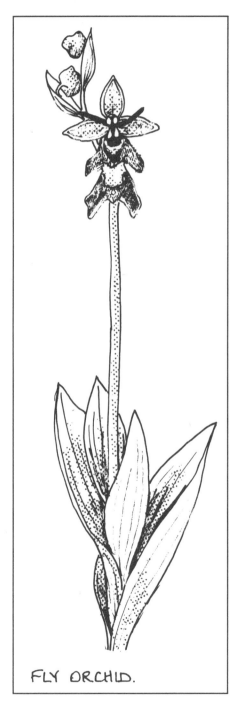

FLY ORCHID.

Speedwell are both so tiny they are hard to find among all the others, but they are there for those who look closely enough. Tall orange and yellow spikes and clusters of Ploughman's Spikenard towers above the brilliant yellow Common Rock Rose. The pale, faded four-petalled Felwort or Autumn Gentian, was found flowering in July despite its name. Yet Autumn is not all that far away and in the gentle blending of the seasons some birds have already finished breeding and casually started the return migration south and fungi will quite soon be appearing.

Fly Orchids are surprisingly difficult to see, for such an outstanding flower, but having positively identified the first one, they do become more visible — exquisite 'insects' dancing on the end of their flower stalks. True insects, as opposed to the mimics, fly in profusion on bright wings and, early in the season, Brimstone and Orange Tip butterflies flutter from one nectary to another. Later in the year Small Pearl Bordered fritilliaries and Large Skipper, both species patterned orange and black, also flit and pose. Two butterfly specialities here are the Duke of Burgundy Fritilliary, which is not really a fritilliary at all, being the only British member of a predominantly South American species. There is also the Dingy Skipper, looking appropriately dull and unimpressive even in his Sunday best! Small Tortoiseshell, Meadow Brown, Red Admiral, Common Blue, Cabbage White and the Green Veined White, Peacock, and Painted Lady butterflies all appear on this reserve during the summer months. In addition to this wide variety of butterflies, I have no doubt that there are many hundreds of moth species also, yet I cannot quite persuade myself to tarry hereabouts after dark with a jar of rum and honey bait and lantern to find out. Perhaps I should drink the rum and honey and rely on just the lantern . . . although I think it is the moths who are supposed to become 'tipsy'?

The reserve at its southernmost point terminates just beyond the Alder Carr, after a short walk across a natural meadow full of wild flowers, including Yellow Rattle, Cowslip, Ragged Robin, Bush Vetch, Germander Speedwell and marsh and spotted orchids. Literature issued with the permit gives strong warnings against entering this swampy carr, particularly alone, and I have always complied with this sound advice.

The return meander northwards through woodland on the eastern side of the reserve is equally delightful. Wrens trill and scold, Robins 'tuc, tuc', Jays scream and cackle and Blackbirds fly away 'quilping' at my approach. Blackcap Warblers sing from deep inside thickets while Woodpigeons soliloquise monotonously. Wild Strawberry suckers under the trees and Black Bryony clambers and twines itself around any available object. Twayblades and a few more Fly Orchids flutter alongside the grassy rides, while the breeze makes restless play with the delicate Wood Mellick and Quaking Grass — marvellous, incomparable Gait Barrows!

One or two intereting insects from the myriads visible along this woodland stretch caught the attention of my eye and camera; a Rosechafer beetle, the whole of his body a gleaming, irridescent metallic green hue — and even this description falls short of adequately conveying his true colour. A green and red Hawthorn Shield Bug was posing on a blade of grass, but the one insect I did not make too close an association with was a black spider of solid build, and I would hazard a guess that this was a male

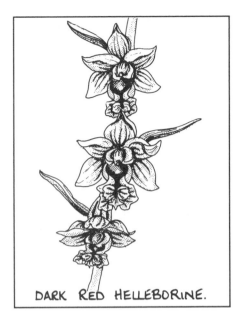

DARK RED HELLEBORINE.

Atypus affinis; he had the largest, most prominent pair of *chelicerae* (jaws) I have ever seen!

And so, after joining the path running parallel with the road on the northern boundary, return to the car park and your vehicle, providing of course, that during your absence the Wood Ants have not dismembered your treasured means of transport and carried it away piece by piece — if so, start searching to the left of the information board, near the Dotted Loosestrife . . !

QUICK GUIDE: Area comprises limestone pavement, coppiced woodland, and wet and dry meadows. No paths on clintfields making walking difficult and tiring. Surrounding woodland has broad grassy, mainly level tracks. Sheltered. *BIRDS:* Common woodland species. *FLORAL HABITAT:* Rich limestone flora, base-rich woodland, meadows and wetland. Open Water (freshwater). *FAUNA:* Deer, butterflies and Wood Ants.

The Knott, Arnside

THIS is an enchanting venue which has everything you could wish for . . a stroll by the sea with all the sights, sounds and scents this implies, plus, with luck, delicious ice-cream to fortify you before setting off on the walk and another as a reward for finishing it! Birdlife and numerous lovely plants can be found, with quiet and peaceful woods to wander around; in fact the whole of the Silverdale and Arnside area has a tracery of footpaths which are well utilised. In spite of this it is a place which seems capable of absorbing many people without becoming overcrowded, and certain spots are idyllically tranquil and overflowing with wildlife. I predict you will run out of time before running out of things to see! Arnside Knott is owned by the National Trust, and administered by a local Knott Management Committee.

The name 'knott' is of Anglo-Saxon origin meaning 'rounded hill' although it is interesting to note that in later Danish culture similar place names, Knott End and Knot Mill derive from the Old Norse 'knutr' or 'knotta' meaning a ball, or knots in a rope, and were used to indicate the speed of a ship. Technology has of course superceded these methods of measurement, yet we still speak of a ship or aircraft's speed in terms of knots — one knot equalling one nautical mile an hour.

AMENITIES: If entering Arnside from Milnthorpe direction on the B5282, the toilets are tucked out of sight on the left of the road, directly after Ye Old Fighting Cocks Inn, with disabled persons toilets sited opposite on the other side of the road. For those persons unable to make the circuit described in the following pages, there is the alternative option of driving direct to the Knott parking spot, which is a marvellous viewpoint. Detailed road directions for this appear at the end of the chapter. Of course, most of the flora and fauna described during my 'Shanks' Pony' method of reaching the summit will be missed by those using 'wheels!' However, although the walk is unsuitable for disabled people, wheelchair-bound 'birders' will be glad to hear that bird-watching can be profitable from the sea front parking spaces and I have watched Green Woodpecker, titmice, Chaffinch and the like from the car park on the Knott. In the village there are shops, cafes, pubs and hotels and the Arnside and Silverdale area boasts six caravan sites for those planning a longer stay. Holiday-makers may also be interested in the bicycle hire firm in Arnside.

MAP REF: SD 456775. Leaving the M6 at junction 35, follow slip road to junction 35a to exit onto the A6 by making a right-turn at the roundabout. Keep left at next roundabout ignoring A6070 going right for Burton-in-Kendal. Follow A6 to take fourth left-turn signposted Yealand Redmayne. Turn right at T-junction in the village. Junction sequence from here is: right, left (ignore minor R) next right, left, finally over railway crossing to bend right into Arnside village. The B5282 joins from the right. Go past the station and curve round onto the front and at bollards and severe left-hand bend, turn-right to find parking spaces facing the estuary.

On leaving your car head westward along the tiny concrete promenade, the wall on your left and the boulders below sporting at least four species of lichen, of which the bright orange *Xanthoria parietina* is perhaps the most well-known. Not so obvious are the paler and more circular crusts of *Caloplaca heppiana* and of the other two, one is black and resembles tar spots and the last one forms round pearl grey patches and is a calcicole or limestone-lover.

Common Solomon's Seal and bright blue Periwinkle were two attractive wild plants noticed blooming in a small garden near the houses, both no doubt planted by human hand — no matter, they were delightful. On the left further along is a tiny patch of nature reserve, Beachwood, tucked away behind a wall, and the steps which invite the curious to ascend and investigate are the only indication from below that it exists. Managed by the Cumbria Trust for Nature Conservation, this small gem hides quite a few treasures which keen eyes may spot and a favourite plant of mine adorns the wall — Ivy Leaved Toadflax. Ramsons, (or Wild Garlic), flowers redolently under the bushes. In the open uncut grass area to the rear of the seats, (which offer pleasing views across the estuary) grow the wild flowers Agrimony, Pignut, Dropwort, Meadow Vetchling, Wild Asparagus and Twayblade — which as its name suggests (twayblade — two blades) has two opposite leaves to each flowering stem. Three species of fern — Black and Maidenhair Spleenworts and Wall Rue protrude from various niches in the wall. According to the reserve's information, an impressive

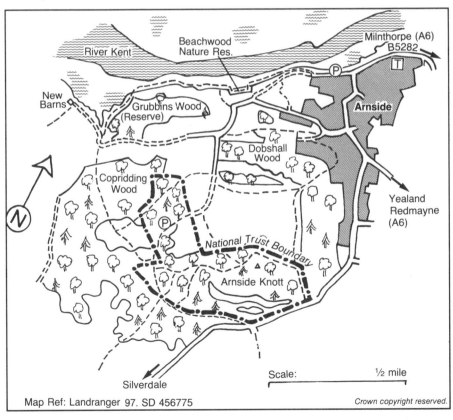

Map Ref: Landranger 97. SD 456775

Crown copyright reserved.

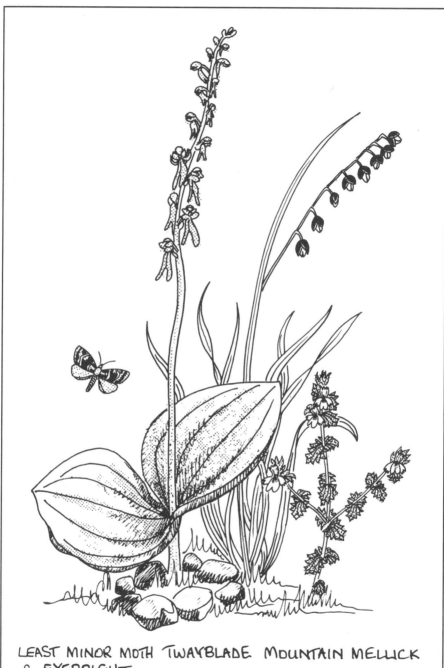

LEAST MINOR MOTH TWAYBLADE MOUNTAIN MELLICK
& EYEBRIGHT.

12 species of ferns have been recorded growing at Beachwood.

Leaving the small nature reserve and returning to the shore, plants with sea-side connections will be found: pink Thrift covers the grassy sward, jostling for space with the cabbage-type flowers of Scurvey Grass in early summer. Sea and Buckshorn Plantain burgeon from niches in the walls and rocks, and that inconspicuous plant Common Gromwell can be found with a little effort under the banking just above the tideline, along with the inevitable Black Bryony. As you wander towards the next creek, waders run and call, or fly in front to sound the alarm that humans are approaching, particularly Ringed Plover and the seemingly nerve-ridden Redshank, which often prompts a Wren to add a staccato burst of angry comment to the general hubbub. You may have noticed that nowhere is sacred from the trilling of Wren and Robin, except perhaps the very tops of mountains . . . and even here I would not be entirely surprised to encounter one or the other shouting abuse!

As you round the corner at the next creek, the grassy banking on the left is ablaze with colour — Common Rock Rose, Hoary Plantain and Salad Burnet with its unmistakeable leaves and unusual petal-less blooms like clusters of tiny green apples sprouting red female styles on top and yellow male stamens below. Keep left on the stone track until an iron gate is seen on the right in the hedgerow; pass through into the field and head towards the wooded slopes of the Knott. In an adjacent rough patch Deadly Nightshade grows — not our commonly seen Bittersweet or Woody Nightshade as it is sometimes called, but the real specimen, Atropa belladona. Once seen, this plant is not easily forgotten, with its dark bell-shaped and sinister yet beautiful flowers, giving way to fatally poisonous berries. Although Atropa belladonna in its wild state is every bit as deadly as its common name suggests, the alkaloid poison (atropine) contained throughout the plant, has many invaluable medicinal uses. Herbalists, homoeopaths and doctors make recourse to this plant in a variety of ways, fo treating certain ailments. Naturally, lesser mortals, with no medical training, would be wise to leave it strictly alone!

Enter the woodland and follow the climbing stone track; the close saplings make the woods dark, but here and there small clearings contain a varied flora competing for these light areas. Blue Moor Grass (Selesria cerulea) tries desperately to dominate the habitat, while odd fronds of Mountain Mellick Grass (Melica nutans) wave delicately above the other herbage, and occasionally Fly Orchids push their insect-imitating flowers up to the sunlight. Mounds of earth, which may be mistaken for mole hills at a first glance, are in fact the nests of Meadow Ants. In the trees, bird-song echoes and ricochets — including everything from our common garden birds, to visiting warblers and Green and Greater Spotted Woodpeckers can all be enjoyed lustily singing or calling.

Having gained the summit, sit and enjoy the spectacular view, starting in the far west at Walney Island and over the dockyards at Barrow, along the Furness coast, over Cartmel Fell and round past Humphrey Head near Grange and Holme Island, to the railway viaduct spanning the Kent estuary. And as if all this coastal scenery is not enough, the backdrop of lakeland peaks adds the final touches and takes your breath away — assuming you have any left to take following your climb to this lofty position!

There are two illustrated plaques naming the hills and peaks of this view, one near the car park and a better and more recent version near the summit — stone built and showing a three-sided panorama, naming 40 or so well known heights in the Lakes. Perhaps some of the most obvious pinnacles, looking from west to east are: Dow Crag, Coniston Old Man, Weatherlam, Helvellyn, Fairfield, Red Screes, John Bells Banner and Ill Bell.

On quiet weekdays I have watched grazing roe deer out in the open near the top and followed Gatekeeper and Small Heath butterflies unsuccessfully with my camera. Reliable sources record that Scotch Argus butterflies breed in the vicinity, although I have not had the good fortune to come across this species yet. Arnside even boasts an unusual moth found only in a handful of other localities (nearby Warton, one spot in Yorkshire and just a few in Northumberland) the Least Minor moth, a small day-flying species, which prefers limestone grasslands and sunny afternoons in June and August. It is easily overlooked because of its size — about 16 millimetres or the width of my thumb nail.

Twayblade is quite common, growing directly from the rocky screes, whilst in the grass the tiny blue flowers of Milkwort strive to exist, alongside Eyebright, Wild Thyme and Harebells. Keen eyes may spot Alder Buckthorn and I have been shown a solitary Barberry bush, normally seen planted in parks and gardens, although here on the Knott it is presumably wild, having arrived without any help from man. The leaves make one think of a weakly Holly, pale and slightly spiny, yet the berries really draw the attention in autumn being bright scarlet, oblong or lozenge-shaped and rich in vitamin C — hence very sharp tasting. Jam can be made from these berries, but it requires large amounts of sugar — enough to make it quite

expensive and very unhealthy!

The easiest way down from the Knott is to follow the rough track from the car park leading towards Arnside village and take the 'Shady Bower' footpath leading to the beach and a short stroll to the car park. Of course, the road is the easiest way up also, especially for people who cannot leave their vehicle and would like somewhere beautiful to have their lunch, in which case the car park, half way up the Knott cannot be bettered. Assuming you have been parked on the sea front in the already mentioned spaces, return to the bollards and turn right into steep Silverdale Road and then right again into Redhills Road; follow the signpost for Arnside Knott — the road meanders a little through housing. Ignore the right turn for Newbarns and go straight up the narrow lane marked Arnside Knott until the parking area is reached. The last part of this track is steep, rough and only wide enough for one car, however on reaching the car park and seeing the splendid panorama you will realise that the effort was most worthwhile.

QUICK GUIDE: Area comprises hilly, wooded limestone and open heathland outcrop. Described circuit involves (at the outset) flat though pebbly beach walking. Gentle meadow uphill. Finally, a very steep, sharp but good path to summit. (Alternative route given in text.) Good viewpoint with an excellent panorama. BIRDS: Waders, seaduck, divers, common woodland species. FLORAL HABITAT: Base-rich woodland, limestone grassland, shingle, saltmarsh, mud, meadows and open heathland. FAUNA: Deer, butterflies and moths.

Morecambe Bay and Hest Bank RSPB Reserve

MORECAMBE Bay and Hest Bank is the first in my selection of three high-tide wader roosts, the other two locations being Southport and Marshside Reserve, and Red Rocks and Hilbre Islands. However, whereas Southport requires the highest tide possible in each month, 31 or 32ft (9.5 - 9.8 mts) to obtain the full sequence of events I describe in later pages, Hest Bank is perhaps better visited during a slightly lower high-tide of 30ft (9.2 mts) or so. Even so, as with all natural phenomena there are no guarantees and for seeing our 'feathered friends' some visits will be better than others, depending on time of day, month and year, certain species being more in evidence during some months than others. Please refer to the Author's Note (see page 3) for details of tide-tables and how to use them.

AMENITIES: There is plenty of choice during the holiday season; there are pubs, cafes, shops, and fish and chip shops both in Morecambe itself and also at Hest Bank. Toilets with disabled facilities are located at several points in Morecambe, and there are toilets without disabled facilities close to the reserve at Hest Bank. Both these venues are particularly suitable for the handicapped and wheelchair-bound arriving by car: wheelchairs can be pushed with ease along the promenade. Those confined to the car will find both sites useful for birdwatching, as you need only to drive and park, wind the window down and use binoculars to see all that is on offer. Dogs are allowed, but must not be permitted to run out onto the marsh at Hest Bank before an incoming tide — it is dangerous, especially for a small dog and

yourself if you need to rescue it, should it get into difficulties.

MAP REF: SD 468665 pin-points the reserve entrance at Hest Bank. If travelling by car, head straight into Morecambe, arriving on the promenade road (the A5105) 2½-3hr before high-tide and find a parking space on the front as near as possible to the stone jetty, which is south of the pier and adjacent to the railway station.

Late August, September and October are perhaps the best months for sheer numbers of waders collecting on our estuaries, before a proportion of the birds depart for southern continents to spend the winter under kinder conditions. They make the same journey in reverse, in April or May on their way northwards to breed, some going as far north as the Arctic tundra. Birds possessed of the breeding urge in spring do not seem to linger on our coasts, but appear anxious to be off — perhaps a bit like newly-weds at the reception! Conversely, in autumn they appear almost too tired from nesting and rearing a family to contemplate the journey ahead and seem to delay as long as possible the dreadful moment of starting out.

Morecambe Bay plays host to the largest population of wintering waders in Britain. During winter 1984-85, approximately 148,000 waders were present; add to this 15,000 more birds a short distance away on the Duddon mudflats and a further 55,000 on the Ribble estuary, to give a total of more than 218,000 waders alone in the region. This total (which does not include wildfowl) comprises around two dozen wader species. Naturally, you are not going

45

to see all 150,000 birds during your visit — these counts are made by different people, simulataneously from the various points around the bay. You will see several thousand birds however, especially of species like Oystercatcher and Knot. How very fortunate we are in the North West to have these marvellous birdwatching habitats sitting on our doorstep; they are freely available and we can visit whenever mood or time allows.

Spending a while overlooking the bay from the stone jetty can be very worthwhile, particularly in rough weather, when sea-going birds, piratical skuas, diving Gannets, Goldeneye, Red-breasted Mergansers and rather uncommon species such as Scaup, which are easily confused with the commoner Tufted Duck, can be seen going about their business. They will occasionally be accompanied by the lovely streamlined Long-tailed Duck and brownish-black Cormorants: even at a distance all are identifiable by their habit of diving beneath the water surface for their chosen food.

If you have arrived by car, you have the choice of leaving it parked and strolling towards Hest Bank on the promenade, or making a series of stops and starts with your vehicle along the front as you work your way towards the reserve. In contrast to Southport, parking is allowed all along the sea front at Morecambe, until the road diverts inland, which means that bad weather need not necessarily spoil your day out at this venue, you can bird watch in comfort from your car — unless a sea fog develops!

A fine day with clear weather, as can be experienced in September and October, when the air is crisp and invigorating with a hint of frost at the outset, is most enjoyable, with lovely views of lavender tinted Lakeland hills, while the huge stretch of in-rushing water, ruffled and driven by the wind into 'white horses' is bespeckled with many gaily coloured small craft. As it fills the bay the sea is patterned and dappled with pigments straight from the artist's palette — turquoise, sepia, amethyst and finally a transparent green, implying shallows overlying pale sand.

Close to the promenade, before the water reaches the sea wall, a variety of small waders feed and in winter and early spring, if the weather has been harsh, they may become very tame and unconcerned about people walking above, so desperate is their search for food, before the water covers their feeding areas and enforces a few hours rest. In spite of their white belly, Turnstones are excellently camouflaged during winter, when their bright colouration fades and it can be quite a surprise, if they are disturbed into flight, to find that the half-dozen you thought you had counted in the muddy shingle turns out to be more than 40 birds. Grey and Ringed Plover dart and pause — visible when running, vanishing the moment they stop — plump, stocky little birds with dark, large watchful eyes. More surprising still may be a few single birds of species not often associated with a mudflat habitat — Common Sandpipers, more likely to be heard flying away, than actually seen, their musical call . . . 'twee-wee-wee' . . . repeated during their low and often zig-zag flight. Common Snipe likewise seem out of place here in the open, instead of marshy fields inland and the adage that 'old habits die hard' certainly applies to snipe, who canon into the air from the sandy mud with hoarse crackling cries, as though bursting out of thick vegetation.

Morecambe Bay is an important place for wildfowl too; during the winter months a large congregation of Pintail Duck gather and may be seen best from the promenade near

Scalestones Point. The drake's milk-chocolate coloured head with its white stripe down a slender neck is easily discernible from the rafts of mallard. Do not linger too long on the promenade or you risk missing the build-up of waders on Hest Bank's reserve. You can always return to Morecambe and find the tide still well in, when it is receding rapidly from Hest Bank, allowing the waders to quickly dissipate and re-commence feeding.

Now return to your vehicle and follow the A5105 in a north-easterly direction (the road diverts away from the sea at the entrance to the Teal Bay restaurant) and continue for a scant half mile, turning left into the reserve entrance over the Hest Bank railway crossing, just before the Pelican road crossing and telephone box on the right-hand side of the road. Go over the railway crossing, turn right and park anywhere along the grassy strip facing seaward,

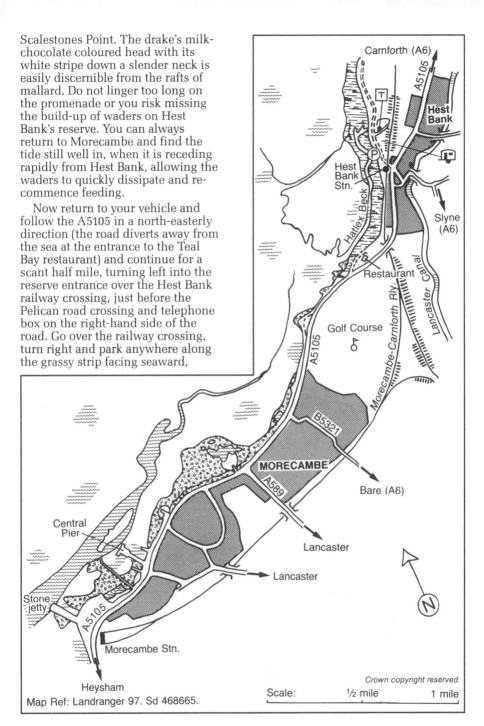

Carnforth (A6)

A5105

T

Hest Bank

P

Hest Bank Stn.

Hatlex Beck

Slyne (A6)

Restaurant

Lancaster Canal

Golf Course

Morecambe-Carnforth Rly.

A5105

B5321

MORECAMBE

A589

Bare (A6)

Central Pier

Lancaster

Lancaster

Stone jetty

A5105

N

Morecambe Stn.

Crown copyright reserved.

Scale: ½ mile 1 mile

Heysham

Map Ref: Landranger 97. Sd 468665.

47

ROOSTING OYSTERCATCHERS.

overlooking a small marsh — this is Hest Bank RSPB Reserve.

Again I repeat my earlier warning: *do not be tempted* to walk out onto the small marsh before an incoming tide; the narrow, innocent looking gutter of Hatlex Beck, just below your parking spot, rapidly turns into a deep, wide, water-filled channel of waist height on an adult, long before the tide reaches the seaward side of the marsh. Perhaps this is also the moment for me to mention that unthinking bird watchers in pursuit of ever closer views of the their quarry, are forcing the waders here to find alternative roosting spots. The strain of in-rushing water on one side and out-rushing humans on the other is putting the birds to flight at a time when they desperately need to rest and sleep. Like Red Rocks, the day may dawn when Hest Bank is no longer famous for its wader roost and the Royal Society for the Protection of Birds will have spent a lot of money on our behalf, buying this strip of land, all for nothing — so *please* remember, reserves are primarily for the wildlife and our

hobbies should come second to their welfare.

Oystercatchers run before the oncoming tide like a liquid chess board; tall and stately Curlew stride and probe on their unhurried way to the grassy marsh; Bar Tailed Godwits, in contrast to the Curlew, fly in towards the shore, some retaining remnants of brick red breeding plumage even in autumn, and a dense, yet smaller pack of Knots than the great conclaves seen on the Ribble, advance robot-like before the waves. Some of these Knot display traces of nuptial dress, shades from russet to salmon pink, while others are already attired in pallid winter grey as early as September. Sanderling, tiny in comparison with the larger species, are a pale and beautiful argent silver hue, accentuated by a sable shoulder patch on each wing; backwards and forwards they rush and bustle, following the advance and retreat of each wave like puppets on elastic.

Providing the tide is not too high, 30ft or so on a calm day, the waders will settle, strung out in a line on the last available strip of sand, although many move up onto the grassy knolls which are covered with typical saltmarsh plants. These include Common Saltmarsh Grass, Sea Aster and Glasswort and, in the drier parts, the dainty Lesser Sea Spurry and Sea Milkwort grows, each with small purple or pinkish flowers. Common Scurvey Grass and Distant Sedge, among others, are found here too.

As the tide slows and turns, the waders sleep, preen or bathe in the emptying gullies, aware that the necessity for dry land has passed for another twelve hours. During a higher tide the waders will move onto thee marsh before being compelled to fly off, usually in a northwards direction, as the water eventually reaches the tiny cliffs at your parking spot, covering the marshland completely. Minutes before this happens all is frenetic activity, then suddenly, or so it seems, the birds have gone! However, the apparently empty reserve may yet yield interest, as clusters of Shelduck rest out the tide, bobbing on the water, the duller birds among them being the current year's young. The adults are in fine garb, freshly returned from their annual moult, completed off Germany's coast. Flotillas of Wigeon sit high on the water and are brought closer to shore by the incoming tide.

Further out, small boats trawl back and forth, followed by hordes of opportunistic gulls, hoping for their equivalent of convenience foods — offal by the bucketful — the darker silhouettes chasing among them could easily be skuas, harrying and robbing the gulls of their catch.

You may also see small numbers of Crows, picking and sorting through the new debris left on the marsh by the retreating tide, together with young Pied Wagtails sporting yellow cheeks, goose-stepping Lapwing and a mixed flock of finches including Greenfinch, Goldfinch, Chaffinch and Linnet — which with bright fluttering wings have on more than one occasion attracted the attention of Peregrine and Sparrowhawk. This causes great excitement among birds and bird watchers — though in the case of the birds the excitement is brought on by sheer terror . . . put it all together and you have the ingredients for several happy hours of birdwatching. If you are a glutton for punishment, or have chosen a morning high-tide for this venue and are now wondering what to do next — why not spend the afternoon at Leighton Moss?!

However, if it is evening time, with the promise of a glorious sunset, and ancient history draws you like a magnet, why not round off your day by sitting on the benches, under the trees outside peaceful St. Patrick's Chapel at the neighbouring and ancient village of Heysham, listening to the strong notes of Wren and Robin and distant Curlew. The interior of the chapel is skilfully lit by hidden spotlamps illuminating the Viking Hogsback gravestone and in the cool silence of the chapel, with the last of the evening light glowing through the beautiful stained glass windows, those ancient times can appear to draw suddenly very close . . .

QUICK GUIDE: Area comprises sea-front promenade and marshland reserve. Described visit involves at worst flat tarmac walking and at best you need not step outside your vehicle! Can be bitterly exposed if you do choose to walk. Excellent bad weather venue. Superb panorama. BIRDS: Waders, wildfowl, seaduck, divers, migrants, raptors. FLORAL HABITAT: Coastal, shingle, mud, saltmarsh and hawthorn scrubland. FAUNA: Rich in seafood — shellfish and mudflat creatures.

The Lune Estuary Path

IN contrast to the three high-tide wader roost venues I describe (Morecambe Bay and Hest Bank, Southport and Marshside, Red Rocks and Hilbre Islands) this walk along part of the Lune Estuary Path is better undertaken at low-tide if birdwatching is your chief interest. Perhaps it should also be kept for when you really feel like 'stretching the legs' for it measures nine miles altogether. It may well be worthwhile considering walking in one direction only (4½ miles) and, boarding a bus for the return journey.

AMENITIES: Toilets, including disabled facilities, are sited opposite the parking area at Glasson, and at the bus station in Lancaster. A cafe, plus a hamburger and chips van, are found at Glasson. Pubs, cafes, fish and chips and other fast foods are available in Lancaster. Paths are good and provide flat walking, though they are a little muddy in places occasionally. Dogs are allowed. This walk is suitable for wheelchairs from the car park at Condor Green — but only as far as Ashton. For Condor Green car park, turn down the track along the front of the Stork pub, and continue until the parking bays are reached, where more toilets will be found, and also picnic tables. This is an excellent venue for cycling and if you carry folding bikes in the car boot, the whole family, including the smallest children, can enjoy a lovely traffic-free ride through pleasant countryside in complete safety. The path utilises the trackbed of the disused Lancaster — Glasson Dock branch line railway.

MAP REF: SD 445561. The car park at Glasson is sandwiched between the B5290 and the marina; a westward turn off the A588 Lancaster — Pilling/Blackpool road.

The start of this walk, alongside the bay-type estuary at Glasson is pleasant and serene, offering attractive views across the River Lune and the marshland overlooking Overton village. There is plenty to see in the dock itself; the marina is usually packed with boats and boating activity, and occasional groups of gulls and feral ducks and geese swim round the craft hoping for scraps to be tossed overboard, or generous visitors willing to part with some of their lunch! Herring, Lesser and Greater Black Back Gulls collecting food in summer will be raising families in places such as Walney and the Bowland fells and they will fly back and forth between Glasson and their nest site many times each day, until the young are fledged and fending for themselves.

Springtime sees a wealth of wild flowers, the edge of the thin ribbon of marsh being colonised by plants which favour the drier conditions. White and yellow members of the *Cruciferae* (cabbage) family are abundant, the flowers bearing four petals, hence the name crucifer — cross shaped. Scurvey Grass (*Cochlearia officinalis*) is a strong antiscorbutic (preventing the deficiency disease scorbutus, more commonly known as scurvey) and is rich in vitamin C. It was used regularly in the days before this vitamin was manufactured in tablet form. Gerrard, writing in the late 16th century, claimed that the leaves, if crushed and applied to face blemishes, would make them disappear in six hours! Other members of the cabbage family which grow hereabouts include Bittercress, Whitlow Grasses and Wild and Sea radish. Sprouting nearer to the ground are three

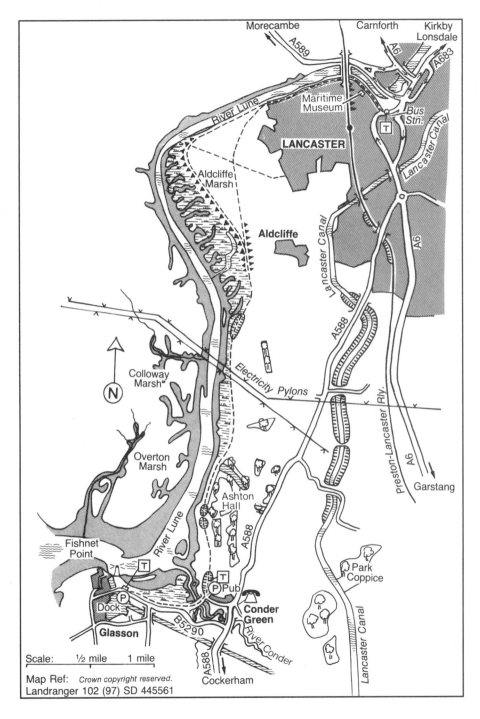

Morecambe

Carnforth

Kirkby Lonsdale

A589

A6

A683

River Lune

Maritime Museum

Bus Stn.

T

LANCASTER

Aldcliffe Marsh

Lancaster Canal

Aldcliffe

A6

Lancaster Canal

A588

Electricity Pylons

Colloway Marsh

N

Preston-Lancaster Rly.

A6

Garstang

Overton Marsh

River Lune

Ashton Hall

A588

Park Coppice

Fishnet Point

T

T

P Pub

Conder Green

P

Dock

Lancaster Canal

Glasson

B5290

River Conder

Scale: ½ mile 1 mile

A588

Cockerham

Map Ref: *Crown copyright reserved.*
Landranger 102 (97) SD 445561

PAINTED LADY BUTTERFLY on BRAMBLE.

members of the carnation family; Sea spurry, Sea Pearlwort and Sea Sandwort. Above the edge of the marsh on the even drier slightly pebbly strip, normally beyond the reach of the tide, except during very severe conditions, grow two types of Sea Lavender, the common variety and Lax Flowered Sea Lavender, along with the nodding pink heads of Thrift.

Alongside the path, species such as the tall yellow spikes of the deliciously fruity-smelling Agrimony were noted still in bloom on the last day of September. A decoction of Arimony is said to cure a sore throat, while boiling and fermenting it with ginger, lemon and oranges results in an admirable tonic wine . . . it could almost be worth being ill for! The same day's ramble produced Wild Carrot, Hop Trefoil, Eyebright and Upright Hedge Parsley and the season's late sunny spell was encouraging a few flowers to put out blooms alongside their own seed heads.

As the tide drops, waders gather on the extensive mudflats opposite, including Curlew, Lapwing and Black Heded Gulls together with a few Cormorants, standing about as though not quite sure what to do next. Knapweed flowers were attracting attention from a small influx of Painted Lady butterflies, sunbathing in the warm late afternoon sun. These insects are strong fliers and migrate to Britain in May and June from Europe and North Africa, distances in excess of 600 miles: those seen in autumn are most likely second hatchings from eggs laid in this country by the early season's migrants, and these second broods will unfortunately die when the first cold weather strikes.

The colours are typically autumnal on this walk late in September: vivid red rose hips occur in such profusion some years that the bushes are weighted down and my thoughts turn momentarily to rose-hip wine. Hawthorn, with its darker, smaller and more bitter fruits also hang heavy and will quickly be devoured when winter conditions in Scandinavia drives Fieldfare and Redwing, those foreign thrushes, into this country to wait out the winter months. The Bracken has turned a rusty red, here and there relieved with the bright blue dots of Harebells. The saffron yellow Ragwort gives evidence, by the great jagged holes in its leaves, of predation by Cinnabar Moth caterpillars, orange and black striped eating-machines, their warning colouration stating clearly that they are inedible. Their bodies store the alkaloid poisons made by their food plants, Ragwort and Groundsel. Sea Aster, the coastal version of Michelmas Daisy has gone to seed (or pappus as the seed or 'clocks' are correctly called) and yet the season is not over, for by its side, Common Cord Grass is just coming into full 'flower', the yellow pollen from its grass heads dusting everything nearby.

The information board at Condor Green car park gives various interesting tit-bits of information, one piece concerning St. John's Wort, which grows along this walk and was believed to be a powerful protection against witchcraft in medieval times and was used in the ancient fire ritual on St. John's Eve (June 23) from whence it takes is name. Interestingly, several old herbal guides claim it is excellent when made into a salve for burns, but only where the skin is unbroken. The display also shows paintings of some locally found birds, Goldeneye, terns, mergansers and common waders.

Soon after Condor Green, a sheltered clump of trees join overhead to make a tunnelled arbour, and at this point a gentleman rode past on a bicycle with a shouted 'Good Evening!' Trotting on a lead beside him was a beautiful, cream-coloured long-legged Saluki; a tall elegant silky-coated dog much favoured by the Arab peoples, and I smiled to myself at the chap's solution to the exercise problem, for here was a breed of dog which certainly needs plenty of it!

At evening time, in early autumn Curlew shout to one another over the estuary and in the fields to the right, rooks and partridges pick and squabble amongst themselves through the freshly cut meadows. Lapwings and gulls dig and scratch in the newly tilled ground for 'leather jackets' — not animal-clad motorcyclists such as myself, but the larvae of cranefly! Without any prior warning a cock Pheasant exploded from the undergrowth near my feet and flew off cackling — perhaps he was shocked at my quiet approach, or maybe he was laughing at adding another startled human to his list. Other pheasants called in response from the woodland as I drew level with Ashton Woods and soon after this, voices on the right told me I was passing the golf course. Apart from this and a few people on cycles, a weekday evening stroll is so lonely that thoughts can be allowed to stray, and it doesn't take much imagination to picture times long ago, when smuggling was a quiet occupation up and down this river. Smuggling it is said, occasionally continues, even in modern times at Glasson, although probably not involving the traditionally romantic booty of kegs of rum, run ashore by men with eye patches and heavily laden donkeys.

For the blackberry pie lovers among us I can recommend the Bramble bushes all along this stretch, those towards the middle being particularly well-endowed with luscious fruit. So be prepared, carry a plastic bag or empty litre ice-cream tub and whilst gathering the fruit in warm sunshine, think about hot pie

OYSTERCATCHERS NEST IN THE VICINITY OF GLASSON.

and custard, fresh as the day you froze the fruit, and consumed before a roaring fire in the snowy depths of winter!

Soon after passing under the electricity pylons, the river curves back to closely join you again, and on the adjacent banking large and colourful clumps of aromatic Tansy grows, used by herbalists, amongst other things, as a poultice to relieve gout and rheumatism. Mixed with the Tansy are a few delicate fronds of sweet-smelling Meadowsweet, spikes of Common Toadflax or 'darling bunny nose' and Bird's Foot Trefoil or 'eggs and bacon!'

Following the footpath out to Marsh Point and keeping to the Lune shore is perhaps the most pleasureable route, delaying drawing close to the City of Lancaster for as long as possible, although staying on the bridlepath is a touch shorter in distance. On reaching the outskirts of Lancaster, keep to St. George's Quay, (the road by the side of the river) passing old quays and warehouses, which in the 17th and 18th centuries did a roaring trade with sea-going craft powered by sail, and emerge in Lancaster centre almost opposite the bus station and toilets. St. George's Quay now houses the Maritime Museum in the former Customs House, which has already attracted several thousand visitors in the short time since it opened. Entrance is free and times of opening are: April — October, 11am — 5pm daily. November — March, 2pm — 5pm daily. The museum is closed from Christmas to New Year. For further information telephone Lancaster (0524) 64637.

If you plan to catch the bus back to Glasson, at the time of writing (1986) services 137 and 139 cover Lancaster to Glasson Dock Post Office and leaflets and timetables are freely available from the city centre bus station. The services are relatively infrequent, and it is worth bearing in mind that the last bus from the city to Glasson leaves at 1735 (5.35pm) during weekdays and 1535 (3.35pm) on Sundays, and this might explain the good numbers of pedal cyclists you will undoubtedly see on this coastal path. On this occasion, I started to retrace my steps back to Glasson before reaching the town buildings, as evening was drawing in faster than I could walk. A splendid sunset was reflected across the water and gulls and a Grey Heron stood like cardboard cut-outs silhouetted on the far bank. It was a tiring walk back and the last of the light faded as I wearily recrossed the bridge over the River Condor, my dark form against the pale sky putting two Greenshank to flight from the muddy creek below, yelping their 'tu-tu-tu' calls. The very next creek disgorged three herons, who flapped laboriously into the air shouting . . . 'frank!' . . . 'frank!' I regained my motorcycle, now standing alone on the empty car park in the gathering darkness, and sank gratefully down with a flask of hot coffee, made earlier in the day in anticipation of this tired moment and I sat listening to sounds of gently clinking rigging and lisping water, the boats bobbing and alight with hundreds of tiny lights.

QUICK GUIDE: Area comprises disused railway line following estuary. Described visit involves excellent level walking over a nine mile distance. (Alternative route given in text). Exposed and sheltered by turns. *BIRDS*: Waders, wildfowl, seaduck, cormorants, herons, terns, wagtails, migrants. *FLORAL HABITAT*: Coastal, estuarine, saltmarsh, mudflat, shingle, heathland, base-rich grassland and copse. *FAUNA*: Butterflies.

Stocks Reservoir, Slaidburn

A North West Water Authority reservoir with the conifer plantation of Gisburn Forest on the north-eastern side, Stocks Reservoir is set in the glorious north Lancashire moors. I must admit to not having explored extensively on foot at this site, as it has been more of a 'staging-

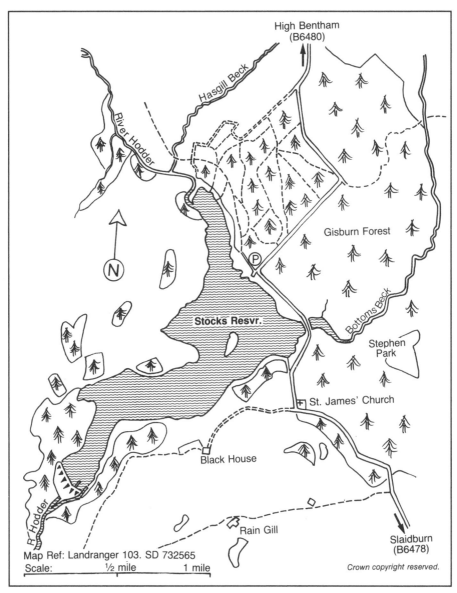

High Bentham
(B6480)

Hasgill Beck

River Hodder

Gisburn Forest

N

Bottoms Beck

Stocks Resvr.

Stephen
Park

St. James' Church

Black House

R. Hodder

Rain Gill

Slaidburn
(B6478)

Map Ref: Landranger 103. SD 732565
Scale: ½ mile   1 mile

Crown copyright reserved.

post' for me between Brungerley Bridge and several favourite Yorkshire sites; a place to take a quick 'gander' at wildfowl rather than have a walk! Also, I remember when most of the land was private, and gaining entry would have entailed climbing in, which I am extremely reluctant to do at any venue — for there is always the remote chance that some places could be game-keepered, and the discovery of this fact, by tripping over a chap with a gun is not an ideal pastime in my opinion!

However, matters are improving at Stocks, with the creation of a car park and three coniferous nature trails of differing lengths, and the designation of part of the shoreline, in a north-easterly direction from the car park as a nature reserve. In the best reserve tradition, there is no entry for humans! 'Birders' will find that binoculars or telescopes, used from the car park, or a little way back along the road towards Bottoms Beck will bring most of the waterfowl into view. The Lancashire Trust for Nature Conservation has a private hide on the shore, for use by Trust members only.

AMENITIES: There is a small car park with a redesigned entrance for safe access on a severe bend. A stone-built information board gives trail details and a map. Unfortunately, the walks are not suitable for disabled or chairbound persons, though there is nothing to stop disabled 'birders' in cars overlooking the water from the road. Nature trail paths at the time of going to press, were poor in places — and very boggy after wet weather. There are no toilet facilities, nearest block being in Slaidburn village, incorporating disabled cubicles. Strictly make and take your own food and drinks. There are some lovely picnic areas with tables, set back off the road, both before and after the reservoir, where you can park safely to enjoy your meal. Dogs are allowed but must be kept under control please, because of the sheep.

MAP REF: SD 732565. Follow the B6478 through Slaidburn in a north-easterly direction — and great care is needed at the extremely severe left-hand bend half a mile out of the village — head for Wigglesworth and Long Preston. Ignore the next two right turns into minor roads, continue to the crossroads and turn left down past a telephone box on the corner. Follow the minor road, where care is needed, especially at the sharp right-hand bend round tiny St. James' Church. Cross over Bottoms Beck inlet and the car park will be found on the left at the next severe right-hand bend. The approach road, which is narrow and requires care at the best of times, was on this last occasion slightly hazardous due to the ice. Farm wagons, Land Rovers and forestry vans towing trailers often appear, seemingly from nowhere, driven by locals who know every inch of this switch-back road, so please drive with extreme caution.

Immediately on leaving the car on my last visit to Stocks, a flock of Wigeon could be heard with their distinct and far carrying 'pee-ooo' calls. A good number of Teal were also whistling and 'blipping' to each other, many out of sight in the water-growing willows, and Mallard were making their flat nasal quacking. Out in the middle of the water, an expanding roost of gulls were gathering, and every few minutes new arrivals were adding their contribution to the noisy mayhem. A little nearer, yet still well away from land, a gaggle of 200 or so honking Canada Geese were playing 'follow my leader', reminiscent of a vintage car rally which has just been shown the green flag!

FIGHTING PHEASANTS.

The light was failing fast and the sun had gone down, disappointingly without the benefit of the expected water-reflected sunset, which was very surprising in view of the earlier lighting and almost clear sky. It was still possible in spite of the gathering dusk to tell the differences between the Tufted Ducks, grey-backed Pochard, larger Mallard and tiny Teal. Overhead, a Great Spotted Woodpecker flew westwards with his undulating, energy-saving and unmistakeable flight, calling 'Jik — Jik!' As we turned to take our leave, crunching through the snow which was already starting to re-freeze in the rapidly falling temperature, two Goldeneye drakes came swimming along the Hodder inlet, forced close to where we stood by ice on the opposite side. Even in the colourless light their yellow eyes were noticeably pale against their dark heads. One was an immature bird, rather ruffled and unkempt with white feathers where only black should be showing, but the second drake was smartly attired with not a feather out of place, a most handsome creature.

While we were drinking the dregs from our flasks, a huge orange moon floated into the sky, paling rapidly, illuminating the landscape with an opalescent glow. Sheep were feeding in the moorland fields, pawing through the snow to reach the grass, their breath rising in damp columns of vapour. At a certain spot not far from Stocks during a night journey home, I always hope for a repeat viewing of a Barn Owl, an experience I had some years ago when one 'wafted' over a wall and into my headlight beam giving me quite a 'turn'. But what a view! Riding over these moors and into the valleys in moonlight is every bit as delightful as the same ride in the middle of a bright, blue day.

News has recently reached me that numbers of Crossbill have been seen in the Gisburn Forest area and that the Great Grey Shrike, presumably the same bird which has previously wintered here, has returned. During an earlier visit in warmer weather, I noticed the grass verges littered with purple Devil's Bit Scabious, among

HONEY FUNGUS.

59

the confetti-like Eyebright. A female Goosander was alternately preening and fishing languidly back and forth across the water, followed by the usual horde of interested Black Headed Gulls, who were hoping no doubt, to divest her of her meal. They were wasting their time, for her catch must have been swallowed before surfacing — each dive came up empty, and I cannot believe she was such a poor fisher that she missed very time. Black Headed Gulls breed here during the nesting season, in a quite large and extremely noisy but sociable colony on the island.

The stone walls were festooned with the lobed common lichen, Crottle (Parmelia saxatilis) and mixed with it were two other lichen species, one a type of cup lichen, the other, Cladonia floerkeana, like thickened grey-green matchsticks with bright scarlet tops. The tawny-coloured caps of Honey Fungus, or Bootlace Fungus as it is sometimes known, (Armillaria mellea) were gaily marching up the trunk of an ill-fated Oak tree, which had been served a death sentence when this attractive parasite chose it as host. A look underneath the bark would reveal a tracery of long black cords, or rhizomorphs, reminiscent of bootlaces, by which the fungus spreads and infects the tree until it dies.

The memory of one spring morning, when I was homeward bound at 0500 (5am) following an enforced stay-over in Yorkshire, is especially vivid. I was high on the moorland before dropping down to Stocks Reservoir, sitting quietly astride my motorcycle, enjoying the atmosphere and watching a pair of Peregrine falcons engaged in a joyous sexual chase, declaring their territory against a back-drop stretching from the purple Lakeland hills, across Leck Fell, Whernside and table-topped Ingleborough to the rising sphynx of Pen-y-ghent and beyond to Fountains Fell and into Craven country around Malham. It's the 'top-of-the-world' on this viewpoint between Crutchenber Fell and Knotteranum at this hour and Red Grouse calls floated up to my ears on the fresh breeze 'Go back . . . back . . . back, back, back!' Curlew 'bubbled' while Skylarks disappeared into the blue, singing melodious songs. Beautiful!

Rounding the bend, on this same morning, into the straight stretch overlooking Stocks, two fighting cock Pheasants spilled onto the road and I braked to a halt to watch, the true meaning of cock-fighting becoming all apparent as they cackled and jumped into the air, grappling with each other, their tail feathers twisting to counter-balance their vilent movements, the backward facing claw of each foot lashing for a toe-hold on the opponent. After no more than a minute-and-a-half of what felt to me like a slowed-down 'action replay', one bird declared defeat and ran, then flew hastily, with the champion in hot pursuit. Both birds vanished back into the undergrowth, the victor 'crowing' and threatening dire consequences should he be lucky enough to catch his vanquished opponent.

QUICK GUIDE: Area comprises hilly, conferous woodland beside reservoir. Described visit involves overlooking water from car park and a quarter-mile of good, flat tarmac walking back towards Slaidburn, followed by a quarter-mile good tarmac walking, gently steepening in the opposite direction towards High Bentham. This venue can be bitterly exposed. BIRDS: Gulls, wildfowl, geese, owls, pheasants, raptors. FLORAL HABITAT: Coniferous plantations, acid heath, wetland, moorland and peat bog.

Brungerley Bridge, Clitheroe

THE limestone pedestal on which Clitheroe stands is the most southerly outpost of this rock in Lancashire, and it is the main reason why the adjacent area is rich in cement and lime workings. The walk from the twin chimneys of the Ribblesdale Cement Works to Brungerley Bridge, on the Waddington Road, is well-blessed with many lime-loving plants.

In years to come, this location is likely to see an increase in dedicated walkers, with their ruck-sacks, strong boots and bobble-caps striding out purposefully, as it has recently been incorporated into the newly-opened Ribble Way. You are told this by a lovely 'squiggly' sign, which features the letters 'R' and 'W' underlined by double waves. The Ribble Way is surely destined to become one of the most popular and picturesque longer walks in a very fair part of the county and one to which I am repeatedly attracted. I have much affection for the Ribble Valley.

AMENITIES: Toilets are at the Brungerley Bridge end of the walk, $1\frac{1}{4}$

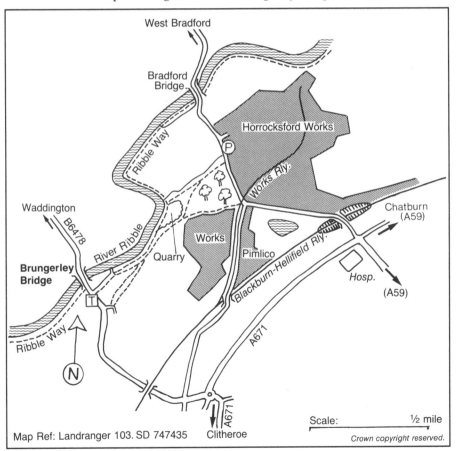

West Bradford

Bradford Bridge

Ribble Way

Horrocksford Works

P

Works Rly.

Waddington

B6478

River Ribble

Brungerley Bridge

Ribble Way

N

Works

Quarry

Pimlico

Blackburn-Hellifield Rly.

Chatburn (A59)

Hosp.

(A59)

A671

A671

Clitheroe

Scale: ½ mile

Map Ref: Landranger 103. SD 747435

QUAKING GRASS BEE ORCHID & HOARY PLANTAIN.

miles away from the start of the walk and unfortunately, parking is impossible at this point, as the B6478 road is too narrow. It is best to make and take your own food, although there are shops, pubs and fish and chis available in Clitheroe. There is a delightful picnic spot at the Brungerley Bridge end of the walk — a lovely grassy play area and seats, though this does entail you carrying your picnic all the way along the walk. Dogs are allowed. The lower path is muddy most of the year, and although the upper path is surfaced this venue is unfortunately, not suitable for the severely disabled or chairbound persons, for most of the interest here is beside the lower path and in the quarry, accessible only to walkers.

MAP REF: SD 747435. If you travel north-east from the round-about north of Whalley, the A59 and A671 converge for a mile with the A59 taking precidence; the A671 subsequently diverts to the left, sign-posted Clitheroe. Ignore this turning, and continue on the A59 towards Gisburn. Pass the next two left turns and take the third left into the far end of the semi-circular A671, sign-posted Pimlico Link Road and follow it over the main railway bridge. About 200 yards after the works railway level crossing, park on the right-hand side of the road just before British Gypsum Gate No. 2, and walk across the road, through a small side-gate leading to works car park (this is strictly for employees only — do not be tempted to park here) and take the path's right fork, beyond the car park and down through the trees.

The opening approach to this Ribble Valley walk, down a gently sloping track, passes several ivy-swathed grottos. Ivy undulates over the pale limestone boulders, weaving upwards round the stunted saplings and flowing across the floor, a living carpet which grasps and suffocates any object standing long enough in its path.

My last ramble here, before writing this chapter was in late November, following an early and unseasonal cold "snap" with a light snow fall, accompanied by freezing fog. The snow, topped by a crisp frost, clung to the dead stalks and seed heads of plants and grasses in a glittering, cold covering. The circular webs spun by orb weaving spiders were encrusted with hoar-frost, like diamond necklaces, provided by nature to adorn the winter countryside. The glossy red berries of Field and Dog Rose, each one with a frosting of crusty snow, looked like decorations for the Christmas cake.

Although the scenery and conditions carried all the hall-marks of winter, I have discovered that in the field the seasons are not always as sharply defined as I once imagined them to be. Some Ivy plants for example were in full bloom, despite the snow and cold, with umble heads of greenish petals and yellow stamens; in others the green petals had dropped, leaving small green 'nubs' which will fruit with prominent blue-black berries in April. A pair of Mistle Thrushes chased each other, shouting in raucous pre-nuptial displays, laying claim to a patch of territory in which nest-building will take place in December or January; the female could be incubating eggs by February.

Slightly hidden away on a rotting stump was a grand cluster of the fungi Velvet Shank, *Flammulina velutipes*, its many shiny orange caps with a crown of snow. This is one of the more noticeable fungal species to exist through the winter and even survives being frozen solid, commencing spore production as soon as it thaws out. Oyster Mushroom *Pleurotus ostreatus* is similar to Velvet Shank, and can also be found all year round on decidious trees. The cap edges are usually split and wavy in older examples, and the colour varies from greyish-sepia to azurine, the beautiful greysh-blue of fresh young specimens.

On the left, 200-300 yards further along, an entrance opens steeply down into the disused Crosshill quarry; do not worry if you miss this opening, for there is another a few yards beyond on level ground. In any case, it is perhaps easier and safer to take this second route, to circle the quarry. This is another place where, during a school trip, I managed to involve myself in a stupid prank, somewhat similar — but even more dangerous — than the one I describe at Jumbles, in Chapter 20. A classmate claimed she could climb to the top of the cliff faster than I could, and she was correct, for I became transfixed with fear half way up and could not move either way, while my friend lolled on the grassy top, grinning down and shouting ribald comments! I did finally climb to the top — but only because I could not retreat — and today 'Old Nick' himself would not get me up there again.

In odd sheltered parts, where the snow had not penetrated, the leaves of Wild Strawberry showed still green, and clumps of darker Wall Rue fern adorned the cliff face. Two types of common mosses grow all along this walk, and in early winter are approaching their most luxuriant time. One variety *Camptothecium sericeum*, has a golden verdant hue, its leaves having a gorgeous silky feel reminiscent of persian cat fur. It creeps over the rocks, sending green fingers of out-growth searching for new places to colonise. The other species is a *Thuidium*, with pale golden fronds growing mat-like on soil, rocks and fallen logs, yet it does not grow quite as opulently as at Silverdale.

Spring and Summer see the quivering Quaking Grass 'flowering', its shivering fronds never still, standing tall above oceans of yellow Lady's Bedstraw, and dotted here and there are the lavender coloured fuzzy heads of sweetly scented Hoary Plantain. In some years, a few magnificent Bee Orchids blaze into glorious bloom: the unique shape of the flower heads (mimicing a bee) being the attraction of this orchid, rather than colour. The yellow *Compositae* (daisy) family is well represented in this area and you can find Rough Hawkbit, Leafy Hawkweed, and Smooth, Rough and Beaked Hawksbeard. Marjoram, that aromatic purple-flowered herb, carpets the quarry floor, while back on the Ribble-side path, the upper banking contains the white umbellifers Rough Chervil, Wood Sanicle and Pignut. The lower banking just above water level boasts clumps of the slightly stiff and glossy Hard Shield Fern.

During our winter wonderland walk, the sun finally managed to break through, only an hour before dusk, chasing the fog quickly away and covering everything with late afternoon gold. The sky was blue and clear, forewarning the freezing conditions which were to return the minute the sun dipped out of sight. Near Brungerley Bridge, a gap in the hedge reveals a flight of steps leading down to the waters edge, on this visit rimmed and dangerous with ice. I sat perfectly still on the top step while a Dipper came foraging and feeding along the frozen edges, plummeting into the icy water in a desperate quest for insect food, while on my left a Little Grebe fished hurriedly, diving quickly to avoid the attention of a half-dozen Black Headed Gulls, who were intent on stealing the grebe's hard-won tit-bits.

The return ramble along the higher path is easy walking on

tarmac, with lovely views on offer through the trees, of Waddington and Easington Fells where Red Grouse roam and chortle in spring. On this ice-gripped occasion, I was grateful for the use of a sturdy four-wheeled, heated mode of transport, instead of my usual draughty two-wheeled version, especially since under these conditions the two wheels seem to favour travelling in different directions! And so, in the last hour of luminous golden light we made a quick dash to see what birds were preparing to spend the night roosting on Stocks Reservoir approximately tne miles further north. (See previous Chapter).

QUICK GUIDE: Even allowing for a circle of the quarry, this is a very short gentle walk of around two miles, on mainly good, level paths beside the River Ribble; a little muddy at times at the outset. Short turf in the quarry. Sheltered. *BIRDS:* Common mixed woodland species. Occasional Dipper, grebes, gulls, swallows and swifts. *FLORAL HABITAT:* Mainly woodland limestone, grassland limestone and riverside wetland.

DIPPER.

Sunnyhurst Wood, Darwen

TO many people, locals and visitors alike, this tree-clothed park, a typical Pennine wooded clough, terminating in a reservoir and moorland, is a pleasant and cheery place to enjoy a walk. I grew up in this area, however, and for me it is so much more than this.

I was not in double years when we moved into the vicinity, and right from the very start we walked here most days and had family picnics near the reservoir during the summer months. It was quiet in those days, as, unlike us, not many people took their meal a scant two miles from home simply for the pleasure of eating it outdoors! My very early and general interest in wildlife sprang from nature walks in and around Sunnyhurst, and this wood has much to offer.

Almost a quarter of a century later, I am still returning to wander and observe its flora and fauna, whilst keeping my mind closely in touch with its 'grass roots'. I see families enjoying this wood today and I hope their children will also be able to look back with pleasure at their childhood spent here, even into old age — one of my ambitions!

AMENITIES: Toilets are next to the Old England Cafe, but there are no disabled facilities. This is a pity for the path, entering from Earnsdale opposite Salisbury Avenue, and keeping in the bottom to the bridge and peacock cage, is particularly suitable for wheelchairs. During weekday working hours (not Sunday), consider visitig the disabled facilities in the town centre's Market Hall building. I recommend that the Old England Cafe's home baking should not be missed, and ice cream and snacks are generally available at the side window, just ring the bell for service.

At the opposite side of the cafe is a small play area with swings, while close by you will find the concrete-bottomed paddling pool, in which children delight. On the right, before the cafe, is a small Information Centre with an interesting garden. The centre is open Tuesdays, Thursdays, Saturdays, Sundays and Bank Holidays, 2 - 4.30 pm. Admission is free, but dogs must be left outside.

MAP REF: SD 676227. The main gates are at the far end of Falcon Avenue. If you travel in a northerly direction towards Blackburn on the A666, not quite a mile from Darwen centre is St Cuthberts Church, on the left at the corner of Earnsdale Avenue. Take the next left turn into Falcon Avenue and park your car, taking care not to obstruct any driveways, or the entrance to a block of garages close by the main gates. If parking is impossible in Falcon Avenue, return to the main road, turn right and then right again into Earnsdale Avenue and park at the rear of the church. A small 'cut-through' across the road leads back to the main gates.

Sunnyhurst Wood was originally farmland; however, in the early 19th century the local gentry envisaged a game park with shooting rights, and trees were planted to provide cover for game birds. A century later it became a public park and was enhanced with a larger variety of trees, and the resulting mixture of approximately 60 species includes, Scots, Corsican and Austrian Pine, limes, Cherry Plum, Hornbeam, Guelder Rose, Whitebeam, Walnut, Rhododendron and New Zealand Daisy Bush, with a predominence of Oak, Sycamore and Beech.

The start to this walk, from the main gates, is rather uninteresting,

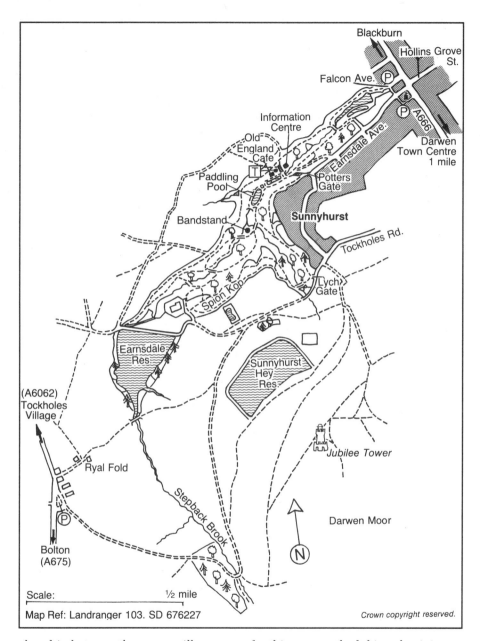

Blackburn

Hollins Grove St.

Falcon Ave. P

P A666

Darwen Town Centre 1 mile

Information Centre

Old England Cafe

Earnsdale Ave.

Potters Gate

Paddling Pool

Sunnyhurst

Bandstand

Tockholes Rd.

Spion Kop

Lych Gate

Earnsdale Res.

Sunnyhurst Hey Res.

(A6062) Tockholes Village

Jubilee Tower

Ryal Fold

Stepback Brook

Darwen Moor

N

Bolton (A675)

P

Scale: ½ mile

Map Ref: Landranger 103. SD 676227

closed-in between the paper mill lodge and private gardens. During bad weather it is also wet and muddy in places, nevertheless, the beauties of the wood itself more than make up for this apparently dubious begining. White Butterbur and Few Flowered Leek find this superficially unattractive part an ideal spot and early risers have caught glimpses of

GREATER SPOTTED WOODPECKER.

Kingfisher and a Heron or two plundering the private fishing of the lodge! *Sulphur polypore* fungus, or 'Chicken of the Woods' as it is known in the country, also alleviates this rather barren stretch — bright yellow as its name suggests and growing from live tree trunks, favouring especially the Oak. Mallard nest on the lodge and flotillas of ducklings following 'mum' are always a delightful sight and a reminder that spring has arrived once more. The lodge narrows at the in-flowing stream at the far end of this stretch of path, just as the woodland begins to open out. The alarm call of the Dipper may attract your attention, or perhaps his white chest will 'catch your eye', looking like an over-fed pied blackbird, as he 'bobs' and rummages among the pebbles in the stream, often disappearing under water altogether for a few seconds.

Over the bridge, botanists may wish to retrace their steps into the lower Earnsdale entrance to view, on the right-hand banking, a lovely clump of Dusky Cranesbill, its dark purple, delicate flowers appearing in June. Turn back to the path and you will enter a long open stretch which in sunny weather is a warm haven, and even in winter is not unpleasant, despite its vulnerability to east winds, which pry into even the most sheltered corners. When snow blankets the landscape, the sheer Christmas card beauty of this wood cannot be beaten, especially when viewed from the top right-hand path, giving views of Darwen Hill and tower. This vista, framed by stark, bare branches is quite superb; yet beware for all paths, except the main route, are hazardous in icy weather.

The tower, as the plaque will tell you, was built to celebrate Queen Victoria's Jubilee, although it also commemorates an episode much closer to 'Darreners' hearts. In 1878 the Lord of the Manor tried to close Darwen Moor and prevent public access, whilst turning the area into a game shoot. Five local men were violently opposed to this and continued to walk the public paths undaunted. They were accordingly served with writs for this supposed tresspass. In due course, the case went to court in London and thankfully the judge ruled in favour of the local people, enabling them once again to walk 'their' moor without hindrance. Two decades later the whole moor was opened for public recreation and placed into the 'hands of posterity' for our children and grandchildren to enjoy.

The view from the tower itself ranges from Pen-y-ghent and Ingleborough in Yorkshire, across Lakeland to Black Combe above Barrow and then down the west coast, by-passing that other tower at Blackpool, over Southport sands and on into Wales and Anglesey at Menai. This view on a clear day must have done the mill-workers hearts a power of good, and was probably the nearest most of them got to seeing these places: how very fortunate we are today in being able to travel so easily.

Love-in-a-Mist, Viper's Bugloss, Wood Spurge, Stinking Hellebore and many other plants are contained in the garden at the Information Centre — planted of course, but lovely to see all the same, together with the herb section containing among others, deliciously lemon-scented Balm. There is also a fern section, slightly hidden away to the right of the Centre. Following your visit to the Information Centre, continue walking towards the Old England Cafe, and with luck, replete with tea and scones, cross the lovely old ornate stone bridge, sparing a glance for the quaint waterfall as you head towards the paddling pool. You may perhaps catch a glimpse of a Grey Wagtail searching for insects beside the stream. Above the pool

Swallows and Swifts scream and twitter as they hawk for insects to feed their growing young.

On your way past or through the bandstand in winter and early spring the nearby stones will have a luxurious covering of mosses, a common and easily recognised species being *Plagiothecium undulatum*, which is noticibly paler, larger, flatter and longer than surrounding varieties. Another common moss found growing around the benches in shady positions is *Atrichum undulatum*, more commonly known as Catherine's Moss, with rosettes of dark, transversely ribbed (hence the latin *undulatum* — WAVY) leaves with strongly toothed margins. The moss *Mnium hornum* found growing near the waterfall outlet of the paddling pool, has equally obvious rosettes, but the pale, lucious apple green leaves are not at all wavy.

Usually in late spring, in the proximity of the bandstand, a male Wood Warbler will be heard singing, quite often in full view and what a lovely sight, his chest a fresh, bright citrus yellow, his gape wide issuing his indomitable song. Nearby, Chiffchaffs sing and male Blackcaps utter their weave of notes — a rich and varied, loud musical warble from the deep cover of Bramble or Rhododendron — while the Willow Warblers descending ripple of sweet notes, floats down from almost every tree. The inimitable Wood Warbler however, eclipses all the other songsters in his territory.

Cross the wicker bridge and between April and June the air hangs heavy with the scent of aniseed from the tall umbellifer Sweet Cicely, which crowds the bank of the stream. By-pass the now-empty Peacock cage (and I clearly remember when it did contain Peacocks and a striking male Golden Pheasant which I believe were all shot by hooligans) continue walking and cross the bridge on your left, which is swathed with my favourite Ivy Leaved Toadflax. Spend a few moments observing a small wet 'flush' (a swampy area, usually on a hillside, where water flows, but not in a defined route) and which in this case plays host to Common Spotted Orchid, Marsh Hawksbeard, Ragged Robin and many more floral delights for keen eyes to note.

Retrace your steps and rejoin the main path, back across the bridge, and pass the solitary Monkey Puzzle Tree. On the left after a short distance you will see another wet area, a shallow pond, which was polluted in 1986 and contained 30 or so breeding Common Frogs, which spawned despite the pollution. This frog is becoming increasingly and worryingly scarce, as their traditional breeding ponds are fouled, filled-in and 'tidied up' countrywide.

From here to the reservoir, bird watchers may encounter such species as Tree Creeper, Spotted Flycatcher, Green and Greater Spotted Woodpecker, Bullfinch, Greenfinch, Chaffinch, various titmice and, in the early hours, Tawny Owl and Sparrowhawk. Once at the reservoir you can if you wish, retrace your steps and return the way you came, or continue across the dam and head for the heathland of Spion Kop. In summer the flowers on the dam banking attract several species of butterfly to sunbathe and feed, with perhaps Small Tortoiseshell and Meadow Brown being the most abundant of these insects. In winter the reservoir itself, if not totally frozen, holds fluctuating numbers of wildfowl, mainly Tufted Duck, Pochard and Mallard, though on occasion the numbers are swollen with a few visiting Goldeneye and Teal.

Follow the track round the hawthorn hedge, where a Long Tailed Tit nested in 1986, and which many people must have passed

DEATH CAP, STINKHORN, BLUSHER, AMYTHST DECEIVER,
'JELLY BABBIES' & ORANGE PEEL FUNGI.

without knowing, so cleverly did the pair hide their small 'football' shaped nest. Go over the stile onto the heathland, Spion Kop, where bird watchers have been observed 'twitching' over a fleeting glimpse of a Merlin, a small immaculate bird of prey, similar to the Kestrel, which also hunts up here. The male Merlin has a slate blue back, in contrast to the male Kestrel's brown spotted upperparts. For those who observe humans, the bird watcher in the grip of a 'twitch' is an unmistakeable sight and so too is the botanist when viewed in the same condition. There is great animation, quivering, muttering, even loud oaths, and the eyes remain glazed even when the initial attack has subsided! Days after the event, mere mention of the special sighting will cause a vigorous renewal of symptoms. Botanists, of course, do not have to contend with the problems of flight, and are usually found on their knees in prayer-like reverence . . .

The surrounding moorlands hosts breeding Red Grouse, which are no longer shot, and on early summer evenings a lonely Cuckoo often advertises his desire for a mate with his distinctive call. I remember, years ago, seeing Hen Harriers gliding over these moors and I well recall the thrill of looking into my first Reed Buntings nest and seeing four eggs which appeared almost hand-painted, discovered during one of our evening picnics.

For those interested in fungi particularly, October is the best month to visit, when many varieties have been recorded including the Stinkhorn, Sulphur Tuft, glistening and Common Inkcaps, Candlesnuff, Wood Wooly Foot, Jelly Babies, the Blusher, many russulas, Coral spot, the Amethyst Deceiver, Milkcaps and boletes, Spotted Tough Shank, White Hellvella, the Death Cap and the Fly Agaric . . . the list is almost endless.

Sunnyhurst is Darwen's gem; it is open at all times to all comers and some of my most satisfying walks in many years have been taken here, sometimes accompanied by a former school friend, who also shares my love of nature and is indeed fortunate to still live close to this most beautiful wood.

QUICK GUIDE: Sunnyhurst contains a wide variety of footpaths, though this walk at its shortest and easiest-straight through the middle to Earnsdale Reservoir and back the same way, is no more than two miles long. There are, however, 11 miles of footpaths within the wood to be explored! In parts there are some sharp, steep climbs and two flights of steep steps. Paths generally good, occasionally muddy. Reasonably sheltered. *BIRDS:* Common mixed woodland species, plus warblers, flycatchers, wagtails and Dipper. Wildfowl. Occasional raptors. *FLORAL HABITAT:* Typical steep-sided Pennine mixed woodland clough ranging from acid heathland through to rich-woodland valley bottom with central stream. Small wetland patches. Open water (reservoir), small coniferous areas.

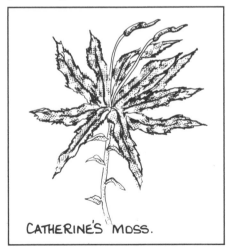

CATHERINE'S MOSS.

Rocky Brook & Roddlesworth Reservoirs, Tockholes

WHILST Roddlesworth is the official title of this venue, local people have always known this Lancashire beauty spot as Rocky Brook, and it is aptly named, being rugged and rocky of path as well as stream! It would be difficult to name another site in the county which has the distinction of playing host to a number of increasingly uncommon bird species such as Redstart, Pied Flycatcher and Kingfisher. The Tockholes area has a fascinating heritage behind it. In the 1660s, the people refused to accept the new Prayer Book and broke away from the Church of England to form a strong pocket of non-conformity. St. Stephen's church in the village has an interesting, if little-known, link with the Industrial Revolution: John Osbalderston, inventor of the Weft Fork, is buried here, having died a pauper while others later went on to profit from his idea. The Weft Fork is a device (fitted to certain power looms) which stops the loom from weaving immediately should the weft thread be broken, thus preventing damage to the cloth.

The enthusiastic and able walker can combine the previous venue, Sunnyhurst Wood with Rocky Brook in a variety of ways. For example, starting out from Falcon Avenue in Darwen, you can ramble through the wood to the reservoir, and walk along to the narrow wooded clough of Stepback, where, according to the eminent Lancashire writer Jessica Lofthouse, Oliver Cromwell is reputed to have uttered the words 'Step back, go no farther'. From Stepback you can climb steeply, yet quickly, to the tower and from the tower a number of paths lead off the moor and down to Roddlesworth and so into Rocky Brook. Given good

weather and an early start on a May or June morning, these two venues can easily rival any trip further afield.

AMENITIES: There are none — strictly make the take your own. No toilet facilities are available in the immediate vicinity — the nearest public block, including disabled facilities, is in the Market Hall at Darwen (open normal weekday hours, closed Sundays) or at the shopping precinct in Blackburn. Unfortunately, this venue is not suitable for the disabled or wheel-chair-bound as paths are stony, with steep steps in two spots and a couple of boggy patches, especially in winter. Dogs are allowed, but please bear in mind that the streams and reservoirs contribute to the North West's drinking water and important notices are posted regarding swimming or fouling.

MAP REF: SD 665215. This walk can be either divided into two visits or combined into one long ramble of approximately 5 miles. For those considering the divided walk, car parking is available in the bus terminus near the Royal Arms at Ryal Fold, on the minor road which joins Blackburn's A6062 with the A675 Preston to Bolton Road. Having parked within the terminus, cross the road and passing through the iron gate, keep left downhill for the stretch along the river towards Belmont village, for one half of the walk. For the other half, in the direction of the three reservoirs and Abbey village, keep right once you have passed through the gate. However, the route I prefer and the one described in this account, combines the whole walk. An un-

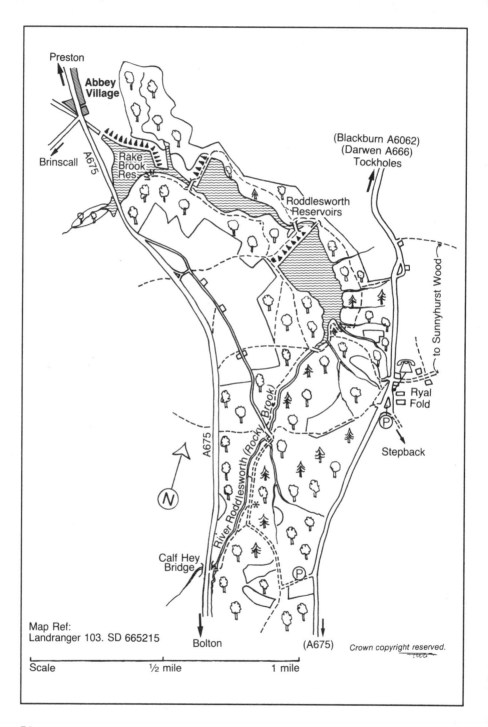

Preston

Abbey Village

Brinscall

A675

Rake Brook Res.

Roddlesworth Reservoirs

(Blackburn A6062)
(Darwen A666)
Tockholes

to Sunnyhurst Wood

Ryal Fold

Ⓟ

Stepback

A675

River Roddlesworth (Rocky Brook)

N

Calf Hey Bridge

Ⓟ

Map Ref:
Landranger 103. SD 665215

Bolton

(A675)

Scale   ½ mile   1 mile

official parking spot on Calf Hey Bridge may be found empty on early weekday mornings. Although for safety's sake I advise using the newly created car park (Map ref: SD 665215) sited on the right, when travelling south in the direction of Bolton, approximately three quarters of a mile, after passing the parking spot in the bus terminus at Ryal Fold. After parking follow the track down into the wood and pick up the walk from the asterisk. For those who wish to take advantage of the new safe parking, yet still cover all the area described, you could either, tack this short stretch onto the end of your walk, or double back at the outset by turning left at the asterisk.

After parking follow the track down into the wood land pick up the walk from the asterisk. Afer stepping through the gap in the wall *Sulphur polypore* fungus on a tree bole was the first thing to catch my eye, glowing dully out of the gloom cast by the thick leaf canopy. A closer look revealed it was an old specimen, faded and tired in appearance, yet still exuding a vigorous and not unpleasant 'mushroomy' smell. I am told it is edible when young and considered a delicacy in some countries . . . thoughts stray . . . and I muse that thin slices fried in butter would compliment a thick juicy slice of gammon rather well. Of course, I *must* advise that fungi should not be eaten, unless you are absolutely sure which species it is — first! The banks of the stream beside the first concrete bridge were packed with mosses, and the liverwort *Pellia epiphylla* looked particularly fresh and succulent on this early June morning. The path is stony and meanders alongside the tumbling stream on your left, which quickly drowns out any traffic noise from the busy road you have just left behind. This first stretch of the walk is usually quiet, almost to the point of desolation. People are rarely encountered and the wildlife is rather sparse too just here, yet this quiet prelude is the very reason why I enjoy the approach from this direction. Large Beech trees, Horse Chesnut and spindly Sycamores are interspersed with Rowan. Bistort, Bluebell and Wood Horsetail carpet the woodland floor, while the open heathy parts support Heather, Heath Bedstraw, Bracken and Bilberry or Whinberry.

A party of young Jays squawked in surprise at my approach and a Grey Squirrel, which had been foraging on the ground, leapt for the nearest tree trunk and sprinted heavenwards with great agility, tail waving like a feather boa. Chaffinch, Robin, Wren, Dunnock and Willow Warbler sang at intervals, though song slowly discontinues as full summer approaches, followed by a brief resumé in late autumn before ceasing for the winter. The song restarts early in the new year and is perhaps heard to best advantage from dawn to lunch-time in any sunlit wood during May.

*The path joins a wide decending stone track, coming from the right, bordered by Silver and Downy Birch, willows and pines. Cross the stone bridge and pass through the small iron gates, with the stream on your right. Red Campion adds bright pink splashes to the Bluebell haze and the pale green tripartite leaves of Wood Sorrell. The right-hand bank of the stream gradually rises to form a steep overhanging cliff, crowded with growth. The trees perch precariously on the ledges, roots reaching over to grasp at thin air before snaking into tiny crevices. Water seeps continuously down the rock face in fine runnels, bathing everything in its path. Near the cliff bottom the liverwort *Concephalum conicum* vies with the bright green starfish-like leaves of the insectivorous Common Butterwort. One wonders, in this wet habitat, how the Butterwort manages to keep the sticky exudate on its leaves long enough to catch any insects at all! As I sat cross-legged on a rock, photographing the Butterwort and being steadily dripped-on from above, the call note of an approaching Grey Wagtail grew louder and more insistant . . . 'see-eet . . . see-eet . . . siz-EET!' Glancing slowly over my left shoulder, I was enthralled to see a resplendent male, with brilliant yellow underparts and a cool, grey back descending a large rock not 40 ft. away, to indulge in a thorough bathe and preen. Ten seconds later, his less-imposing female joined him and not a half-minute had passed before a Spotted Flycatcher launched itself into a pool closer still. As on many other similar occasions, I longed for a telephoto lens like those seen on newspapermen's cameras — the sort where the business-end equals the dimensions of a good-sized dinner plate. The male Grey Wagtail would have looked superlative, filling the frame with every feather in focus, the clear

sunlit filled water droplets flying outwards — frozen on film for ever.

Leaving the cliff behind, the path asends and subsequently descends steep steps, followed by a small bridge over a gully. Continue to the next concrete bridge and cross over, with the stream back on your left again. On both sides of the path near the wall large clumps of Sweet Cicely filled the air as I passed with aniseed fragrance while a Blackcap warbler sang from nearby thick cover. Another Grey Wagtail flew past and on the return journey I discovered there were actually two pairs of wagtail nesting in this area, when a territory dispute occured, as the two male birds engaged in a lively scuffle before retreating — each to his own end of the stream. A pair of Great Spotted Woodpeckers were anxiously 'jikking' at top volume, close to where the inlet starts to widen towards the first reservoir and I presumed they had newly fledged-young, fresh out of the nest. The widening stream contains large shoals of Minnow and young Brown Trout (or parr as they are called at this age) with clearly visible red

GREY WAGTAIL.

spots along their flanks. These 4 in. and 5 in. trout are capable of a mind-boggling turn of speed and are vigorous swimmers even at this early stage in their development.

The water dominated panorama gradually unfolds on your left through the pines, and for me this evokes images of Scotland, especially in winter when numbers of Goldeneye plunge for fish in the un-frozen corners of the reservoir and snow carpets floor. Step across the next inlet at its narrowest point. At the time of writing a new small footbridge is under construction here, along with a new short stretch of path which will lead up to the main track. Until this is completed keep to the waters edge until the next inlet is reached, then turn right, away from the reservoir to scale the short gradient, turning left onto the main stoned-up access track and continue on this in the direction of the first dam.

Here and there, Herb Robert sports its ubiquitous and evil-smelling small pink flowers and reddening leaves, along with patches of Ivy and Honeysuckle. A clump of Large Bittercress protruded from a damp gulley and is an obvious relation of Cuckoo Flower, or Lady's Smock as it is sometimes called. The Bittercress has four white petals, and there is nothing unusual in this, but the noticible peculiarity are the violet-coloured pollen sacs, or anthers as they are properly known. A tiny flash of orange on a nearby pine stump turned out to be the fungus *Dacrymyces stillatus*, the main mass comprising tiny jelly-like lumps and bumps, although the growth continuing down the side of the stump clearly showed the minute 'tuning forks' described in Roger Phillips' 'Guide to Mushrooms'.

The path meanders pleasantly under pines, through dead and new Bracken, late Bluebells and small Sycamores with only the wind in the

CINNABAR MOTHS.

tree-tops for company on early mornings in summer. The faint voices of the fishermen on the far bank, on this occasion, was the only indication that the outside world was still there, waiting. A Cuckoo's lonely lament floated off the high moorland from the direction of Stepback's copse — where Ring Ousel have recently been watched — the first Blackburn record for Ring Ousel in more than 100 years! Presently, two Crows came winging over the water to investigate what I was doing conversing with each other in harsh guttural barks, amplified by the surrounding silence. Yet what a different personality this venue wears on Saturday afternoons in summer, full of families enjoying a break; laughing children, barking dogs, picnics in full swing . . . my memories echo enjoyment such as this from chilhood . . . I particularly recall catching 'tiddlers' with a knotted 'hankie'.

Cinnabar Moths were found in some quantity on reaching the marshy overflow of the first dam; several were posing on the wall waiting for the sun to reach round and warm their bodies. One had a crumpled forewing — was it newly hatched I wondered and still pumping blood into the delicate vein-netted wing to extend it, or was it permanently damaged and doomed to die without achieving its life's single aim — propagation of the species? The moths were cold, drowsy and easily moved onto the plants in the sun where I photographed one or two — yet how quickly they warmed up in sunlight and became lively and decidedly unco-operative! The overflow herbage contains Lesser Spearwort, much resembling a buttercup and in fact hailing from the *Ranunculaceae* (buttercup) family although possessed of lanceolate (spear shaped) leaves as its name suggests, instead of the typically lobed buttercup foliage. Odd plants of the frail looking Ragged Robin, delicate Cuckoo Flower and the straight green spines of Water Horsetail were mixed with the spearwort. A pair of Blue Tits had a nestful of young in the wall and were constantly arriving with food, squeezing through an unbelieveably narrow gap, a few scant feet away from where I was kneeling, photographing the moths.

What I guessed was a young Tawny Owl was plaintively begging for food nearby, while I tucked into my lunch of beef and onion sandwiches — and this at only 10.30 in the morning — this nature watching business is hungry work! The two Crows returned with their hacking coughs to see if I was going to discard anything worthwile and I told them 'Sorry boys — too hungry to spare any today!'. A mighty, fallen Beech with only a third of its roots still in the ground was beautifully green and leafy despite its predicament. The branches were slowly re-organising themselves to bend round towards the light. The roots contained three complete Wren nests, one of which was new and un-used, together with the remains, or maybe the unfinished beginnings, of four very old structures, which made a total of seven Wren nests in this one beech tree.

Other years have seen Redstart

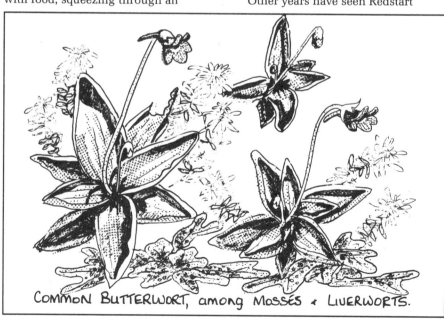

COMMON BUTTERWORT, among MOSSES & LIVERWORTS.

favouring the warm, raised heathy area of bracken and birches to be found half-way along the northern side of the middle reservoir. I noted this was not the case this year, for I had already heard the males 'whee-tic-tic . . . whee-tic-tic' snatch of song near the second bridge, as approached from the A675. Other observers reported five singing males in 1986 in the Hollinshead/Wishing Well area — an excellent record for this site.

The white stone track finally curves round and down to the dam at the end of the second reservoir. Green Woodpecker and Pied Flycatcher are frequently seen and heard from here and I caught a glimpse of a female Pied Flycatcher in the trees below the banking whilst half way across. Cross over the new wooden bridge and turn right for a quick look over the third reservoir before retracing your steps for the return walk. On this occasion, I discovered a pair of Common Sandpiper with chicks on the nearside bank, the parents shrilling acute anxiety at my sudden appearance, as all good parents should when danger threatens.

Come back past the new bridge, from where I have been told you may enjoy excellent views of the resident Kingfisher, however, the bird was being less than obliging when I visited, and this delightful turquoise and orange-coloured, bullit-shaped bird did not materialise for me — despite prolonged and hopeful lingering. Keep straight along the southern boundary of the middle reservoir and as you approach the wall the path forks at a concrete post bearing the word 'water'! Take the right fork and head towards a gap in the wall, crossing a tiny gulley spanned by a stone slab bridge. Go up the hill to join the tarmac surfaced track coming from the right. Ignore path going down-hill left at this point and keep on tarmac track with the wall on your right, by-passing as you go, the stone building which deals with fishing return documents. Draw alongside the first reservoir again, keeping to the outside of the fence and finally pick-up signs for the nature trail diverting right into the woodland, avoiding the private area marked for anglers only — they will be fly fishing for trout and their lines reach well back over this path, when casting, making walking hazardous. Rejoin the earlier track by turning right just above the second concrete bridge and return to your vehicle beside my most favourite Rocky Brook. The Redstart I noticed on my return had stopped singing near the bridge and was being replaced by a Wood Warbler giving a slow and sad sounding rendition — the tail end only of his song . . . 'schree-e-e-e . . . tip — tip — schree-e-e-e-e . . .'

QUICK GUIDE: The walk alongside the brook and round the reservoirs is of medium length (approximately 4-5 miles) yet moderately difficult if taken in its entirety. Paths are reasonable — some stoned — though there are a couple of severe boggy patches at the outset of the full walk. Several short, steep climbs involved and, unless the walk is reversed by starting at Abbey Village, the outward journey is steadily downhill — with a long, steady climb on the return. Sheltered.

BIRDS: Common mixed woodland/coniferous species coniferous species. Scrub and tree warblers, flycatchers, chats and redstarts, Kingfishers, Dipper, wildfowl, swallows, swifts and House Martin.

FLORAL HABITAT: Moorland edge mixed/coniferous woodlands and heathland scrub. Mainly acid-type species. Some acid bog. Open water (three reservoirs and streams).

Lytham, Fairhaven Lake & Local Nature Reserve

FOR the enthusiast who really enjoys walking, these three areas can be combined into one long walk of approximately 8-9 miles. However, I recommend dividing them into two or even three visits and travelling between them by bus or car, as the stretch from Fairhaven to Ansdell has little to see in summer, apart from people, deckchairs and flat expanses of sand — and in winter, just the sand! Lytham is another place where our family 'put down roots' for a while and it was here, 17 years ago, that I began bird watching in earnest. I started with a brand new pair of binoculars and bird guide, both of which I quickly found to be unsuitable, as the book was bought more for its superb paintings, than to assist identification, and I soon found I could not distinguish between similar species. The binoculars were grossly over-powered at a massive 16×50 magnification, and very heavy and tiring to use . . . I'm sure had I been able to hold them steady, I would have found myself counting the feather lice on Southport's resident Peregrine Falcon — perched on the gas works tower!

AMENITIES: As with most seaside resorts, the major problem is choice:

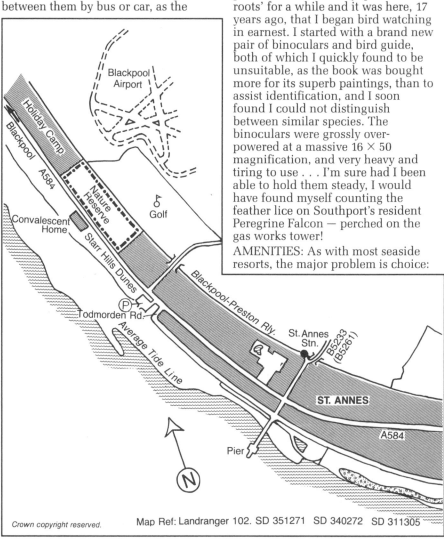

Blackpool Airport

Nature Reserve

Holiday Camp

Blackpool A584

Convalescent Home

Golf

Starr Hills Dunes

Blackpool-Preston Rly.

Todmorden Rd.

Average Tide Line

St. Annes Stn.

B5233 (B5261)

ST. ANNES

A584

Pier

N

Map Ref: Landranger 102. SD 351271 SD 340272 SD 311305

food available during the season varies from a-la-carte to fish and chips and sandwiches to pub grub, in addition to the usual endless supply of ice-cream and candy floss. Toilet facilities are plentiful with Lowther Gardens making full provision for the handicapped and aged. The toilet block in central Lytham is at the foot of some steep steps and not suitable for the disabled. More toilets are located at Fairhaven Lake with reasonable access but no special facilities. There are no toilets near the reserve. Lytham and Fairhaven are very suitable for wheelchairs, and the local disabled people, in their battery-cars, are frequently encountered enjoying this round trip. Botanists need to leave the tarmac paths, but birdwatchers (disabled or not) need only pause at intervals along the front to see all that is on offer. The nature reserve is, unfortunately, only accessible on foot, and is more suited to the avid botanist than the bird watcher. Dogs are allowed on the reserve, on leads please.

MAP REF: SD 351271, SD 340272, SD 311305. Follow the A584 towards Blackpool, by-passing Lytham centre, keeping instead to the coastal 'green' road. After the sharp bend at the Blackpool end of the green, take the next left turn into Fairlawn Road and park your car at the bottom of the road on the left.

Lytham, with its famous white windmill and green, not to mention the hordes of visitors, does not at first glance appear to be a good place for nature observation, but look again, and you may be amazed at the abundance of wildlife encountered here throughout the year. I wonder what species flourished in and around Lytham in 1086 when it was known as 'Lidun' and was included in the Domesday Survey? Would there have been more to see, or less? A windmill was recorded on this site in the early 12th century and may even have been the first English windmill in existence. All in all, quiet, peaceful Lytham has more than a little to boast about, — but it is far too dignified for that!

You can, if you wish, park at any of several places along the green and begin your walk sooner than

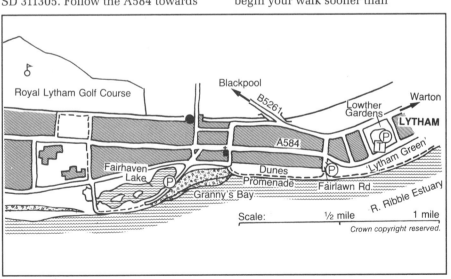

Crown copyright reserved.

Fairlawn Road: many people like to walk out on the wooden jetty at the Lifeboat station for a closer look into the estuary. Cormorant fish out in the river in winter, and a Heron or two stalks along the waters edge for unwary fish and crabs when the tide is low. Flocks of wildfowl, Wigeon, Pintail and occasionally small numbers of Common Scoter make use of the Ribble estuary in winter too, although they are often a long way out and difficult to distinguish without the aid of a telescope. I notice, with some amusement, that when I am on the Lytham side of the Ribble the interesting birds appear to be close to Southport, and when I am on the Southport side, everything looks equally close to Lytham — something to do with Murphy's Law perhaps!

If you have parked your car in Fairlawn Road, walk towards the sea and if the tide is coming in you may notice small numbers of waders gathering on the tiny pebble-covered promontory just to the left of here. Dunlin, Ringed Plover, Redshank and maybe a few Oystercatcher and Shelduck will continue feeding, seemingly unconcerned by people strolling along the promenade. Turning to botany the strip of grass-covered sand-dunes sandwiched between the promenade and the high wall of the private gardens is a botanical paradise. An apparently aimless wander back and forth across this area, on your way towards Fairhaven, will bring many species into view and allow a bird-watching eye to be cast over the estuary occasionally. Perhaps the most noticeable plant at the start of the walk (during May) being the bright yellowish-green umbel-type flowers of Cypress Spurge, giving way after a few yards to large patches of the mouse-ear Dusty Miller followed by Spring Beauty, Bulbous Buttercup, Common Dog Voilet, Spring Vetch, Hedgerow Cranesbill and Sea Radish. Further along still, there are great eye-catching swathes of Wild Pansy, some all-yellow, others all-purple and the rest a delightful mixture of both shades. Later in the year, the same area is covered with swathes of Yellow Rattle, Lady's Bedstraw, Rest Harrow, Smooth Hawksbeard, Haresfoot Clover, Large Flowered Evening Primrose and, beside the wooden benches, a few tall stalks of Crow Garlic. There is something magical about this short stretch of land — and there are no half measures, most of the plants which flower here, do so lavishly.

The niches of the promonade wall host Sea Sandwort, Buckshorn Plantain, Bird's Foot Trefoil, Biting Stonecrop and several scurvey grasses jockeying for position. Whilst looking down at these, you may become aware of 'comic' terns hunting with shrill cries along the estuary, 'comic' being the nick-name applied when they are not close enough to distinguish whether they are Common or Arctic, the former having a black tip to the red bill and whiter underparts, the latter having a wholly blood-red bill and greyer underparts giving a suggestion of a paler stripe below the eye and cap. Close to the garden wall in one spot, slightly hidden, grows bright blue Periwinkle with lovely glossy leaves and below it is a small amount of Common Star of Bethlehem, its light-reflecting petals increasing the temperature on the flower head and encouraging insects to sunbathe. These will be covered in pollen, which will hopefully be transferred to the next Common Star of Bethlehem visited by the insect, thus ensuring cross-pollination. A male Whitethroat scratchily advertises in song his desire for a mate in the bushes above, while the flat, tuneless nasal twanging 'schreeeee!' of several male Greenfinch floats over the wall. Spring also finds the House Martin gathering mud on the beach

MARRAM GRASS
CROW GARLIC &
WILD PANSY.

to construct the cup-shaped nest and in the town I noticed two pairs of House Martins had chosen a very auspicious site on which to build — under the Police Station eaves!

Fairhaven is more of a birdwatching or boating location. Wildfowl are mostly feral and present on the lake all year round. Yet rarities do sometimes stop here to rest during migration in spring and autumn. One year saw both Grey and Red Necked Phalarope present together, during a week which caused quite a stir amongst local and visiting birdwatchers alike. The widening estuary at this point can be full of waders, particularly in winter: Redshank, Grey Plover, Dunlin, Curlew, Sanderling, Knot, Ringed Plover, Bar and Black Tailed Godwit and Oystercatcher — a high tide will push them closer to your binoculars, allowing you good views before they fly off to roost. Several plants found here worthy of a special mention are, the tiny Sea Pearlwort growing from cracks in walls and pavements, and Hoary Cress (a member of the cabbage family) growing in noticeable clumps near the lake in May and June, plus Sea Buckthorn, Lesser Burdock and Common Storksbill.

Now, retrace your steps to your vehicle or take a bus and alight near the Convalescent Home. Car parking is allowed on the left-hand side of

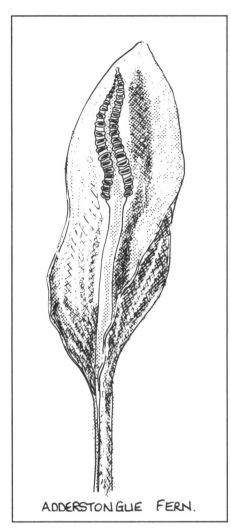

ADDERSTONGUE FERN.

the road beyond the home: however I recommend using the free parking place marked down the last road on the left before the traffic lights (see map). The A584 is busy and dangerous and the kerb is very high, so parking is not recommended here.

Starr Hills and the Nature Reserve stand on the northern shore of the Ribble estuary, as do Fairhaven and Lytham, and even in the Bronze Age, man was passing this coastline. Irish traders used the Ribble and then travelled overland through the Aire Gap to Bridlington, as a short cut to the Danish metal markets. Today, the interest in Ansdell centres on natural history and this area is yet another heaven for botanists. Leave the parking place through a small exit onto the beach, turn right and circle the wire-enclosed compound and once in to the dunes, head towards Blackpool. Most of the interesting plants will be found in the flattish strip between the road and the dunes — known as Starr Hills. Fortunes are reversed here, July being the better month for a variety of flowers and Opium Poppy, with deep voilet petals, is found growing directly out of the sand. Where there is some grass you will pass great swathes of yellow-coloured Kidney Vetch, known sometimes as Lady's fingers for the flower head resembles a woman's glove. Also dotted about are clumps of Lucerne, which is widely cultivated as alfalfa, its pea-type flowers coloured from pale purple to blackish-mauve.

When you draw level with the signs for the Nature Reserve, cross the road and once again I draw your attention to the dangers of this busy carriageway. Once into the reserve, please stay on the narrow, grassy tracks and even here watch where you put your feet, for some of the orchids have colonised the paths, free from competition with the surrounding herbage! Also, some patches (known as 'slacks' when they occur in mature dunes) are marshy and straying from the path can rather suddenly mean wet feet. Common plants abound such as Wild Thyme and Marsh Pennywort. The pennywort has minute 'pinkish' flowers which are well-hidden beneath its leaves. In many places you will notice the dunes have a dense and impenetrable carpet of Creeping Willow — a very typical duneland bush. Not so universal are the Common Spotted and Marsh orchids and their hybrids, for these plants can and do produce orchid crosses — noticeably taller mixtures of the two parent plants.

A few Pyramidal Orchids bloom splendidly, and beautiful Marsh Helleborine flutters delicately in the breeze — what a pale and gorgeously understated plant this is. Isle of Man Cabbage is one of the specialities of this reserve, its deeply divided leaves making it unmistakable. Another interesting 'find' is the Fare Dune Helleborine, while a few Bee Orchids bloom gloriously, which for all their showy splendour are not easy to spot. Even more difficult to see in the undergrowth are the tiny spikes of Adderstongue Fern. Moonwort, a relative of adderstongue, made an appearance here in 1983, however, I do not believe it has been seen since, although again it is not a conspicuous plant and it may yet re-appear. This being an afternoon visit, the Goatsbeard was living up to its country name of 'Jack-go-to-bed-at-noon' and all blooms were firmly shut — one of the few plants which goes in for regular 'early nights'! Common Centuary flowers in abundance here, and even more interesting is the white variety of common Centuary, growing alongside the normal pink examples.

A great diversity of moths have been recorded at the reserve, though most are only visible towards evening, or are attracted to lights during darkness. A few day-time fliers are well in evidence, however, in July: the pristine white male Satin Moth is very obvious and I can't help but feel that there is an ecological mistake here somewhere, white hardly being a candidate for warning colouration. On the other hand, the hundreds of black and red Six Spot Burnet Moths, seen mating on top of flower and grass heads all over the reserve, imply quite clearly by colour that they are poisonous. Perhaps the satin moths were merely disturbed

from cover, yet they made no rush to return to the undergrowth, posing openly on herbage and, in one case, on a gentleman's shirt collar! His shirt was blue by the way — so the moth was not trying to hide!

In this vicinity, many years ago, was the site of a small chapel or oratory, where monks were sent to do penance, and which, like many buildings on this coastline, has since disappeared, probably into the sea. According to local folklore however, a phantom bell still ecoes from the depths of the sea on New Years Eve . . .

If it is a particularly clear evening as you drive back towards home through Lytham, do stop and admire the view from the sea front; the panorama is majestic, as it sweeps across land from Anglesey, 60 miles distant, past Llandudno's twin Ormes and Snowdon's range, to Southport and onwards over Parbold towards Winter Hill with its television mast glinting in the evening light. The distant skyline skims the moor and Darwen's tower, before plunging to rest among Preston's highrise flats.

QUICK GUIDE: The proceedure I recommend here is to split the four sites into two visits and car or 'bus-hop' between. The Lytham — Fairhaven circular ramble of roughly three miles (including dune stroll) is level walking on either short turf or surfaced path and pavement. The Starr Hills — Reserve circular ramble of approximately two miles (and including a mile or so wandering in the reserve) is also level walking, but comprises some loose sand (Starr Hills) and short turf in the reserve. Can be exposed. Panoramic views. *BIRDS:* Waders, wildfowl, terns, gulls, Cormorant, Heron and various migrants during spring/autumn passage. *FLORAL HABITAT:* Coastal species, rich duneland and slacks. Open water (Sea and freshwater lake).

Southport — High Tide

THIS strip of coastline, from the pier to Crossens Marsh provides the bird watchers dream — I cannot think of anywhere better for sitting spell-bound, whilst observing thousands of waders. Add the other bird species and flora which occur here for good measure and if you have followed my advice in the Authors Note, (see page 3) you should plan a visit to Southport on any one of the highest tides of the year. There are usually at least one or two tides of 32 ft. or more each month, from autumn through winter to spring, which will provide the bird-watching bonanza I describe in this chapter.

AMENITIES: You will be spoilt for choice during weekdays with bar meals, fish and chips and bakeries providing a wide variety of food. Toilet facilities are dotted around Southport (particularly on the promenade) though unfortunately, the block which is most conveniently sited for this venue (on the right before the traffic lights at the junction of the A565 and the B5244 at Churchtown) are locked at weekends. Making and taking your own refreshments will enable you to bird-watch and eat simultaneously — a state of affairs which always makes me happy! Making and taking your own hot foot and drinks is almost compulsory on Sundays in Winter. The beauty of this venue is that if you do not wish to, or perhaps cannot, leave your vehicle you can still bird-watch to your heart's content and see just as much (if not more on some occasions!) than those who expend lots of energy dashing up and down the sea front with their telescopes! Having said that, I have recently purchased a telescope which, used sensibly, has revolutionised my 'birding' and I am slowly having to 'eat my words'!

MAP REF: SD 352204. Arrive at Marshside sandworks two to three hours before high tide and park on the recently created car park south of the works on the seaward side of the road, opposite the Marshside Road junction with the Coastal Road. If this area is full, head towards Preston and find rough parking spots on the landward side of the road, then walk back past the sandworks towards Southport. *Do not* be tempted to park anywhere on the road itself, or the pavement, as parking restrictions are taken very seriously around Southport.

Whatever the extent of your interest in bird-watching, you must visit Southport and experience one of the North West's great bird spectaculars. Poor Southport has been the butt of jokes for years, due to the sea receeding so far out at low tide that it almost disappears over the horizon, leaving the resort high and dry!. However, it more than makes up for this sad state of affairs when the tide comes in, pushing thousands of elegant waders landwards to congregate on the sandy foreshore. I will name a few to whet your appetite: black and white Oystercatcher, Curlew with long sturdy legs and down-curving beaks, Redshank with trilling calls, restless quirky personalities and red legs and beaks — although I note that immature Redshank have pale, almost flesh-coloured legs and beaks. Knot, medium-sized greyish-brown waders are packed tightly together whilst alternately sleeping and moving in unison before the on-rushing tide as though obeying a shouted command. The smaller Dunlin dash hither and thither, feeding right up to the very last moments before water covers the entire shore, while their hyperactive

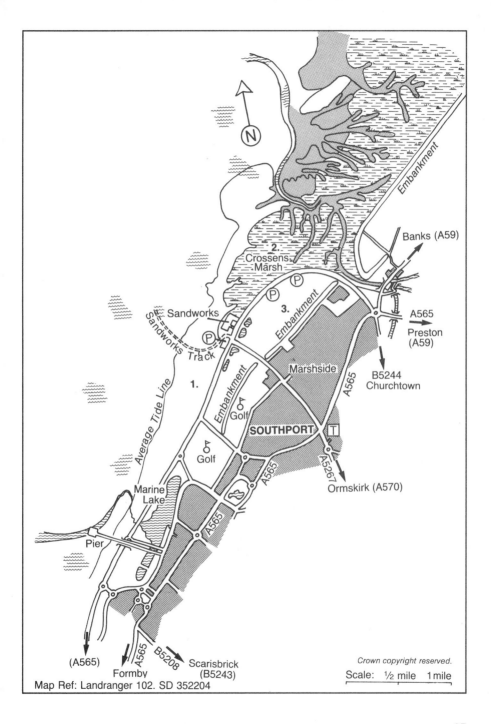

Banks (A59)

2.
Crossens
Marsh

Sandworks

Sandworks Track

P

P

P

3.

Embankment

A565
Preston
(A59)

Embankment

Marshside

B5244
Churchtown

1.

Average Tide Line

Embankment

A565

Golf

Golf

SOUTHPORT

T

A565

A5267

Ormskirk (A570)

Marine
Lake

A565

Pier

(A565)

Formby

A565

B5208

Scarisbrick
(B5243)

Scale: ½ mile   1 mile

Map Ref: Landranger 102. SD 352204

cousins, the Sanderling run so quickly that their legs are a blur of continuous movement. Mixed in and around this advancing hubbub may be seen Bar Tailed Godwit, similar to the Curlew except the Godwit's bill is straight, or ever so slightly up-tilted. Grey Plover stand out, being dumpy waders, with distinctive 'pee-ooo' calls and black 'armpits' (or underwing patches, as they are correctly called) showing clearly during flight. Their smaller relative the Ringed Plover often appear to be quite tame, feeding close to the road, unperturbed by the traffic.

Rare sandpipers appear from time to time, blown to the English shore by gales from foreign countries, and occasionally our less common waders, the tiny Little Stint, the elegant and beautiful Greenshank and the equally lovely Spotted Redshank call in at this estuary. Various species of tern including Common, Arctic and Sandwich, not to mention the rarer Roseate and Little Tern on occasion, and may be seen and heard hawking for food up and down the tideline during the migration times of spring and autumn. Small numbers of Black Tailed Godwits have taken to feeding very close to the Marshside Road, usually just over the fence in the field on the Preston side and good views can sometimes be had — though do not step outside your car or they will fly away.

June and July are the two months when this exciting wader pageant does not occur as the tides are at their weakest, leaving mud uncovered far out in the estuary and the non-breeding waders that remain on the coast throughout the nesting season, continue feeding or roosting out there, without needing to come to the inner shore. The breeding majority are scattered miles inland, busily engaged in family life and at this holiday time, you may well be far away perhaps, watching nesting

Curlew and Greenshank high on Scottish moorland, incubating their eggs and tending chicks, surrounded by vastly different scenery from their wintering quarters on our esturies.

September and October are perhaps the best months for sheer numbers of waders gathering, the winter population of Ribble waders being swollen by birds on migration who will eventually land and winter in Africa and other warmer climes. Select for your visits the highest tide in each month, at a time of day when you can arrive on the front at least two hours before the tide reaches its zenith (see the Authors Note, Page 3 for an explanation of tide tables). An extra word of caution too — a strong west wind will not only make the tide come in earlier than predicted in the tables, but it will also rise much higher and miscalculations under these conditions may have you arriving just in time to see waves washing over the promenade and the last skein of waders vanishing north towards the marsh. Do not despair, for all is not lost: although you may have missed the initial build-up of waders on the foreshore, (numbered 1 on the map) the show is by no means over and you now follow the birds, past the sandworks to their next collection point (2) either by walking or by car. If you have been parked near the sandworks, move off towards Preston to find a parking space on the right-hand side of the road, in one of several rough spots on the grass verge. The waders will be quite a long way out on the marsh at this stage, but the advancing water will gradually push them closer, and if your calculations are right and you picked a high enough tide, the marsh will eventually be completely covered. As a result the birds will fly to the only dry roosting place left — the fields on the landward side of the road (3), bringing them into close range with your binoculars and

KNOTT & GREY PLOVER.

cameras as they fly overhead.

The added attractions brought by the marsh flooding are that any raptors (birds of prey) roosting on the ground in the marsh, will be forced into the open to sit on fence posts. Alternatively, they may fly around — and then the action really starts, as panic-stricken waders explode skywards in a frenzy of fear and thousands of birds stage a magnificent aerobatics display. I have watched Merlin and Peregrine Falcon fly over and 'stoop', or dive, at the waders, I am sure, just for the fun of causing mayhem. On other occasions, however, the dive has apparently been in deadly earnest — particularly for the wader or duck whose life came to an adrupt end in the grip of a Peregrine's talons . . .

From January to March the diversity increases. The marshland may have lost many of its waders to southern continents, but it gains replacements such as Whooper and Bewick swans, and bird watchers 'flock' from miles around to see these two species of relatively rare swans in a natural setting — grazing in the fields with the cattle! Several thousand Pink-Footed Geese arrive to graze the marsh, having sooner or later exhausted inland crops of carrots and grain. Many thousands of duck also congregate; the grass feeders such as wigeon take their toll of the marshland habitat while tri-colour Shelduck and Shovelar and the delicate Pintail are also present in good numbers. Very dark duck seen flying out in the eastuary will most likely be Common Scoter, although these birds seem to favour

DUNLIN.

Liverpool Bay rather than the Ribble. Raptors tend to increase during the winter months too: I have counted four female Hen Harrier flying lazily over the marsh, together with two Short-Eared Owls (which look like pale large bats in flight) and a Peregrine Falcon all in the air at the same time, causing pandemonium among birds and bird watchers alike. A short time after this incident, when all had become settled, and nervously calm, a large female Sparrowhawk appeared, causing renewed panic all over the marsh. After flying among the waders, she settled on a passing grab — talons lowered — in the midst of a group of finches, mainly Greenfinch, Twite and Goldfinch, but on this occasion she missed. Little wonder the Redshank are such nervous birds! Even species as large as geese react with horror and take noisily to the sky, flapping and cackling with panic, when sythe-shaped raptor

wings appear in the sky.

Before turning for home, when the waders have dispersed back out to the mudflats, it may be worthwhile to scan the Marine Lake, particularly following periods of severe gales. Species such as Cormorant, Goldeneye, Long-tailed Duck and rare divers and grebes may be seeking refuge on the calmer waters of this man-made lake, though I would point out that rarities should not be hounded or over-watched by people anxious to add another tick to their 'list'. This sort of behaviour bears no relation to the true spirit of bird watching and I doubt that this sort of people-pressure helps wind-battered and storm-damaged birds to recuperate and return to their true element.

When the tide is out, Southport is such a quiet place and without first-hand experience one would never suspect that this exhilarating exhibition occurs twice a day, regardless of daylight or darkness and is particularly evident when the tides are higher than normal.

QUICK GUIDE: There are two recommended procedures for Southport — either one long route (approximately 6 — 7 miles) of flat, surfaced walk or, alternatively, there is absolutely no reason to step outside your vehicle — the whole of this outing can be achieved by nothing more strenuous than winding the car window up or down! Excellent bad weather venue — if you are using a car. Can be bitterly cold and exposed if you have arrived by public transport (or motor-cycle) and are forced to complete the walk.

BIRDS: Waders by the thousand! Also Wildfowl, geese, swans, raptors, owls, terns, finches, larks, buntings and various other migrants at spring/autumn passage. FLORAL HABITAT: Coastal and saltmarsh. Wetland — a mixture of fresh and saline pools. Open water (sea and marina).

Entwistle Reservoir, Edgworth

QUITE apart from natural history, the area around Entwistle, Wayoh and Jumbles reservoirs is fascinating because of its ancient history. The Roman road from *Mamucium* to *Bremetennacum* — Manchester to Ribchester in todays language runs on the eastern side. Constructed in the late 70s AD, it was the main Roman military route north for the following 20 years. Entwistle Reservoir is administered by the North West Water Authority.

Turton Heights encompasses the site of a prehistoric stone circle overlooking the reservoirs while nearby Affetside has a stone column marking the half-way point on the old coaching route from London to Edinburgh. Two 15th century towers remain, one at the traffic lights in Bradshaw; the other, Turton Tower is now a museum and is well worth a visit, especially if the weather changes suddenly and dampens your enthusiasm for a nature ramble.

AMENITIES: There are none, you must make and take your own. The nearest toilets are at Jumbles Country Park just over 4 miles away going via Turton Bottoms to join the A676, then turning south to Jumbles. Dogs are allowed but must be kept under control — remember please that this is a source of drinking water. Wheelchair access is available at each end of the dam and all the way round the reservoir, though path narrow in one spot.

MAP REF: SD 722173. Travelling southwards on the A666 Darwen to Bolton Road, make a left turn, after

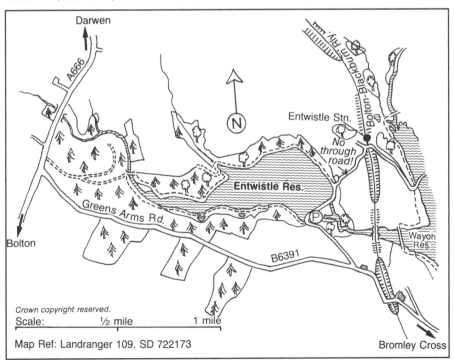

Crown copyright reserved.
Scale: ½ mile   1 mile

Map Ref: Landranger 109. SD 722173

AESHNA GRANDIS DRAGONFLY and GREAT CRESTED GREBE.

the dip approximately two and three-quarter miles from Darwen centre, into Greens Arms Road, the B6391 for Turton Bottoms and Bromley Cross. After approximately one and a half miles turn left into the minor road, taking special care, as it is narrow in places with a steep, sharp bend just above the two car parks, one on the left, the other on the right before the start of the dam. This is the only approach to Entwistle reservoir, as the road at the opposite end of the dam, leading to Entwistle station and Edgworth village, is privately owned and closed to motor traffic.

Entwistle is like Lancashire's own little corner of Scotland; it takes only a very short leap of imagination to conjure images of Glen Trool Forest in Galloway, when admiring the view across the water from the dam. This scene has changed for the better, in the aesthetic sense, since I first saw it more than 20 years ago as a child, during family picnics taken after school. The forest was, like myself, quite young and much less extensive, with ample bare moorland visible. Over the course of two decades however, the nakedness of the hillsides has given way to a heavy clothing of deep green fir trees, planted by the North West Water Authority. This has bestowed on Entwistle the kind of serenity found only where majestic evergreens stand silent guard, around an unruffled sheet of silver water. It has other moods of course; baking under a shimmering heat haze in high summer or when spring gales whip the water into sizeable waves with wind-blown spume leaving patterns like torn net curtains on the choppy surface. In winter, hard weather takes a firm grip and mallard stand forlorn on the ice making the similarity with Scotland even more pronounced.

Circuit the water by whichever route takes your fancy most; a meander in September will reveal large clumps of the garden escape (cultivated and now doing well growing wild) Dotted Loosestrife, with brilliant spikes of erect yellow bells, and the wild purple-coloured Devil's Bit Scabious at the sides of the approach road. The Bilberry (or as I have known it since a child, Whinberry) bushes are heavy with shiny, lucious fruit and many walkers carry polythene bags and boxes filled with the days rich pickings . . . more winter pies, hidden in freezers — the human equivalent of squirrels?

Other signals of autumn, with mauve flowers are the patches of Heather, Foxglove and Self Heal, sprinkled with the bright yellow four-petalled Tormentil. Self Heal and Tormentil are much favoured by herbalists; Self Heal as an astringent and healer of wounds (both without and within) while tormentil is said to calm the stomach and intestines when food of dubious freshness has been eaten. I have had rescourse to this herb myself, having eaten unwisely, and I can personally vouch for its efficiency.

Several interesting ponds are encountered on the way round the reservoir, and while all is apparently quite among the water starwort and duckweed in September, earlier in the year the ponds were doubtless full of activity and diverse species, some requiring specialist knowledge and microscopes for accurate identification. 'Pond dipping' as it is known and indulged in by many junior schools as a forerunner to senior school biololgy classes, can be a fascinating experience. Water Fleas, algae, Freshwater Shrimps and larvae of all kinds provide a very important food for birds like the Dipper and Grey Wagtail. There may also be Water mites, water beetles, water worms, snails and even an air breathing, yet fully aquatic spider, which lives under water in its own home-made silk bell tent, which it fills with air bubbles carried below the surface trapped on its body hairs. As the Water Spider uses up the oxygen in the bell, diffusion takes place from the oxygen dissolved in the surrounding water, so the spider does not need to keep re-filling it. Raft spiders may also be found round the edges of these ponds; I prefer their latin name of *Dolomedes* as it seems to express their character, — large, imposing spiders with seemingly shrewd and judicious expressions in their clearly visible eyes. The female *Dolomedes fimbriatus* can measure up to 22 millimetres in body length, excluding her legs — a truly marvellous sight, although this thought may just have discouraged you from 'pond dipping' for life!

Bright autumn sunshine dazzles and sparkles on the wings of a large Brown Aeshna dragonfly as it hawks for insect prey with 'clickity-clackaty' flight back and forth across the shallow, weedy, western bay of the reservoir above another lone hunter, a Great Crested Grebe, diving in search of fish. Deciduous trees surround the small inlet at this end, primarily beech and sycamore, and under the beeches, fungi will be found in the latter part of year — the Beechwood Sickener *Russula Mairei*, which as its name implies is poisonous. Along the northern side of the reservoir, back under the edges of the plantation, grow many brightly coloured *russula* fungi, their caps all manner of lovely shades; yellow, purple and red, their stems pure white and of a typically crumbly texture. Colonies of bright Sulphur Tuft Fungi sprout from any left-over stumps and dead logs, while the smaller fallen dead branches sport splashes of Coral Spot fungi, resembling drops of congealing blood.

Goldcrest and Coal Tits, characteristic inhabitants of pines,

can be heard twittering and 'tseeping' to one another, while Swallows gather in excited chattering flocks over the farmland, obviously preparing to take their leave of us for another year.

Normally, the combination of forestry plantation, deep reservoir and acidic conditions would not lend itself to an abundance of wildlife as the lack of food variety and light in their environment precludes many species. However, Entwistle's bird population is enhanced, if only on a passing basis, by its situation adjacent to farmland, and the other reservoirs at Wayoh and Jumbles, and the proximity of houses and gardens with mixed trees and bushes; the not-too-distant Rivington complex of water and wooded moorland and of course, Bolton itself with its high proportion of tree-covered, almost natural parks and stream valleys, all combine to make Entwistle a more interesting place for wild life than would otherwise be expected with this type of habitat.

That Entwistle has more than a passing resemblance to Scotland has been amply verified, in my view at least, by the visitation in one recent year of a Golden Eagle. It was not a figment of my artist's imaginative mind, it was real enough, recorded and photographed, albeit a fleeting shot, by the surprised but wholly-pleased warden! It was possibly a young bird slightly off-course from its migration route, following the Pennine chain of hills.

The Goosander, another bird strongly associated with the 'land of tartan' often spends time at Entwistle during winter. The males are resplendent in contrasting plumage, the white underparts becoming flushed with pink during the breeding season, while the upper parts are black with a white stripe down each side just above the wings, which also have a white patch visible in flight. The plumage is completed with a dark, bottle-green head, sporting a scarlet beak and red eyes. The Goosander's torpedo-shaped body, with legs set well to the rear, makes a formidable fish-catching machine, as graceful under water as it is ungainly on land.

Entwistle is a peaceful place for a reflective ramble and I keep it in my repertoire for just this reason.

QUICK GUIDE: A visit to Entwistle comprises a circular walk around the reservoir over approximately three miles of level, good paths. Pleasing panorama. *BIRDS:* Coniferous woodland species, wildfowl, grebes, wagtails and finches. *FLORAL HABITAT:* Coniferous plantation, heathland, base-poor to acid species, small wetland patches. Open water (reservoir, fresh-water ponds).

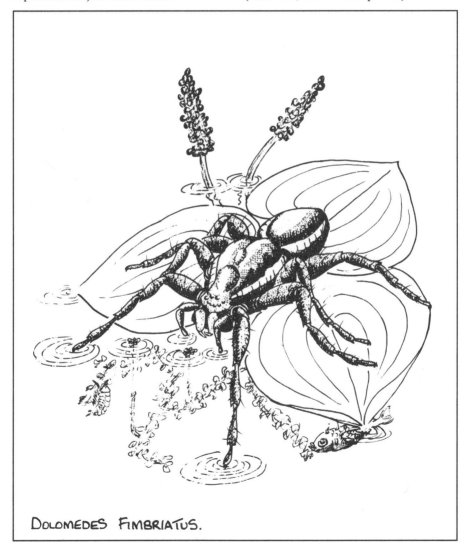

Dolomedes Fimbriatus.

Wayoh Reservoir, Edgworth

IN contrast to Entwistle, Wayoh has quite a different character even though they are close together. It is slightly lower lying and surrounded by farmland, rather than open moor and pine afforestation, with a richly divergent flora colonising the edges. The inlet at the northern end, being shallow with muddy margins, is particularly rich in wildlife — not a state of affairs normally associated with northern reservoirs. Of the three waters, (Wayoh, Entwistle and Jumbles) Wayoh in my opinion is the least attractive in appearance — though it is certainly the best from a natural history standpoint. Wayoh is destined to become a protected reserve besides being a reservoir and source of drinking water, and will be jointly administered by the North West Water Authority and the Lancashire Trust for Nature Conservation.

AMENITIES: You must strictly make and take your own food at this location. Dogs are allowed but keep them under control. Paths are good as at Entwistle, but wheelchairs need lifting over the locked gates and can only be taken for a limited distance along each side of the water. The paths become rugged towards the northern end, terminating in steep steps leading up to the road on the left-hand side of the reservoir.

MAP REF: SD 734162. Travelling south towards Bromley Cross on the B6391 car parking is possible in the third road on the left, after leaving the approach road to Entwistle, taking care not to obstruct any of the driveways, or the entrance gate to the water-works. Parking is also possible on the northern dam; however, the approach road down from the Edgworth side is very narrow, and the section beyond Entwistle station

to the start of Entwistle dam is private and closed to motor traffic, as indicated in the previous chapter.

Although there are stands of spruce trees here, unlike Entwistle they are not the dominant feature, and parts of the woodlands at Wayoh contain a large proportion of deciduous varieties; Sycamore, Ash, Alder, Silver and Downy Birch, Oak and Hawthorn are just a few that I noticed during my warm September afternoon stroll.

A nearby Rook colony quickly impressed itself on my conciousness, the birds 'cawing' and 'cackling' to one another in their sociable way. Meanwhile, another genial group of birds were diving and feeding together on the water — Tufted Ducks, the male birds a little bedraggled in appearance, their moulting incomplete. In another month or so, their pied plumage will be faultless, and their numbers will increase on our inland waters throughout the winter. In cold weather they feed by diving often, thus keeping a small patch of water un-frozen and together with other wildfowl, Coot and swans, they mill around in a tiny opening, when all the rest is thick and stilled with ice. Two other diving duck species are also winter visitors to Wayoh; the Goldeneye in his spectacular white and black dress and greenish triangular-shaped head and the equally smart Pochard with grey back, cheeky black bottom and chesnut head, glinting and sparkling with auburn fire on bright frosty mornings.

From a bird-watching standpoint the whole of this area, from Bradshaw Brook to Turton moor, taking in the three waters has a very impressive checklist, compiled between 1977-87 and includes 147

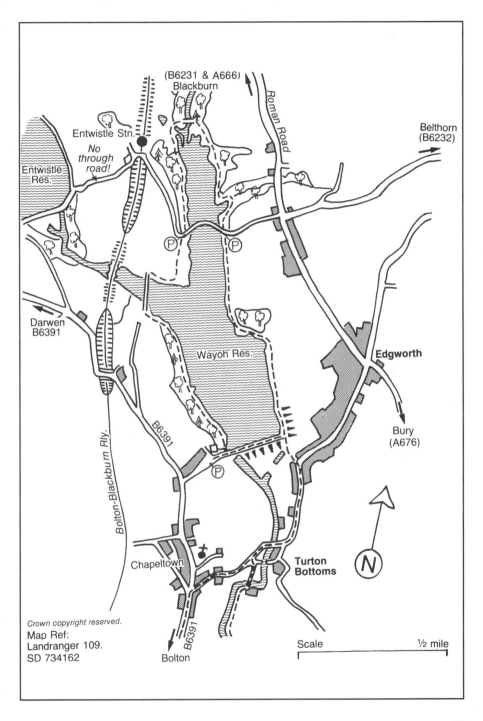

(B6231 & A666)
Blackburn

Roman Road

Belthorn
(B6232)

Entwistle Stn.

No through road!

Entwistle Res.

Darwen
B6391

Wayoh Res.

Edgworth

Bury
(A676)

Bolton-Blackburn Rly.

B6391

Chapeltown

Turton
Bottoms

N

Bolton

B6391

Crown copyright reserved.
Map Ref:
Landranger 109.
SD 734162

Scale   ½ mile

97

ROSEBAY WILLOWHERB.

species. Winter visitors have included: Bittern, Whooper Swan, Wigeon, Pintail, Jack Snipe, Water Rail, Iceland Gull, Goosander, Siskin, Brambling and even Crossbill — giving further credence to my Scottish theory! Species such as Scaup, Shelduck, Cormorant, Hen Harrier, Peregrine Green Woodpecker and the previously mentioned Golden Eagle are irregular visitors, seen by a lucky few, and may be encountered again in the future. Summer residents, and possible breeding birds, have included such delights as Little Grebe, Teal, Little Ringed Plover, Redshank, Common Sandpiper, Blackcap and Chiffchaff. Although these species are present all summer, they will not all raise families, for some will be single birds — non-breeders, too young, too old, perhaps even sickly, yet quite a few of these do indeed nest in the vicinity. Four species of tern have been recorded on passage during migration, also Ring Ousel, Green Sandpiper, Dunlin, Wheatear, Yellow Wagtail and even a Grey Phalarope — worth a 'twitch' in any 'birders' book! Altogether, this noteworthy collection of records gives clear proof that keeping special places for wild creatures to visit or live in is indeed worthwhile — both for them and us.

However, to return to my less productive September wander; the expected goldcrests and col tits were going about their business in the fir trees on the western side of the water. Growing in the damp shade under the spruce trees were clumps of the fragile and enchanting Wood Horsetail, a mimic in miniature of the fir trees above. Horsetails are perennial herbs which reproduce by means of spores (as do ferns, mosses and fungi) and they are often overlooked, or regarded merely as weeds. Closer scrutiny reveals a delicate beauty especially in the frail-looking Wood Horsetail. Herbalists both ancient and modern have favoured the horsetail. The famous herbalist Culpeper, writing in the 17th century, recommended it to staunch haemorrhaging 'either inward or outward.' Centuries earlier the Greek Physician Dioscorides, writing in Asia Minor around AD 78, also knew horsetail, and proclaimed it to 'perfectly cure wounds' when crushed and laid on the injury. Dioscorides was the originator of the *Materia Medica* (first published in 1478 in Latin) in which he described over 600 plants.

In the boggy waterside patches, standing tall above the surrounding herbage, are clusters of pink Hemp Agrimony — a member of the *Compositae* (daisy) family, its rather flat-topped heads made up of many single florets, tightly packed into a compound head. Growing nearby is a close relative, the bright yellow Golden Rod and in the very next marshy patch can be found the pale spikes of Meadowsweet and Sneezewort; also radiant yellow Ragwort, Leafy Hawkweed and large stands of pinkish-purple Rose-bay Willowherb, also known as Fireweed, for its habit of being one of the first colonisers of burnt ground. It even added colour to London, when devasted by the Blitz. *Funaria hygrometrica*, a characteristically curly, twisted moss is another burnt ground lover, and is resplendent in lustrous orange and green during the fruiting season. In winter sunlight, it almost glows, and together with the fireweed, it provides a natural and speedy covering to charred areas of the landscape.

Just before the steps are reached, the banking on the left has a lovely mixed show of Broad Buckler Fern and Mountain or Lemon-scented Fern, so-named for its fresh citrus fragrance if the leaves are crushed or even brushed against while you walk by. On gaining the road at the northern end, cross over and circuit the quiet inlet. During late summer, if water levels are low, this corner frequently dries out, exposing extensive muddy borders which migrant waders find attractive. Consequently, stealthy early-morning human visitors may be fortunate enough to watch Greenshank probing and feeding in this rich insect-laden region or even indulging in courtship display during the spring. The early 'birder' walking past this inlet may also startle a Heron into the air.

On reaching the road again, cross over and return by way of the eastern side path, which is sparsely wooded at first with a mixture of deciduous species. However, once round the corner, the final leg of the walk back to the southern dam is more open, with a steep-sided sandy bank to your left, which houses a good assortment of plants. Tufted Vetch is here with brilliant purple flowers; also, its near relative Bush Vetch, with shorter flower spikes of slightly larger and discoloured-looking bluish-purple, almost faded flowers — even when seen at its best. Another purple member of the *Leguminosae* (pea-flower family) is the Wild Lupin, plus my old favourite yellow 'tinfoil' or more properly Bird's Foot Trefoil. Wood Sage also grows in profusion, its greenish flowers inconspicuous until you take a close look and see the protruding dark red stamens adding unexpected points of colour.

A family of Pied Wagtail called and cavorted on the dam wall amidst splashes of the yellow lichen *Candelariella vitellina*, a commonly found species on stone walls and rocks. The parent wagtails were trim, sharp and well-refined in shades of black and white, the young birds less clearly marked and, in common with young Lapwing and several of the tit-mice family, displaying prominent yellow cheek patches, which will be pristine white when maturity is reached.

Globe flower, that lovely member of the *Ranunculaceae* (buttercup) family can be found growing at Wayoh, I understand. In spite of its appearance of brilliant yellow globe-shaped flowers, it is in fact a petal-less plant in botanical terms, consisting instead of 10 incurving petaloid sepals (resembling petals). Sepals are the outer or lower part of the flower, found below the petals and in most plants where both are present, the sepals are usually green or brown in colour. Another, and perhaps better known member of the buttercup family to show this same characteristic, is Marsh Marigold (or 'May Blobs' as they are sometimes known), and this yellow sepalled plant also grows at Wayoh.

Wayoh reservoir, with its thriving natural hinterland, gives proof that not all man-made development need preclude the existence of wildlife. For not only is the natural balance preserved, but without the creation of the reservoir much of Wayoh's flora and fauna would not be here at all!

QUICK GUIDE: A circular, mainly level walk (approximately five miles) of which paths are reasonable at the outset, becoming rugged towards the northern end. Steep steps up to the road on the left-hand path. As at Entwistle, stile entrance/exits at western and eastern sides of the dam. BIRDS: Wildfowl, waders, terns, swans, common woodland species, scrub and swamp warblers, buntings, raptors, cormorant, grebes, finches, wagtails and Heron. FLORAL HABITAT: Mixed woodland and coniferous areas, heathland, wetland, marsh and scrub. Open water (reservoir).

Jumbles Country Park, Bolton

THE flooding of Bradshaw valley in 1970 to make Jumbles reservoir and country park has turned a fairly ordinary, slightly industrial clough into a pretty scene when viewed from certain spots, for there are few more pleasant vistas than the sun glinting off blue water dotted with brightly striped yachting sails, set against the backdrop of farm and mixed woodland. This is a family place, as all good country parks should be; it caters for fishing, picnicing and walking while still retaining an abundant wildlife — which is quite an achievement. Jumbles Country Park is owned by the North West Water Authority and covered by the West Pennine Countryside Ranger Service.

AMENITIES: Toilets, including disabled facilities are provided and the main car parking area is on the left, beyond the toilet block. Disabled persons parking bays, overlooking the water, are on the right at the end of the approach road. These bays are ideal for handicapped bird watchers with binoculars or telescopes to watch wildfowl on the reservoir. Wheelchair access to eastern perimeter track, from main car park is possible at all times. Near to this track is a bird hide with wheelchair access. Make and take your own food if planning a prolonged visit, and while dogs are allowed, they must be kept under control. Guided walks are arranged by the rangers and programmes are posted on the information board at the main car park. A second car park is located at Ousel's Nest, just off the B6391 on the western side of Jumbles — no facilities other than car parking. Information Centre sited on the right at the bottom of the access road. Opening times are as follows: Easter to October; Wednesday and Saturday 13.00 - 17.00. Sundays 11.00 - 18.00. Bank Holidays 10.00 - 18.00. Winter, Sunday 11.00 - 17.00.

MAP REF: SD 736140. Following the A676 out of Bolton in a north-easterly direction, the signposted entrance road to Jumbles is on the left approximately one mile from Bradshaw traffic lights and directly opposite the lane leading to Brown Barn Farm. Turn left and continue to the end, keeping left to reach the main car parking area and toilet block.

Jumbles, opened in 1971, is the most southerly of the three reservoirs and the newest. Entwistle was built in 1831, enlarged in 1840 and taken into public water supply in 1876 when Wayoh was completed. I can hazily remember a school biology field trip to this valley bottom, more than 20 years ago before it was flooded and I confess at this time to showing more interest in a 'dare' with one of the lads. This involved crossing a large pipe spanning a deep gulley, and was more interesting than listening to the tuition of the teacher, who was by this stage quite a distance ahead, completely unaware that two of the party had stealthily detached themselves and were up to no good. The teacher in spite of my admission much later to this foolish prank, became a good friend and my natural history mentor.

Circuit the water by whichever way appeals most; if you go clockwise, the steep steps are downhill and take you away from the water for quite a distance, before regaining it again on the western side. If you go anti-clockwise, you remain at the waters edge for most of the walk, but the steps then come at the end and may seem much steeper

101

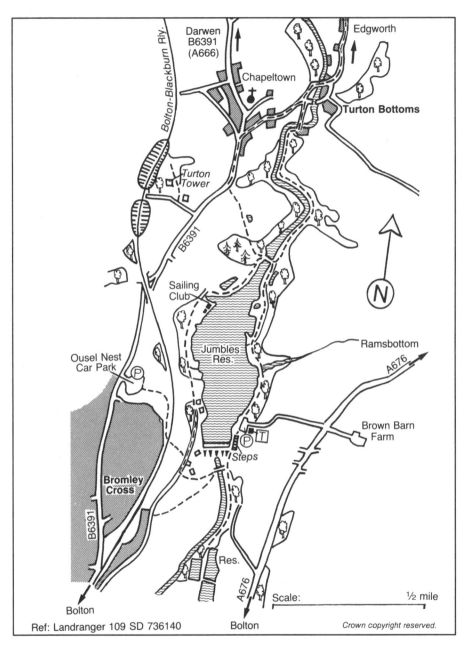

Darwen
B6391
(A666)

Chapeltown

Edgworth

Turton Bottoms

Bolton-Blackburn Rly.

Turton Tower

B6391

Sailing Club

Jumbles Res.

Ramsbottom

A676

Ousel Nest Car Park

P

Brown Barn Farm

Bromley Cross

B6391

P T

Steps

Res.

A676

Bolton

N

Scale:

½ mile

Ref: Landranger 109 SD 736140

Bolton

Crown copyright reserved.

when your legs are tired! In spite of this I prefer the second route, as the start is high above the water, when any wildfowl will be more easily seen and identified. You will notice conservation areas at intervals fenced off and accompanied by 'do not enter' signs; these are sensitive places where certain aspects of wildlife, especially plants, receive special protection from many tramping feet. Permission to enter, for purposes of photography or specific study, must be sought from the warden *before* venturing into these extremely important areas.

Spring and summer produce an interesting number of thriving plants in the marshy places, and I was surprised and delighted to find the enchanting and almost-smiling blooms of Monkey Flower, a member of the *Scrophulariaceae* (figwort) family. Foxgloves, mulliens, snapdragons, speedwells and the figworts all belong to this genus. Growing beside the Monkey Flower was Brooklime, a member of the speedwell family with typically joined four-petalled blue flowers and two projecting stamens. It is a fleshy plant, liking wet conditions and bearing lustrous, glossy leaves. Just slightly higher and marginally drier are many tall-pointed columns of Common Spotted Orchids and the even taller Marsh Thistle, both purple-coloured, although the thistle had a sprinkling of white heads. This is not an uncommon occurence, as purple-flowered plants occasionally produce white specimens — I remember my puzzlement in the past on discovering a single, pure white specimen of Black Knapweed — which should have been a rich reddish-mauve colour under normal conditions! Jumbles boasts yet another relation of the figwort, Common Cow Wheat or 'cowbells' as they are sometimes known, a hemi-parasite which grows on the roots of other plants and is particularly partial to Heather and Bilberry or Whinberry. Its hooded, two-lipped yellow flowers sprout in pairs from the stem, much resembling tiny cowbells.

A cold, dull day at the end of October found autumn colours flaring; bronze Bracken; Oak and willows turning a burnished yellow and the Purple Moor Grass *(Molinia)* deepening into an unbelievable shade of red, the backdrop of overcast grey sky accentuating the autumn tints. Herb Robert, Knapweed and the umbellifers Hogweed and Sweet Cicely were still flowering on the eastern side, the Sweet Cicely giving off its unmistakable aroma of aniseed. The seeds have been utilised for hundreds of years amongst other things, as a flavouring in sweets, a constituent of cough linctus and as a carminative, which in other words in a cure for flatulence!

Steps on the right-hand side near the northern end of the reservoir lead to a hidden lodge pool covered in green duckweed, where Mallard were secreted away under the tree boughs on the opposite side, half-dozing, but casually observing my movements. Retrace your steps from here, to the path, and continue northwards up the stream, beyond the second concrete and iron bridge. The path becomes rugged along this pleasant tree enclosed, narrow river valley; a typically northern wooded clough with Oak, Ash, Holly, Sycamore, Hazel, Willows and, in the damp parts, Alder bushes. The banking here sports reddish-gold Bracken and a myriad shades of green in the leaves of Bilberry, Wood Fescue Grass, Woodrush, Hairmoss, Dog's Mercury, Opposite-leaved Golden Saxafrage and pale apple-coloured Wood Sorrel leaves, like an army of tiny three-sided umbrellas. Here and there, clusters of the dark Hard Fern are growing, characteristically stiff and unyielding, some with long, spiky fertile fronds standing tall from the centre of the plant.

The stream divides beyond this point, one branch being a man-made channel, probably built originally for the mill which disappeared when the valley was flooded. The path winds back and forth across the right-hand side of the valley and passes over a wooden bridge crossing an old goyt. On a dead silver birch stump, a magnificient Birch Polypore (Razor Strop Fungus) one of the bracket species, the size of a dinner place was sprouting. In times past it was cut into strips, dried and used to sharpen cut-throat razors. Later, I discovered a near relative, Beefsteak Fungus *(Fistulina hepatica)* which having been removed from its host, an Oak tree, was dying on the ground. Live specimens resemble prime steak in texture and even 'bleed' a reddish juice.

A party of two dozen or so energetic Long-tailed Tits flitted through the branches, tame and unconcerned about my presence, followed by a sprinkling of Blue Tits, Coal Tits and Great Tit. Further ahead, a Bullfinch signalled my approach with his oft-repeated single anxious notes and I caught sight of his blue-grey back and conspicuous white rump patch flying on ahead. Nearing the bridge at Turton Bottoms, beyond the secluded stone cottages, an overhang on the opposite side of the stream holds an exquisite display of graceful Lady Fern, and in the lower wetter recesses grows the common liverwort *Concephalum conicum*, its leaf-like appendiges resembling many spreading damp green tongues.

Emerging from the trees into daylight at Turton Bottoms bridge, it is possible to walk to the western side via the road; however, I prefer to return along the stream the way I came, rather than venture into the noisy carbon-monoxide world. There is time enough for this on the homeward journey! Also, you may spot something different and new which you missed on the way up; the inmates of habitats are constantly moving, especially the birds, and instead of a family of titmice, you may catch a glimpse of a flock of Siskin or perhaps a Sparrowhawk may flash by. It is the uncertainity and surprises of a nature ramble that appeals so strongly, in my view.

Return to the most northerly concrete and iron bridge, cross over and meander along the western shore. The hillside to your right here contains a mixture of larch and pine, and close by, in the Hawthorn hedgerow, the prominent rutile berries of a lone Guelder Rose were vividly lit, as I passed, by a tantalising shaft of sunlight, before fading into the background as the sable sky dissolved into a fine weeping drizzle.

Pass the fishing lodge on your right and follow the track round the inlet over the green iron bridge, where on my visit the view and its lovely autumnal colours were rendered subtle and blurred by gentle rain, the water pockmarked by the dripping trees. Pass Jumbles Sailing Club on the left and climb the stile. As I walked by, an extensive area of thistles and cleavers on the right expoded with a flurry of wings with prominent yellow stripes and patches, giving evidence of Greenfinch, Goldfinch and the flutey 'chirrups' of Linnets, which had been feeding on the thistle heads or pappus, until I disturbed them.

On approaching the farm, dogs *must* be kept on a lead, as the path passes between two cattle shippons with small gates at either end — *please close* these gates, behind you. Soon after, a track runs off to the right, uphill to Ousel's nest car park. Keep going, straight through the wide arcade of Lime and Horse Chestnut trees, multi-coloured and lovely even in the rain. Protruding from a stump were the black and white 'antlers' of Candlesnuff fungus, *Xylaria hypoxylon*. Turn left at the stile and sign-post for Jumbles reservoir and follow the descending stone track through the open field, to

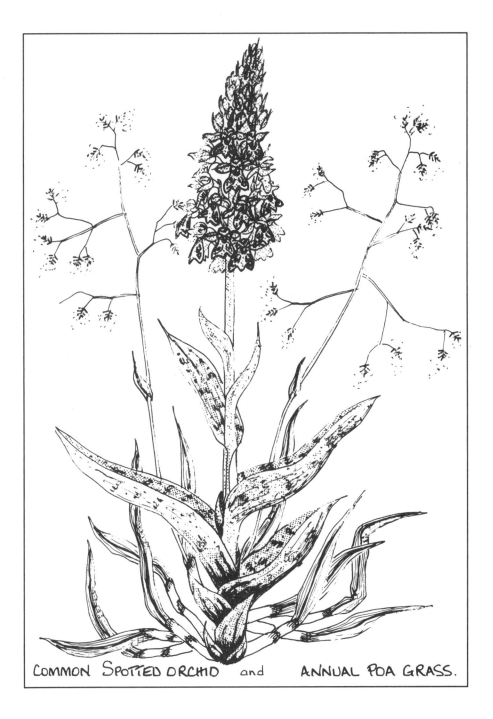

COMMON SPOTTED ORCHID and ANNUAL POA GRASS.

the green iron bridge at the bottom of the dam, diverting left up the steep steps leading to the main car park and welcome 'cuppa' from your flask! On this occasion, my sandwiches returned home with me, as rain-sodden bread is rather unappetising — such are the joys of the motor-cycling naturalist rambler!

QUICK GUIDE: Jumbles is the third and last of the three circular reservoir walks, (See previous chapters) and measures roughly three miles on reasonably good mainly level paths — though they become a little rugged towards the northern end beside the stream. A few stiles are encountered at intervals and one flight of steep steps near the car park. Can be cold and exposed. Pleasing panorama. BIRDS: Very similar to the preceeding chapter of Wayoh;. Though watch out particularly for common woodland species, wildfowl, grebes, finches, buntings, wagtails and warblers. FLORAL HABITAT: Mixed woodland, scrub, marsh and small wetland patches. Open water (reservoir).

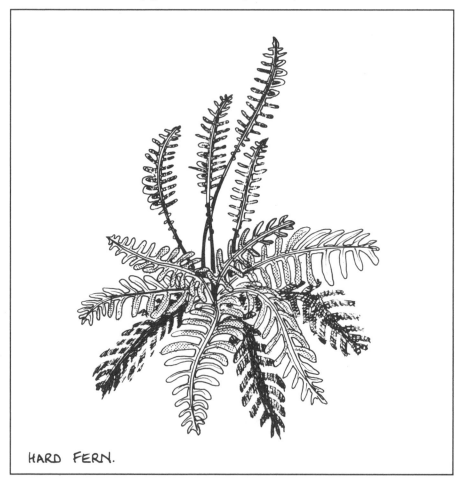

HARD FERN.

Mere Sands Wood Reserve, Rufford

THE woodland here, incorporating once-used sand pits, was not a recognised reserve when I first visited several years ago. Yet even then it showed promise for wildlife, which at that time was doing its best to survive whilst contending with much human interference and disturbance. Once the working life of the pits ended, the Lancashire Trust for Nature Conservation took over, by prior agreement with the sand company, to protect and enhance the area. Since then, things have improved substantially, both for resident wildlife and visitors — including nature's migrant visitors, as well as the human variety!

A number of hides have been provided, allowing watchers to observe without causing disturbance. The woodland walk, from one hide to the next, brings pleasant interludes in between periods of comfortable inactivity. As I write, work is going on, particularly with hide-building and I forsee, when this work is completed and the reserve only requires management, yet another welcome sanctuary wrought out of man's industrial left-overs. Mere Sands has been appointed as a Site of Special Scientific Interest, due to its unique geological history.

AMENITIES: The car park is open every day from 9.30 am to 5 pm. The gate is locked before and after these hours, though car parking is possible on the right hand side of the lane, before the gate, with access for able-bodied folk only (over the stile) out of opening hours. There is a toilet with no disabled facilities at the time of going to press. An Information Centre and Wardens Office is provided. Tel: Rufford 821809. The first hide, adjacent to the office is suitable for wheelchairs. Unfortunately, the circular walk at this venue is unsuitable for chairbound persons. You should make and take your own food if planning a prolonged stay. Dogs are allowed, on leads at all times please.

MAP REF: SD 447158. Travelling towards Preston, from Ormskirk, on the A59, turn left into the B5246 at the Hesketh Arms. The Mere Sands entrance track is on the left after approximately one and a quarter miles. Turn in and continue to the car park at the far end of the track, in the wood.

Over the last couple of years I have developed the habit of dropping into Mere Sands late in the afternoon to round off a day spent watching the high-tide wader activity at Southport. Although there has always been plenty to note in the afternoon at this water and woodland habitat, I aim periodically to reverse this itinerary and call into Mere Sands early, before dashing off to Southport to catch the tide!

Having parked in the lane I usually make the circuit in an anti-clockwise direction, climbing over the stile at the main gate and turning right along the path leading to the second hide. But first I have a quick look in the hide beside the information centre, which over-looks the now disused and transformed sand workings. Cockle shells have been liberally ladled around, partly to disguise the man-made devestation, though mainly to make these islands a suitable breeding site for Ringed and Little Ringed Plover, both having bread here intermittently in the past.

A recent look from this first hide found Teal and Coot milling around the pools, while a Little Grebe was

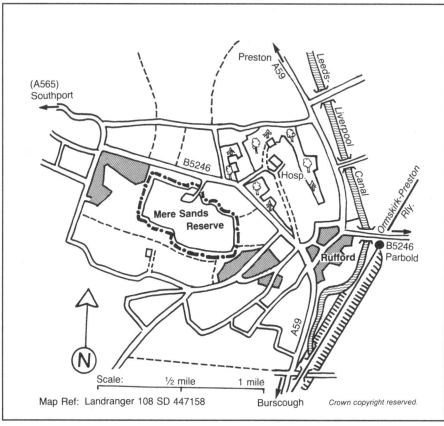

Preston
(A565)
Southport

Leeds

Liverpool

B5246

Hosp.

Canal

Ormskirk-Preston Rly.

Mere Sands Reserve

B5246
Parbold

Rufford

A59

N

Scale: ½ mile   1 mile

Map Ref: Landranger 108 SD 447158   Burscough   *Crown copyright reserved.*

working hard to feed its single chick, which was creating a fuss about meals 'arriving on time'. Its thin, high 'steeping' provided a continual backdrop of sound in the hide and a feverish prompt to the parent to catch food faster. This being middle September it did not have a great deal of time left in which to grow up and prepare for the harsh weather ahead.

A female Goldeneye appeared, swimming and diving, back and forth across the pool in front — another warning that winter is running to catch up with autumn. Further reinforcement of this thought was brought by the shrill, spine-tingling call of a Green Sandpiper . . . 'weet-a-weet . . . weet-a-weet' . . . which appeared flitting and flying in its typically nervous, jerky fashion, white rump positively glowing as he made several quick reconnisance glides, before settling in silence, out of sight to the rear of the main island. The Green Sandpiper is such a secretive species, and seeing one walking and feeding is an uncommon though delightful experience for the 'birder'. Normally all you would see and hear would be the bird suddenly canoning into the air, shrieking with alarm.

My attention was next attracted by a female Pheasant 'goose-stepping' up a small sandy rise, while a young Coot ambled, head down, up the opposite incline, until they came face to face at the top. Stillness followed for a second or two both within and without the hide . . . and as neither bird was willing to step aside and let the other go, a couple of head lunges led to a fully-blown fight, involving much jumping in the air and kicking. During this few seconds fraccas, a Hare appeared and ran past the opponents and I have yet to decide whether he was coming for a closer look or trying to get out of the way! Amazingly, the young coot won, despite being the smaller bird, and the pheasant had to retreat and go elsewhere. Minutes later, the wild flutey calls of Golden Plover were heard approaching and six birds were seen flying high overhead. They did not land, but continued, and judging by their direction, seemed to be heading directly to Martin Mere, the Wildfowl Trust Reserve — a scant two miles away for those flying in straight lines!

A heavy downpour abruptly resolved the question of whether to proceed further, or return home for the evening meal, and we decided to call it a day. Less than a week later, we returned in better weather and as only volunteer workers were visible from the hide nearest the office, we started out immediately along the track to the second hide, which overlooks part of the main mere. A very warm autumn afternoon found many Mallard dozing, while several robins lusty songs bombarded our ears and a Wood Pigeon flew overhead. Such was the strength of the sunshine that two Moorhen were observed deeply involved in protracted courtship rituals. Although the breeding season is technically over by September for many species, prolonged mild, sunny weather at this time can occasionally lead to an unexpected batch of chicks! Which has in fact occured this year (1986) when a female

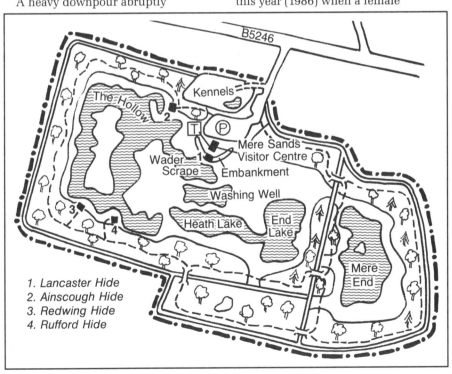

1. Lancaster Hide
2. Ainscough Hide
3. Redwing Hide
4. Rufford Hide

Mallard presented nearby Martin Mere with a very late surprise clutch of ducklings! These youngsters were assured of food and human assistance should the weather turn suddenly nasty, although, birds in the wild are not so blessed. However, the courting moorhens were not aware of this fact, and continued their tender preening around the neck of the other, whilst fanning their white-edged tail feathers. They were stood on a patch of green mud — which was probably beached duckweed when the water level dropped — and I speculated what a marvellous photograph this would make . . .

Coot, Tufted Duck, Pochard and Little Grebe were going about their business on the water and our arrival in the third hide brought clear views of the mere and several Pochard into close viewing range, their chestnut heads aflame with the lovely crystal lighting that only seems to occur in September. This hide would be better visited either early or late in the day, for by lunch time the sun is directly in your eyes. The path to reach this hide is screened on both sides by rhododendrons and Silver Birch and many of the birches on the reserve play host to the white Birch Polypore fungus, *Piptoporus betulinus*. One or two Foxgloves dangled a few listless, late flowers, while a patch of rowans were splendidly eye-catching — awash with pellucid autumn gold.

Swallows were dipping to the water and I wondered whether they were drinking, as it often supposed, or snatching insects trapped in the surface tension of the water. A few Ruddy Duck and Teal bobbed and circled on the mere, moving rapidly out of the way as a small flock of tufted, mallard and one Wigeon flighted in and skidded onto the water. Hoarse crackling cries . . . 'schiipe . . . schiipe'! . . . foretold a bevy of Common Snipe fast

approaching and they plummeted down to melt into the waterside rushes, while more wood pigeons passed hurriedly overhead. Perhaps a gun was being used not many miles distant. The loud weave of notes suddenly filling the hide from behind prompted us to exchange startled glances and a quick word . . . 'Garden Warbler — our back'! We went to investigate, but the irritating little bird refused to show itself.

We then set out to discover the fourth hide, on the left after crossing the bridge, enjoying on the way the serenity and naturalness of this scrubby woodland, where Redpolls were 'chupping' in the top-most twigs. Family parties of tit-mice played in the lower branches, in an apparently half-hearted quest for food, with much chasing and bouncing about. They were delighted no doubt by autumn's bounteous supply of insects. How different will be their demeanour within a few short weeks, when winter's hand takes a throttling grip and sends them out of the woodland and onto our garden bird tables, which help many birds stay alive in icy weather. Many would not survive without these 'handouts'. Besides peanuts, seed, fat and bread, bruised apples, bought at knock-down prices in the local market, will attract Fieldfare and Redwing, also Mistle Thrush and Blackbird, giving you the opportunity to bird-watch without leaving the warmth of your house, while also keeping these species from starving. If you have space in your freezer, during the summer you could pick a few bunches of elderberries, blackberries or hawthorn fruits, which will also be much appreciated by a variety of birds when defrosted and added to the fare on the bird table in the depths of winter.

Turning to plants fungi are abundant at this reserve in autumn, and Common Earthballs sprout by

COMMON SNIPE and SWALLOWS.

the hundred. Splashes of Coral Spot decorate many of the fallen twigs and the noxious stench of ripe Stinkhorn wafts over the path and, unbidden, up the nostrils at frequent eye-watering intervals! Others include the Blusher, Brown Roll-Rim, Common Inkcaps, Sulphur Turf, the Deceiver and 'plums and custard' its latin name an engaging mouthful — *Tricholomopsis rutilans*, which trips off the tongue rather splendidly! Add to these quantities of red, purple and yellow russulas and Ugly Milkcaps

(*Lactarius turpis*) which is difficult to see under the bracken and dying leaves — and you soon realise that taking your eyes off the floor for even a moment is likely to result in fungi being missed.

Although well hidden, the plaintive begging cries of young Coot and Little Grebe informs you that the water is not far away and we rounded the corner into the fourth hide, which also overlooks the mere, providing on this occasion a look at two Gadwall, the leaves of water lilies and stalks of fruiting Common Bulrush, though very little else. We moved away quite quickly, shortly to be confronted by a massive oak tree, its trunk evenly branched into four arms, reaching skyward, followed immediately by an equally impressive beech of matching proportions to the oak, its fine-grained silvery bark corroborating its great age.

The trail divides beyond these two lovely trees, and you can either walk straight on for the shortest route, or turn right over the ditch and rustic bridge for a slightly wider circuit. In the event I covered both routes, feeling that choosing one over the other would result in my missing something. This supposition proved correct, for Turkey Oak leaves on the floor at one spot led me to identify its owner towering above. Taking the other path, I found the common liver-wort *Lophocolea heterophylla* creeping over a dead log. The lichen *Cladonia conoicraea*, made up of bluish-grey scales, with pale twisted projections, was noted on a tree trunk. These projections are slender hollow stalks, coated with plant's powdery re-productive structures (soredia) containing algal cells trapped in fine fungal threads (hyphae) which result in vegetative reproduction of the plant. The moss *Orthodontium linare* was also recognised by its habit of growing round the bases of live tree trunks,

its fruit hanging downwards like a lot of green elongated clubs.

We were almost to the end of the circuit when my attention was attracted by 'plopping' noises at the top of an oak tree; it was a red squirrel, plucking acorns by throwing them to the floor. He was collecting for his winter store by emptying the tree first by throwing the acorns to the ground, then cramming them into his cheek pouches to carry them away . . . it saves all that running up and down the trunk, doesn't it?

The small lake, visible as you return to the car park, plays frequent host to Goldeneye and on occasion, Goosanders. The adjacent open land finds many plants flourishing in summer, although public access is not permitted to this sensitive area. However, the edge of this land, close to the public path, still had a prolific show of Century, many with tiny pink buds reay to burst into bloom, despite this being mid-September. Most had already seeded earlier in the season, assuring that this part will see more century flowering next year. One of the day-flying species of moth — Silver Y was fussing over the Ragwort as we came back to the main path, en-route for home and another late-evening meal caused by prolonged lingering in delightful Mere Sands Wood.

QUICK GUIDE: A pleasant circular woodland ramble, overlooking several meres. Paths reasonable, mainly level (a little muddy at times), with a choice of birdwatching hides. One stile to be negotiated if visiting 'out of hours'. Walk measures at most one and a half miles. Reasonably sheltered. BIRDS: Waders, wildfowl, grebes, game birds, common woodland species, tree, scrub and swamp warblers, buntings and finches. FLORAL HABITAT: Mixed woodland, heathland, scrub and wetland. Open water (sand pit floodings).

Martin Mere Wildfowl Trust

IN common with Leighton Moss, Martin Mere is a well known bird reserve, especially since the 'Mere' was the subject of the BBC's live 'Birdwatch' programme on New Years' Day in 1986. This gave most of the country an opportunity to take a peep at a reserve which everyone in the North West is privileged to have within easy reach for 363 days each year.

Time passes easily and quickly on a good day when five hours slips past like five minutes, for not only are there the truly wild birds to observe from a choice of nine hides, there is also the pen and pools section, containing both English and foreign pinioned wildfowl. These are maintained as breeding stock and are an invaluable aid for the world's rarer species. Autumn and winter are the best seasons for viewing wild waders, ducks, swans and geese at Martin Mere, although a trip or two during spring and early summer to view the antics of the captive ducklings, goslings and cygnets is a delightful and informative experience for all ages to enjoy.

AMENITIES: Admission charges are: £2; OAPs £1.30; young persons under 16 £1 and no charge at all for children under four years old. Admission is between 9.30 am and 5.30 pm in summer and 9.30 am — 4 pm in winter; the grounds are cleared at 6.30 pm in summer, and dusk in winter. Car and coach parking spaces provided, and disabled persons are allowed to disembark directly opposite the main entrance. Both sets of toilets incorporate disabled facilities. Ramps up to the hides are provided for wheelchairs, together with lower viewing slits in the hides for chairbound persons. A special trail caters for for the visually handicapped. There is also an information desk and Art Gallery, upstairs in the main concourse. A children's playground has been constructed and there are excellent educational facilities for all age-groups, by prior arrangement with the Trust's Education Officer. The coffee shop provides refreshments, although keen bird watchers like me may wish to make and take their own food, hot soup or stew in a flask being most welcome in winter. The reserve shop is well-stocked with a selection of tempting items, and an interesting book section full of wildlife titles. And don't forget the bags of 'duck-buns', available for feeding the occupants of the first pool who are always waiting to divest you of anything edible — including your packed lunch! . . .

MAP REF: SD 428145. Following the A59 in a northerly direction from Ormskirk towards Preston, go over Burscough's twin bridges, turning left into Red Cat Lane just over the summit of the second bridge. The entrance to the Trust car park is on the left after approximately one and a half miles.

Martin Mere shares yet another similarity with Leighton Moss — that indefinable air of keen tension emanating from the bird watchers sat hunched over their binoculars, telescopes and even a few high-pedigree cameras. Their excitement is well-founded, for the sights and more particularly the sounds of hundreds of wildly 'whooping' swans, clearly distinguishable above the softer Bewick's babble and strident honking klaxons of thousands of Pink-footed Geese, is indeed a magnificent live audio-visual display, which will brighten any winter afternoon.

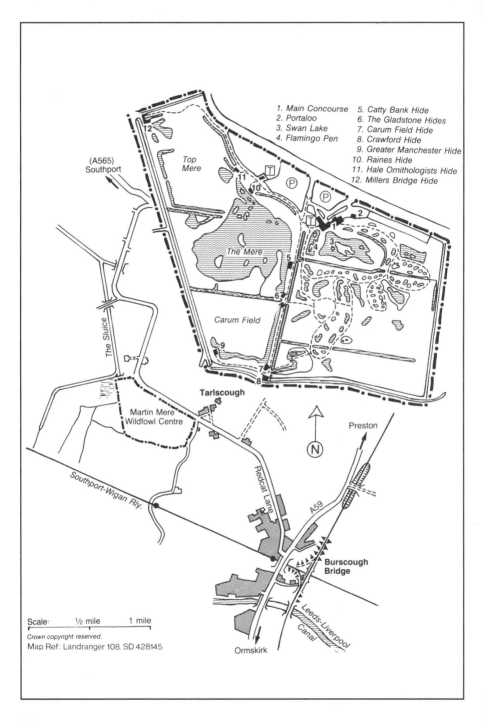

1. Main Concourse
2. Portaloo
3. Swan Lake
4. Flamingo Pen
5. Catty Bank Hide
6. The Gladstone Hides
7. Carum Field Hide
8. Crawford Hide
9. Greater Manchester Hide
10. Raines Hide
11. Hale Ornithologists Hide
12. Millers Bridge Hide

(A565)
Southport

Top
Mere

The Mere

Carum Field

The Sluice

Tarlscough

Martin Mere
Wildfowl Centre

Southport-Wigan Rly.

Redcat Lane

Preston

N

A59

Burscough
Bridge

Leeds-Liverpool
Canal

Ormskirk

Scale: ½ mile   1 mile

Crown copyright reserved.
Map Ref: Landranger 108. SD 428145

You can visit the hides in any order you wish; however, I always make my first stop at the Catty Bank Hide to scan the main water and obtain an overall idea of what may be on the 'bird watching menu' before moving off to other viewpoints. Many visits over the years have left lasting impressions on me . . . that close view of a Kingfisher posing on the fence in front of Millers Bridge Hide . . . both male and female Hen Harrier flying leisurely together along the out-lying ditch . . . the tired and bedraggled Ruff feeding round the edges of one of the pens, not 10 ft. away from where I was standing . . .

Then there are those occasions of which bird watching dreams are made — the Mere's main water covered with a startling variety of wildfowl, the immediate impression being a kaleidoscopic panorama of dazzling drakes; Mallard in sunlight with heads the colour of green bottles . . . Goldeneye trimmed in white and black, the angular head giving off a deep green glow . . . Tufted Duck sleek with more black than white on show and a purple irridesence to the black head which sports a cheeky dangling crest . . . Scaup, a confusing mixture of the two latter species, having tufted body shape, while the head is a dark greenish-black, no crest and the white sides merge with the grey back. This is indeed a lovely place.

The drake Pintail, as his name suggests, shows longer tail feathers, adding an extra eight inches to his body length, while his small chocolate-coloured head sits atop the long delicate white neck; in direct contrast, the Shoveler is large, dumpy, bull-necked and almost ungainly with the massive beautifully designed bill. Wigeon are more likely to be observed grazing the grass with the geese than swimming on the mere, and they are a lovely combination of grey and pink while the chestnut head and blue short bill is topped off by the striking buff crown stripe. An echo of the Scaup is found in the Pochard's black chest, bottom and grey back; however, the Scaup's dark head is replaced in the Pochard by a vibrant chestnut colour. The Gadwall, neat and grey, becomes almost non-descript among all this finery and likewise the Garganey — his most noticeable asset being the wide white eyestripe. Nevertheless, the prize for the smallest, most cheerful looking wildfowl must go to the Teal, his chestnut head, green eyestripe, pinkish breast and yellow bottom all contriving to make him resemble a child's toy.

Now, to distinguish the females — well its easy she's the brown duck with each drake; however, the identification problems crop up when she is viewed alone without her characteristic mate! (and qualified in 'birding jargon' as 'unidentified brown jobs') I soon came to realise that they are all perfect replicas of the drakes for shape and facial expression — merely lacking the bright colouring. Mallard ducks are large, ubiquitous birds with conspicuous violet-coloured lower wing feathers (secondaries) which are correctly termed the speculum in female wildfowl. The Goldeneye female is a perfect, if duller, reproduction of her mate, showing greyer shades and a drab chestnut head. The Tufted Duck is dark brown and wears an expression uniform with her drake — a bright, intense yellow-eyed stare — while her sides show the faint suggestion of paler patches. Although the female Scaup strongly resembles the Tufted Duck, she is in fact larger, and less compact-looking with a starkly noticeable white patch around the base of the bill — a characteristic the Tufted Duck displays to a much lesser degree.

Female Pintail are also slender-necked; however, the tail is pointed rather than long and perhaps the most characteristic feature is the grey bill on a small head. Shoveler ducks are a brown mirror-image of their drakes, carrying a similar impressive huge beak. The dumpy, rounded-looking duck (which always reminds me of a football with a tennis ball stuck on one end!) is in fact a female Wigeon. Two further characteristic Wigeon features are the high forehead in comparison to other duck species, and if visible, the pale shoulder patches. The poor Pochard duck is very nearly an insult to the immaculate drake, being a pale and rather scruffy replica of the male.

The Gadwall is perhaps the closest in appearance to the female Mallard, except she is smaller, neater and slighter and a glimpse of her white speculum avoids any further confusion. Garganey duck, in common with the Gadwall, are slightly bewildering and perhaps the best pointer to indentification is their greyness with noticeably paler edges to the feathers, particularly across the back. She is also quite small. Similarly, the female Teal is hard to confuse by virtue of size alone — she is toy-like in her tininess, with a conspicuous green speculum which also assists identification.

Having absorbed those guidelines, return to Martin Mere in late summer and early autumn for increased fun and headaches, when the drakes will be moulting and appear extremely similar to their females, except for very subtle differences, and the recently fledged young look like 'nothing on earth' . . . and you will appreciate why I said that five hours can pass as easily as five minutes!

Once you have mastered the art of 'duck-spotting', there are always the identities of the geese to sort out; Pink-footed and Greylag, Canada and Barnacle and occasionally Bean Goose and White-fronted, while even more rarely, one appears which cannot possibly be mistaken for anything other than what it is — a Snow Goose! Even so, I must admit that individual geese do not fire my bird-watching enthusiasm, though collectively they are a magnificent spectacle. It is simply a matter of personal choice. Of the 36,000 or so geese wintering in South West Lancashire each year, 16,000 are normally present at Martin Mere towards the end of winter — which more than justifies the upkeep of this mossland reserve. It is incredibly impressive when a raptor (be it Hen Harrier, Short-eared Owl or Peregrine Falcon) passes overhead, causing terrific alarm and sending the whole shrieking, babbling flock of thousands of birds en-masse into the sky.

Besides wildfowl, waders are much in evidence at Martin Mere and a collection of Lapwing several hundred strong were supplemented during our last late winter visit with 40 to 50 visible Ruffs — and it is quite likely that there were many more Ruffs hidden in odd corners. I also saw 20 or so Oystercatcher and a varying number of feeding Snipe, appearing and disappearing among the marshy hummocks, looking like so many well-oiled sewing machines as their long bills jabbed the mud with measured precision. In the spring, the arrival of large flocks of Golden Plover, many belonging to the northern race, showing the dividing white band around the black chest, evokes images of wild and fantastic places far to the north, their ethereal call proving a more magical and hair-tingling experience even than the sight and sounds of the geese.

Shelduck, Moorhen and Coot were noted in front of every hide apart from the Crawford Hide, which overlooks adjacent farmland. This hide, like the argicultural land it

PINTAIL.

observes, was suffering from a shortage of both birds and bird watchers on this cool winter's afternoon, providing a chance to sit and reflect in solitude — an unusual occurrence at this busy venue. In the far distance, a flock of Wood Pigeon was taking to the air, presumably in answer to the twin reports of a shotgun, the sound of their 'clapping' wings and noisy comment dulled by the distance between us. Rather nearer, the demented screaming of a Water Rail, that shy and elusive member of the crake family, floated clearly up to my ears from the neighbouring ditch. Late summer and early autumn should see much activitiy in front of this hide, as a variety of finches begin congregating to spend the winter in communal parties: Linnet, Corn Bunting, Greenfinch, Goldfinch, Redpoll and Brambling, while Pheasant and Partridge patrol the bare, fallow fields. The thought of all these small convenience meals-on-wings, doubtless cheers the

outlook for the local Sparrowhawk, making raptor life near Martin Mere a most desirable prospect.

The ditches bordering the paths to the hides hold their own interest in summer; dragonflies with their noisy 'clock-work' flight both hunt and breed here, as does the Moorhen. A spring visit revealed a female Moorhen incubating eggs, almost within hand's-reach — a gift for the camera — yet I noticed quite a few people passed by, without apparently seeing her, such was their hurry to reach the next hide.

The naturalist's day here is enhanced by two interesting plants, one of which has been deliberately introduced by man — Greater Spearwort, for it is no longer a common species due to the steady cultivation of our native wetlands. The other, Whorled Caraway (Carum verticillatum) is in its original and natural environment at Martin Mere, and unless it is discovered elsewhere in the county, this appears to be the only example growing in Lancashire.

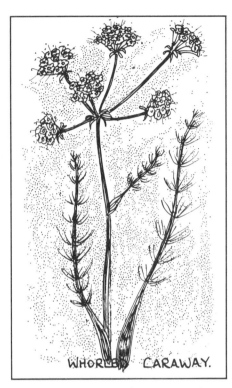

WHORLED CARAWAY.

Unfortunately, the caraway cannot be seen as it flourishes only in the Carum Field actually in the reserve, thus benefiting from the protection afforded to the wildfowl; a welcome bonus for conservation.

An outwardly hilarious incident coloured my last visit to the Mere, and will go into my memory along with the other high-lights — hilarious to us that is, but taken seriously, no doubt, by the birds involved. I had noted five Goosander keeping company on the Flamingo Pool at the outset of the visit and whilst photographing geese from the Gladstone Hides, the male of the party arrived on the water, to the left of these two hides, with the four females in hot pursuit. He seemingly did his best to shake off the four hussies, who were displaying their attractions to the point of 'working up a storm', heads and necks held out-stretched along the water and tails raised in invitation. The poor drake, one could almost say he looked haggard, showed not the slightest interest, in fact rather the opposite, and when the four suceeded in trapping him in a corner of the pond, he dived to escape and all four 'ladies' went down with him. As he emerged towards the middle of the pond, he shook off excess water and took to the air — with his four 'suiters' still in pursuit, leaving us chuckling and simultaneously and silently contemplating future cine cameras to replace our present slide 'stills'.

In conclusion, I can think of no better place this side of the famous Slimbridge for the novice to become proficient and knowledgeable about wildfowl in all its feather stages. Visits to Martin Mere can transform bird watching from a hobby into a specialised skill, eventually resulting in that deep, warm feeling of satisfaction generated by being able to correctly identify a pair of ducks seen flying in silhouette, or a small flock half a mile away in the middle of a lake, or two drakes in moult plumage at your local reservoir or pond.

QUICK GUIDE: A visit to Martin Mere comprises short walks between the various hides on good, flat surfaced paths and can be as long or as short as you wish depending on how many times you circle the reserve! There is a comfortable, warm, main concourse with all facilities, together with a variety of hides dotted around the reserve area. Excellent bad weather venue. *BIRDS:* Wildfowl, swans, geese, waders, raptors, Heron, Bittern on occasion, Kingfisher, game birds, finches, buntings, larks, and a variety of migrant species in spring/autumn. *FLORAL HABITAT:* Wetland and scrub. Open water (Meres, pools and ditches).

Ainsdale and Birkdale Local Nature Reserve

THIS is the second venue in my chosen trio of duneland habitats (see also chapters 16 and 24) and it is another botanists paradise. However, there is also a variety of breeding birds and the dune slacks contain water life, insects and plants which are a study in themselves. Whereas the adjoining National Nature Reserve (just south of this local reserve) requires a permit in advance to enter, the local reserve does not, but please keep to the marked footpaths, to avoid disturbing and destroying these invaluable wildlife places. Many careless, tramping feet wreak havoc in this constantly changing habitat of loose shifting sand, particularly the newer dunes on the seaward side, where sand colonising grasses have not yet established sufficient hold with their root system to 'fix' the habitat and hold the dune secure. This nature reserve is administered and protected by Sefton Borough Council.

AMENITIES: You must make and take your own food and refreshments. Toilets are near the entrance to the beach and also in Formby shopping centre, although both are quite often locked — especially on Sundays! Consider using the facilities in Southport before arriving here. Please keep dogs on leads in the reserve area. Unfortunately this outing is not suitable for wheelchairs and the walking is quite laborious even for the physically fit — the paths are hard-going in parts due to loose sand, there are slatted board-walks in places, although they are not extensive.

MAP REF: SD295117. Free car parking is available at the boating lake, opposite Pontin's Holiday Camp at Ainsdale: drive as though you were heading for the beach, and the opening to the car park is on the right, immediately following the large traffic island and pub. Walk to the beach, turn left and cover approximately half-a-mile, until a white-topped post is seen on the left, with an information board, and enter the reserve through this first row of dunes. Alternatively, you can pay to drive onto the beach during the season and park on the hard sand quite close to the information board and entrance of the reserve. Beach parking is normally free in winter — but beware — a high tide may just reach your parking spot!

This small reserve is a marvellous example of duneland habitat and information boards at intervals along the paths give explanations as to how the dunes are formed. Starr Hills and Ansdell Reserve near Blackpool are similar to this location, but the progression there from newly-formed dunes through to slacks (the wet depressions landwards of the dunes) and on to drier and more settled areas, furthest from the sea, is not as clear at Ansdell, partly due to the Blackpool road which divides the new dunes from the fixed areas. Here at Ainsdale and Birkdale, there are no such divisions to divert the eye and there is the added interest of pine woods.

The more I visit duneland habitat, the more I marvel at the number of species present; botanically these places are a treasure-house and after a while it becomes almost as interesting to note what does not grow here, rather than what does! Calcium lovers (calcicoles) grow in profusion, attracted to the heavy lime deposits of the broken shells in the sand. Yellow-wort is abundant, yet I have rarely found this attractive yellow flower with its petals fully opeed. Like Goatsbeard, which is also plentiful, it appears to be always either in bud of gone to seed! Other yellow-flowered varieties include ample spikes of the pale, flimsy and lovely Large Flowered Evening Primrose, the sulphurous and shiny-petalled Lesser Spearwort, the buttery gold of Kidney Vetch, and the greenish-yellow of the Wild Parsnip. All the shades from pale-pink through to the most brilliant purple are well represented too — Centuary, Marsh Pennywort, Marsh Willowherb, Purple Loose-strife,

Early Marsh Orchid, Common Spotted Orchid, Early Dog Violet, Rest Harrow and Tufted Vetch.

In the wetter parts, bordering the slacks, grow stands of bright green Spike Rush and the darker shades of various sedges. Closeby, the tall branched spikes and tiny white flowers of Brookweed appear and a few small blooms of pale blue Forget-me-Not and Blue Fleabane can be found. Pale flowers have a place here too, including the deliciously delicate Marsh Helleborine, the pale beige rosettes of Carline Thistle and the tightly packed head of the umbellifer Tubular Water Dropwort with its unusual characteristically double row of thin leaves. As

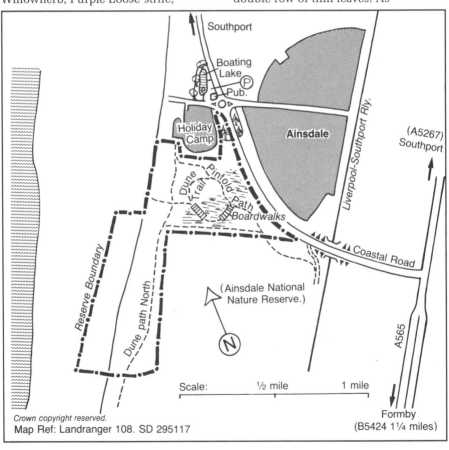

Crown copyright reserved.
Map Ref: Landranger 108. SD 295117

120

Autumn approaches, the creamy blooms and heavenly fragrance of Meadowsweet drifts on the fresh tangy air. Late in the season the Sea Buckthorn puts on a heavy dress of sparkling orange berries, beside the Hawthorn's blood-red fruits. Those unusual plants, the spurges, grow abundantly in this habitat; Sea Spurge is an obvious seaside plant with fleshy leaves which conserve water in this salt laden atmosphere and Cypress Spurge, with thinner leaves, which turn bright scarlet as the season advances are both in evidence. Neither plant has either sepals or petals; instead the male and female parts of this plant are housed in a greenish cup-shaped bract. Bugloss grows nearer to the holiday camp, in the sandhills, and early in the year under the pines between the camp and the main road, masses of Spring Beauty blooms. Its last pair of leaves, immediately below the flower, are joined and completely encircle the stem, causing the flowers to look as though they are sat in green saucers!

The so-called Common Frog, which in reality is not common anywhere nowadays, also flourishes in this habitat; so too I suspect, does the occasional snake. That snakes are undoubtably present is indicated by the unmistakable s-shaped tracks found in the firm sand before the wind has a chance to rearrange the dunes and cover the evidence. Like the frogs, perhaps the snakes live free from most interference in the settled areas which are densely clothed with Bramble, Creeping Willow and the very spiny Sea Buckthorn which affords protection to birds and mammals alike. You will also find the tracks of voles, mice, rats, birds and foxes-fox droppings can be found by the keen-eyed, together with owl and kestrel pellets — indigestible portions of the birds food comprised of feathers, fur, bones and beetle-cases which are

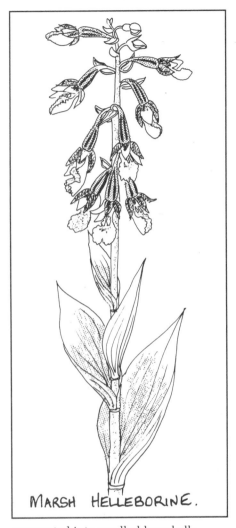

MARSH HELLEBORINE.

compacted into small oblong balls and regurgitated. In recent years, observations have shown that many species of birds can resort to this method of ridding themselves of inedible matter, not just birds of prey and owls.

If you have parked your car at the boating lake, you should make your return along the beach and if, like me, a frustrated beachcomber lurks in your soul, take a look along the tide-line, for it tells an interesting

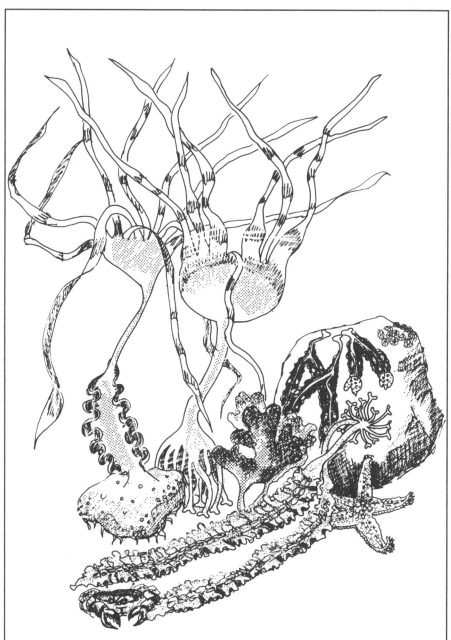

FURBELOWS, OAR WEED, BLADDER WRACK, HORNWRACK, and SEA BELT.

story about a part of life most of us will never have the opportunity to view firsthand — deep sea life. Many empty shells are washed-up, including Common Whelk, Thin Tellin, Variegated Scallop, winkles and Necklace Shells, Mussels, Razor and Tower shells. The tellins and necklace shells are often beautifully coloured in shades of pink and rose, yet for all their pretty colours and delicate looks, the necklace shells are both carnivorous and cannibalistic, feeding on other bi-valves (species with double shells) such as cockles.

The empty egg cases of skates and rays, so-called Mermaid's Purses, and the spongy round balls of empty Whelks egg cases are also a very common sight washed up on any shore. So too are the variety of seaweeds, torn-up by rough seas and left behind following stormy weather; kelps and wracks — some with lovely sounding names — Furbelows, Dabberlocks and Bladder Wrack! One species commonly encountered — Hornwrack — has pale flattened forked branches, resembling a seaweed, except the branches consist of small compartments, thus distinguishing it from the seaweeds. These tiny divisions hold minute animals (zooids) which have feathery antennae, filtering and traping small food particles floating in the water.

Amongst the dead flotsam and jetsam washed up on the shore are the live insects busy cleaning up the debris; Sand Hoppers, Bristletails and crustaceans resembling woodlice. These in turn are fed upon by wading birds, particularly Turnstone, in winter when there a few people to disturb them away from the cold and windy foreshore.

Once back at the boating lake, a short stroll round the accessible part at the southern-most end (the Southport end being impassable as it is boggy, with thick vegetation) will reveal an unexpected array of flowers, not great swathes as can be seen on the reserves, but a selection of many of the species associated with this coastline. You will see Marsh Helleborine, Common Spotted and Marsh Orchids and their hybrids; Kidney Vetch, Grass of Parnassus and an abundance of Yellow Rattle, plus Common Club Rush and occasionally Black Nightshade. This is also a very useful and interesting spot for any botanist who is unable to walk very far.

In some years, the poplars at the lake play host to Puss Moths, large pale moths with a three inch or more wingspan, and covered, as their name suggests, in cat-like 'fur', the forewings streaked with darker zig-zag markings. The hindwings are white with an outer ring of faded spots. The older caterpillar of this moth is an incredible sight, with a strange hump-backed posture, green-coloured with white spots below and black above, divided by a white line, the six forelegs alternately striped black and white. If provoked, it rears up, withdrawing the head to inflate a scarlet collar with two black false 'eyes' glaring malevolently, accompanied by whip-like curved filaments which can be protruded from the divided tail and waved menacingly. If all this actually fails to frighten, glands behind the head spray jets of formic acid at the intruder — accurately aimed at the eyes for maximum smarting effect! The early bird tackling this particular 'worm' would not find it a particularly easy 'victim'.

One visit to the reserve and boating lake in mid-September, following several hours watching waders at Marshside, revealed most plants to be still flowering, although not as profusely as in mid-summer. Common Scurvey Grass, Centuary, Yellow-wort, Grass of Parnassus, Water Forget-me-Not and great clumps of Water Mint, releasing aromatic menthol vapours whenever

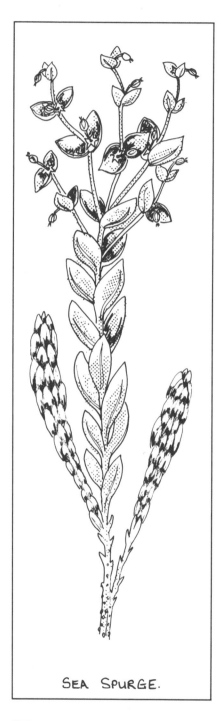

SEA SPURGE.

accidentally trodden on, were all in evidence. The tide was receeding quickly over the large area of flat sand, yet with the aid of binoculars we picked out a distant and solitary Manx Shearwater over the sea — unmistakable with dark 'uppers' and white underneath, flying with easy charming grace. A Great Skua was also distant, but heavy-looking, and displaying the obvious pale wing crescents and somewhat erratic flight. A slim, dark, long-winged bir flying with supreme ease was without doubt a Sooty Shearwater. All were quite a long way out, but silhouttes and modes of flight are very characteristic for many species and are an indispensible aid to indentification. Meanwhile, a flock of Oystercatcher were heading north, whilst the other rarities mentioned were all, without exception, flying south on migration. The Oystercatchers however, were returning from their roost to feed on the fast uncovering mudflats.

QUICK GUIDE: The interest of this quite small reserve is mainly centered on a circular stroll in the central area. The walk is of short duration (especially if you are parked on the beach next to the entrance) and measures $1\frac{1}{2}$ miles at most. There is an extension of the reserve heading south and traversed by the public Dune Path North, which you can follow for a mile (and return the same way) without leaving this local reserve. Walking however, is 'up and down' and rather difficult due to loose blown sand on the footpaths. Sheltered. BIRDS: Scrub swamp and tree warblers, Wren, Magpie, Kestrel, woodpeckers, thrushes, raptors, gulls and waders. Keep a look out for passage migrant seabirds, sea duck and divers on your way to and from the reserve. FLORAL HABITAT: Coastal, duneland, slacks (fresh water further inland, ranging to slightly brackish towards the beach) Lime rich flora.

Ainsdale National Nature Reserve

SPRING and Summer at this venue brings variations on the theme described in my previous two accounts of duneland (see chapters 16 and 23). The route I have chosen to write about, following the public footpaths which circle the outer edges of the National Reserve, removes the need to obtain a permit before setting out. Of course, if you do wish to explore the reserve in greater detail by 'straying' from these public rights of way, into the private areas, you must have a permit first, (issued free of charge) by writing direct to the Nature Conservancy Council, North West Regional Office, Blackwell, Bowness-on-Windermere, Windermere, Cumbria, LA23 3JR. The National reserve contains a number of specific and well publicised attractions, the most notable being the Natterjack Toad and Sand Lizard colonies and the Red Squirrels. For those feeling fit and energetic, this walk with the addition of a portion of the Ainsdale and Birkdale Local Reserve (no permit needed for the local reserve), can bring great interest, pleasure and diversity, and fill many hours, the distance being a little over five miles.

AMENITIES: There are no toilet facilities; the nearest public conveniences are in Formby (locked on Sundays) and Southport. Shops and a cafe are opposite the parking area, but you may be best advised to make and take your own food, especially 'out of season'. Dogs are allowed on the public paths but not anywhere on the reserve. Users of wheelchairs and cycles will not experience too much difficulty, by keeping to the stone track between Freshfield and the Coastal Road, close to Woodvale airport (see map). Unfortunately, the circular walk will not be possible for the handicapped because of the duneland terrain. Great care must be excercised with wheelchairs, prams, children and dogs at the railway crossing — this is a busy electric line.

MAP REF: SD 290100. Travelling south from the boating lake and holiday camp on the Coastal Road at Southport, turn right at the traffic lights onto the A565, and continue approximately two miles, turning right at the traffic island into the B5195. Drive straight on to the T-junction and turn right into minor road, continue round severe left-hand bend, cross the next junction, and then turn right at next T-junction. Take the first left turn and park your car on the spare ground on the right-hand side of the road, sandwiched between Freshfield Station and the bus turning circle.

Winter is a fitting time to consider the circular walk, which is invigorating in cooler weather, with plenty of interesting aspects which cannot be seen during summer, such as Crossbills and great parties of mixed finches, titmice and flights of waders. During summer, although the whole area boasts a superb flora, there are also sandflies, and worse, horseflies, together with lots of people: in my experience there is nothing more energy-sapping than toiling up and down sandhills, with the sun beating a tatoo on head and neck, followed by lukewarm fizzy drinks and gritty sandwiches! Yes, a winter visit has much to offer!

The Natterjack Toads are aptly named, for the males do indeed make a rumpus during their nuptials and the sound projects quite a distance, particularly at night. The word 'natter" is actually thought to be of Anglo-Saxon origin, meaning 'crawling creature', while 'jack' refers

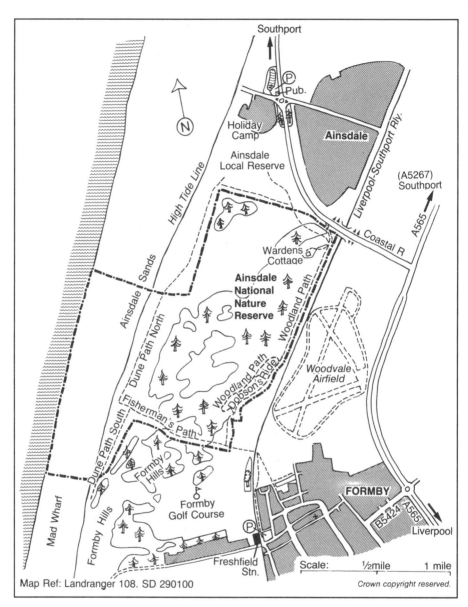

Map Ref: Landranger 108. SD 290100

Crown copyright reserved.

to the smaller size when compared with our Common Toad. The croaking chorus is, of course, not idle gossip; the males are advertising for mates and making very sure that their lady friends know exactly where to find them — quite an important point if one happens to be a rather slow moving reptile, living in thick undergrowth, (though they can run when the occasion demands). The male Sand Lizard adopts a slightly different approach to the serious matter of courtship, using bright colour, and a broad band of green passes along each side of his body. At its palest it is a lime green shade, at its richest, a brilliant emerald hue, reaching from his nostrils, down each flank, including both front legs and finishing above his rear legs; the remainder, like his female, is brown.

Our Winter-day walk, on New Years Day in 1986, dawned bright and promising, but as so often happens at this time of year, it deteriorated into dull dampness with a chilling breeze and finally rain. After parking your car, follow the track northwards, keeping the railway line on your left, until the crossing is reached — again extreme caution is required here, particularly for the hard-of-hearing and the elderly, for the trains are frequent, fast-moving and appear with little or no warning. Also, the line is electric, so keep both children and animals under control here and make sure you close the gates. Follow the path bisecting the golf course, and at the intersection with the Woodland Walk keep straight ahead for the beach on Fisherman's Path. You can, of course, make this circuit in which ever direction you wish, but by going clock-wise, the path close to the airport, which provides easier walking, comes last when my legs best appreciate it!

On the way to the beach I noted Scots and Maritime Pine growing along this stretch; Maritime Pine is easily recognisable in that its twin leaves, or needles, are the longest and the broadest in the pine family. Sea Buckthorn is prolific over most of the reserve and I saw a huge patch towards the seaward end clothed with pale orange berries which were past their prime, some almost white, yet a month or so ago they would have been scarlet. A tiny 2 inch patch of Yellow Brain Fungus sometimes known as Golden Jelly (Tremella mesenterica) captured my

attention, growing on bare twigs, the only splash of colour in several yards of drabness. Soon after, partially hidden on a stump, were a few remaining Brick Cap Fungi (Hypholoma sublateritium) — the red edition of the same family which includes the common fungi Sulpher Tuft.

Crossbills were shouting their loud double notes in the trees and a party of Goldcrest came searching every nook and cranny in both the pines and the willows, a few feet away from where we stood, giving lovely views of their acrobatics and tiny yellow-striped heads. A Collared Dove was singing monotonously — a harbinger of spring — and I suddenly recognised a spot in the reserve where two years before one of the wardens had pointed out countless spikes of the tiny Adder's Tongue Fern, which I had been unable to relocate on subsequent visits.

Our arrival at the beach was deliberately timed to coincide with high tide and as we 'bobbed' over the last dunes, flocks of Bar Tailed Godwit were streaming past, travelling south to roost, with a few Sanderling trailing in their wake. Just prior to this last row of dunes, the Dune Path North diverts off to the right in a northerly direction and we doubled back from the beach and turned into this grassy track, marked with white-topped posts. Once into this track I realised my mistake — what I had thought to be grass was actually the bright green lushness of a moss, Rhacometrium canescens, which clothed the sand in a lovely greenish-gold to both right and left of the path. A Greater Spotted Woodpecker flew overhead, calling loudly, and it felt odd somehow to see him so close to the sea. I smiled at my companion's description of his flight as 'two flaps and a glide' — most apt! A Kestrel was hovering above the reserve and several Magpies were bemoaning his

COMMON EARTHSTAR FUNGI.

presence, while a Blackbird and a Wren both complained stridently about everything!

Towards the northern end of the National Reserve, a series of settled mature slacks are found and in summer this coastline's fabulous plants bloom in and around these wet areas — though to see most of these you will need to leave the paths, and wellington boots might be required. You will also need your permit. A once-common plant, now becoming scarce elsewhere, but abundant here is Cuckoo Flower or Lady's Smock; the lovely wine-red, star-shaped flowers of Marsh Cinquefoil are a delight. While the tiny white flowers and unusual

dangling s-shaped style of Round Leaved Wintergreen gives me a pronounced 'botanical twitch' as does the beautiful white petalled flower Grass of Parnassus, with its green-veined snowy flowers. This is really in a class by itself — both figuratively and literally — belonging to the genus *Parnassiaceae*. Add to these the orchids and helleborines and, botanically speaking, this reserve its sheer heaven!

However, I digress from my winter walk; near its northern end the Dune Path North diverges, one continuing into Ainsdale and Birkdale Local Reserve, the other turning right to follow the fence towards the far reaches of the Woodland Path. The first path is easier, if a little longer, whilst the latter becomes confused and difficult in places, requiring a scramble through a clump of Sea Buckthorn — not very pleasant, due to its thorns! The easier path undulates through the Local Reserve and when you arrive at a cross-roads in the paths, turn right to follow the often indistinct track (covered by loose blown sand) towards the northern end of the conifer belt, near the Coastal Road. Fieldfare and Redwing were disturbed from their feasting on the buckthorn berries and flew away 'chacking' and 'tseeping.' Another, or possibly the same Greater Spotted Woodpecker we encountered earlier could be heard hammering a tree bole in the distance and a party of Long Tailed Tits came twittering from one bush to another, their calls reminiscent of two or three pebbles being stuck together.

A fungi found at this northern end provided the botanical 'twitch' of the day — I was especially delighted with

NATTERJACK TOAD.

my discovery of Common Earthstar, *(Geastrum triplex)*; a pity they had darkened and gone beyond their best, although they were still quite recognisable. Their appearance is not unlike the puffballs, except that there is the added attraction of the 'spore bag' sitting in a 'saucer' on top of a star-shaped structure — lovely.

Follow the track round to the right at the end of the pines, past the entrance lane to the wardens house and join the broad stone track of the Woodland Path southwards back to Freshfield, sandwiched between the fir trees and the railway. The open rough ground all along this stretch is marvellous for flora during Summer, with great stands of Large Flowered Evening Primrose towering on the right-hand banking. Oil from the cultivated variety of Evening Primrose is now popular, sold in capsule form and said to be successful in dealing with stomach and intestinal problems and also ladies disorders. Red Bartsia, Common and Viper's Bugloss and the 'furry-feet' of Haresfoot Clover, along with Yarrow and Ragwort accompany your stroll on Fisherman's Path in the Summer months. You may also be lucky and come across small amounts of Black Nightshade, Wild Asparagus, Wild Carrot, Tuberous or FyfefieldPea and Broad Leaved Everlasting Pea.

Dune Helleborine grows in the reserve and in Autumn I came across its dead seed heads in a number of spots. Many varieties of fungi fruit here, and perhaps the most obvious and well known is the Fly Agaric — those red toadstools with white spots portrayed in fairy tales involving elves and dwarfs! There are many bright russulas, various boletes (some quite large) and several species of puffball and milkcaps, which all help make this an attractive venue for a fungal foray in Autumn: I am informed at least 430

species have been recorded here.

One area on the return stroll holds many bunches of the lichen *Cladonia portentosa*, at first glance resembling yellow scouring pads! Pixie Cup, another variety of *Cladonia* grows in sheets, while two mosses draw the eye here too, one richly green and hair-like, most of its fronds pointing in the same direction is *Dicranum scoparum*. The other — *Leucobryum glaucum* is a pale 'bluish' hue when wet and almost white when dry. *Leucobryum*, more so than any other moss (except perhaps the sphagnums) has a great capacity for holding water — it can literally be squeezed out like a sponge!

This New Year's Day walk ended in the dwindling twilight of a mid-winter afternoon with the promise of imminent rain. The prospect of a waiting flask of hot coffee and a 'nip' of rum back at the car, hastened our return footsteps!

QUICK GUIDE: The described circuit just inside the perimeter of the reserve is slightly longer than five miles. If you obtain a permit in order to 'wander at will' this walk could quite easily exceed eight or nine miles. Paths vary from level to undulating and good to non-existent! I would classify this walk as moderatley difficult owing to sandhill terrain and it can be tiring. Consider visiting a section at a time — one day Woodland Path and another Fisherman's Path, for example. Can be bitterly exposed in winter and hot and airless in Summer. *BIRDS*: Titmice, Goldcrest, Crossbill, scrub and tree warblers, waders, seabirds. Occasional seaduck, raptors and passage migrants. *FLORAL HABITAT*: Coastal lime-rich duneland, slacks, buckthorn scrub and pinewoods. *FAUNA*: Toads, lizards, Red Squirrel, foxes and a rich variety of insect life.

Nob End, Farnworth

NOB END is only a very small part of the Croal-Irwell Valley, although it is certainly a rather unusual part. It has not been over-tidied or made 'pretty' as is too often the case in town-based country parks, resulting in unnatural looking placid areas of closly-shorn bright green grass which in the context of this book are relatively useless for wildlife. At Nob End, any kind of beautifying or alteration would destroy the unique habitat — even though it was originally man-made by the dumping of lime-rich spoil, discarded by former industry. In the 18th century Wilson's Willow Works concentrated on manufacturing soda crystals by the Leblanc process and this operation resulted in the dumping of lime-rich vat wastes, giving rise in later years to Nob Ends fabulous lime-loving flora. Consequently, the attractions of this venue will be best appreciated either by botanists, or by folks who wish to view part of our fascinating industrial metamorphosis. I must admit that the scene was robbed of something important when the cooling towers which so dominated and complemented this urban landscape

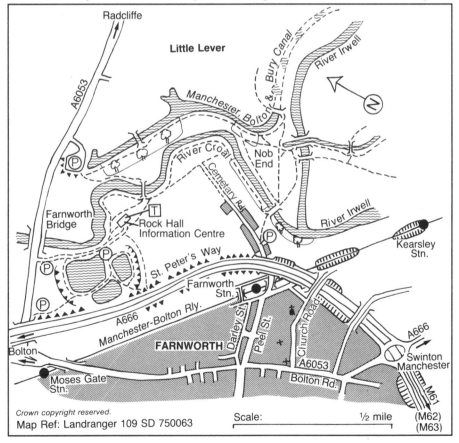

Map Ref: Landranger 109 SD 750063

Scale: ½ mile

were demolished and my mind's eye cannot quite reconcile itself to the 'empty space' on the skyline. However, if you prefer to visit aesthetically rural places for leisure then this venue is probably not for you.

AMENITIES: No special facilities are available here — you must strictly make your own. Unfortunately, although the actual area is flat enough for wheelchair pushing the access path is steep, un-even and not suitable for chair-bound persons. Dogs are allowed — but on leads please. Toilet facilities and official car parking are available at the Rock Hall Information Centre — a right turn from the A6053 Hall Lane, before Farnworth Bridge, when travelling in an easterly direction towards Little Lever, from Farnworth. For further details telephone the warden service at Rock Hall on Farnworth 71561.

MAP REF: SD 749062. Travelling from Bolton to Kearsley through Farnworth, make a left turn into Darley Street, adjacent to the building society premises. Continue to the T-junction and turn right, by-passing the Rawson's Arms public house. Take the next left turn over the railway bridge adjacent to Farnworth Station, continuing under the A666 St. Peter's Way, finding a parking space anywhere in Cemetery Road, being careful not to obstruct residents access to housing or garages. Follow the track down the grass verge, over the iron bridge and into the open "vee" of land sandwiched between the Manchester, Bolton and Bury canal and the rivers Croal and Irwell — to that small area called Nob End. Leaders of car-borne parties may be better advised to park at the Moses Gate centre and walk the short distance to Nob End, rather than cause annoyance to the residents in Cemetery Road.

Early July is probably the best time to view the flora and because this is such a compact venue, around two hours is ample time to see everything of interest, even for people like me who, sometimes feels inclined to conduct a fine-tooth-comb search! This site, perhaps more so than any of the others I have covered, could easily be dubbed the 'botanist twitchers' paradise — flower lovers are often encountered and are easily recognised by their glassy-eyed expressions and reverential tip-toeing gait!

However, the most surprising thing about this site is not the rarity of the plants, but the fact that they are in this industrial wasteland at all. Without man's original intervention in dumping the lime-rich spoil they would not be here. Industry, it seems, is not always detrimental to some forms of nature — particularly plants — which have the ability to rise from 'man-made' ashes and many might even survive a nuclear holocaust. The same cannot be said for us . . .

My descent towards the iron bridge found the path in August bordered by thick growth; bracken and balsam along with Great and Rosebay Willowherb were particularly evident. Honey bees were abundant over the whole area, and their choice of flowers was cosmopolitan. I wondered if there was a local 'Croal Valley' honey for sale somewhere close by and this is not as crazy as it might sound — read on for a selection of gorgeous flowers the bees were collecting nectar from.

Rosebay Willowherb and August bring another insect to mind — the fantastic caterpillar of the Elephant Hawk Moth, which may be found by the fortunate — or those who search diligently during this month on Rosebay. The threatening posture of

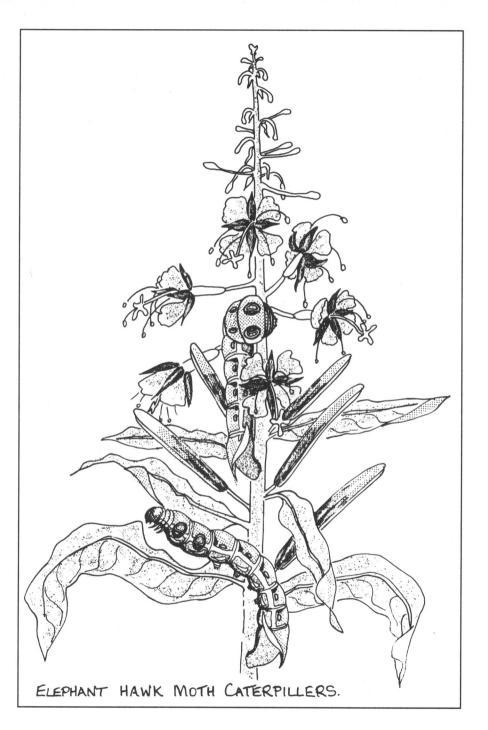

ELEPHANT HAWK MOTH CATERPILLERS.

this caterpillar — showing false 'eyes' — is spectacular, if a little less colourful than those of the Puss Moth.

The iron bridge spanning the River Croal is quite high and a good vantage point to see and hear passing Kingfisher, Grey Wagtail and occasionally a Heron, surprised whilst wading the murky edges. Even so, the Croal, in common with Lancashire's other rivers, is slowly becoming cleaner owing to lessening industry and the acceptance of more enlightened ideas about the effects of pollution. A male Blackcap was singing lustily in spring from the thick undergrowth beside the river and he sounded just as confident of attracting a mate, as any Blackcap heard in more traditional country surroundings. We may feel after visiting that it was not a lovely countryside walk with all the sights, sounds and scents this implies, but nature unlike us, really doesn't mind where it is and our desolate and abandoned industrial left-overs are a heaven-sent opportunity for natural life to rush in and take over once again, each species trying to reproduce and gain a foothold faster than the next. Autumn shows, by the characteristically shiny red berries, that the small bushes to the left of the bridge, as you start to cross, are Guelder Rose, if you visit earlier in the year, the flowers in Spring are just as impressive as Autumns' fruit - scented halos of wholesome white, the outer flowers of each bunch being much larger than the inner florets. Rowans are dotted about the banking too and their berries were pale and anaemic in early August; nevertheless, a couple of weeks will see them ripe and speedily disappearing as food for thrushes and blackbirds, among others!

Once over the bridge, I usually keep to the right-hand paths, shallowly zig-zagging back and forth until the river Irwell prevents further progress. Hemp Agrimony is making a fierce stand for independence on the banks of both rivers in 1986, rapidly spreading its tall maroon-stemmed clumps of pinkish-mauve flowers, much favoured by butterflies, for sunbathing as well as feeding, especially the Small Tortoiseshell species.

Paths — and regrettably, motorcycle tracks — criss-cross lower Nob End, although much is being done to prevent disturbance by people who do not yet understand that this is not another peice of forgotten waste land abandoned to dereliction. The Fragrant Orchids for which Nob End is also so famous will not benefit at all from the disturbance caused by the motorcyclists — especially during the flowering season. Only one or two orchids were still in bloom on my last visit, the majority having set seed and I noted with curiosity that these Orchids appear to be gaining in height as the years pass. At Hawes Water the Fragrant Orchids remain a constant size with neat spikes of an unvarying height, whilst Nob End seems to me to be fathering expanding giants! Marsh and Common Spotted Orchids also add to the riot of colour here, though their flowering time is a little earlier than the Fragrant species.

The lime-rich soil deposits host an otherwise predictable cast: Carline Thistle, Purging Flax, Blue Fleabane, Centuary and Eyebright are prominent. However, there must be pockets of a more acidic soil here and there, for a variety of species occur which might not normally be considered as compatible with the plants I have already mentioned, including Tormentil, Devil's Bit Scabious, Sneezewort, Yarrow and (in Autumn) the huge leaves of Coltsfoot and Butterbur. There is also Tufted Vetch and Meadow Vetchling, cinquefoil, hair moss, and Heather and I therefore conclude that the soil must vary from heavily alkaline to partially acidic — and all the shades in between. Blue Fleabane has a characteristic clock or pappus, small tight and milky-coffee coloured in appearance. There was more of it dotted around than I had first thought too.

Several friends tell me that Blue-eyed Grass is to be found at this site. However, I have yet to be lucky and come across this species, which only opens in full sunlight — perhaps it is always cloudy when I visit? In fact, it is not a grass at all, but a member of the *Iridaceae* (Iris) family. Furthermore, neither does it have a 'blue-eye' — the flower centre is yellow — it is the petals that are blue . . . small wonder that we amateur botanists occasionally become confused!

At least four species of fungi were making a fresh appearance, pushing through the ash. Two species were clearly *Hygrocybes* or 'wax caps' as they are more commonly known, both for colour and shape. Some were bright yellow, shading to orange round the cap edges, while others were paler and of a more citrine colour in both cap and stem, and all looked like so many tiny rockets. The Deceiver, *Laccaria laccata,* was also found and is aptly named — it always fools me at first! It has a particular tawny shade, wavy cap edges and irregular, widely-spaced gills. The final species I identified was *Leptonia lazulina* and is small and dark and not very outstanding, yet a closer look reveals its distinctive striated cap, bluish flesh, and 'pinkish' coloured spore dust. It also has a strongly appetising smell, although, *be warned* this mushroom is poisonous.

At the top of the 'vee' of land turn left, where you will find the herbage changes from stunted Hawthorn and bare ashes clothed in orchids, to willows and lush grass full of clover and vetches. These clovers and vetches play host to another Nob End speciality, the parasitic Common or Lesser Broomrape. Like the Toothwort at Hawes Water, this plant is a member of the *Orobanchaceae* (broomrape) family and lacks both leaves and the colour green, taking its nourishment directly from the host plant, instead of synthesising its own food, like the majority of plants do.

Part of the canal which butts into this eastern end of the 'vee' is worth a look in passing. Both Hedge and Marsh Woundwort grow, the former sprouting from the dry banking and the latter, as its name suggests, preferring the parts where the canal is silting, yet still wet. The low growing umbellifer Fools Watercress was crawling and scrambling about the water edges, helping to clog things further, while Common Duckweed added to the jumbled tangle building up between the reeds and Sweet Flag. The crumbling brickwork sported the fern Black Spleenwort out of the cracks illustrating that all things man-made are speedily reclaimed by nature given just half a chance — a fact appreciated by many a gardener!

The sun peered out weakly but warmly for a short spell during my last call here, prompting a dragonfly into noisy flight — it was instantly recognisable as the species *Aeshna grandis*, owing to its brown wings and long, slim body. It hawked, rather surprisingly, over the ground ignoring both rivers and canal, settling during cloudy spells, not in the water grasses as might be expected, but in the various willow bushes. Each time the sun briefly reappeared, the dragonfly burst forth into renewed action.

Of the other plants there seems to be an almost bewildering array of the yellow dandelion-type species, although I finally narrowed them down to four on this occasion. The tall Perennial Sow Thistle, Autumn

WAX CAPS, the 'DECEIVER' + LEPTONIA LAZULINA.

and Lesser Hawkbits and Spotted Hawkweed, all with yellow blooms. The purple shades from this family, Creeping and Spear Thistle and knapweeds, added to the distinctly autumnal atmosphere, much increased by several parties of both juvenile and adult Linnets, flitting and 'chuttering' about the herbage. The flock of Lapwing gathering in the adjacent fields also sounded the knell for the end of Summer and the slowly decaying slide of the third season into the chilly embrace of the fourth.

Those with time to spare should explore more of the Croal-Irwell Valley, after a visit to Nob End, and although the country park as a whole does not improve in scenic beauty, its natural history is rich and varied and well worth looking for. Past visits have produced such unusual plant delights as Chicory, Creeping Jenny, Vervain, Greater Knapweed, Fig-leaved Goosefoot, Zig-Zag Clover and Marsh Cudweed, none of which can be said to be everyday discoveries. As far as birds are concerned, the valley boasts interesting records of waders resting at the Clifton sewage pools during migration. Bird-watching at the old type sewage beds is often rewarding

— providing your sense of smell is poor, or better still, non-existent! Natural air pollution however, is not the problem at Clifton, rather noise and carbon monoxide — for one of the busiest sections of the M62 motorway runs close by, and given a choice, I prefer to do my wader-watching whilst inhaling the 'fumes' of our coastal ozone!

QUICK GUIDE: Undertaken as a walk, Nob End at best measures no more than a mile, including tracing any one of the footpaths which criss-cross this small area of grass, ashes and scrubland. There is a steep descent from the Cemetery Road approach to the iron bridge (and it appears even steeper on your return!) Paths are reasonably level after the bridge and usually dry, this being a mid-summer outing for the best results. BIRDS: Common garden species, tree and scrub warblers, finches, buntings, larks, wagtails, Lapwing. Occasional Heron, Kingfisher and Kestrel. FLORAL HABITAT: Lime-rich, highly alkaline with neutral to slightly acidic pockets and bankings. Open water (two fast-flowing rivers, and canal — part containing static water.)

136

Wigan Flashes

IN common with the Pennington area before the creation of the country park (see following chapter) the panorama of Wigan's flashes (a 'flash' being the correct term for these expanses of water caused by mining subsidence) at the time of writing holds nothing pastorally pleasant or scenically attractive to the human eye. Instead, as at Pennington, it testifies to man's ability to create an industrial moonscape of desolation. Thankfully, wildlife appears to lack our 'inner eye' and indicates by its abundance and diversity that it is flexible enough to attempt and suceed in the colonisation of the most unlikely sites.

The amount of flora and fauna found at this venue, accompanied by the appearance of twice-yearly migratory avian species, is awe-inspiring and the potential of this wildlife haven is incredible. It cries out for recognition and protection. Back in the 1950s, Sir Peter Scott visited this location and advocated that a reserve should be made of these waters. Unfortunately, his recommendation was not acted upon at the time, for in those days nature reserves and country parks were virtually unheard of. Now, at last, in 1986, changes are on the way for Wigan's waters, though none so sweeping or great as to threaten the fantastic wealth of life which is already here, or ruin the potential for more to arrive. At the time of going to press, the whole area was under discussion to become a country park incorporating an ecological reserve and I foresee, if the development is properly achieved, an unbelievably rich and varied wildlife park which will rank high among the country's other outstanding reserves. It will, give Wigan another 'feather in its cap' to add to its already famous and redeveloped pier complex.

AMENITIES: There are no special facilities at the time of writing (late 1986) so you would be advised to make and take your own hot food and drinks, particularly for winter wildfowl visits. Unfortunately, this venue is not suitable for chairbound persons at present, although development plans for the future park will doubtless include all the associated amenities of toilets, including disabled facilities, car parking, hides, lecture and educational resources, reinforced by a wardening scheme. Dogs are allowed.

MAP REF: SD 580040. Travelling west towards Wigan on the A577 from Hindley and Leigh, turn left into the B5238 (Poolstock Lane), which connects the A577 with the A49. Pass under the railway and keep straight at the traffic island. Continue for approximately half-a-mile, turning right into Pool Street, immediately before St. James church, and then turn first left to find a parking space anywhere in the street, wedged between the gardens and the church frontage. After parking, retrace your steps, turn the corner back to the busy B5238, cross over and ascend the canal banking, turning right at the top for the walk beside the canal bisecting the two largest waters, or 'flashes' — Scotsman's on the right and Pearson's on the left.

People who know from previous experience what awaits at this venue, have two very different wildlife motivations, at opposing times of the year, for visiting what sounds and looks otherwise like a rather unappealing spot. Folks who have not already discovered this place tend to give you some odd looks when the conversation goes

137

something like this:

"Where are you off to today then — somewhere good?"

'Yes — Wigan Flashes . . .'

They frown and you can see them thinking 'how thrilling . . .' — and *that's* the funny part about it — it *can* be thrilling!

A winter wildfowl walk, though often a bitterly cold experience, exposed to every vicious blast of arctic wind, can be rewarding, provided Scotsman's Flash still has some open water and is not completely frozen over, in which case a panorama of duck will be seen going about their business. Setting off well wrapped up may allow you to linger just long enough to carry out a duck-count, when you may suddenly become aware that one of their number turns out to be a Great Northern Diver or a Slavonian Grebe. Not that an appearance by either of these two rare birds can be guaranteed, but they have put in

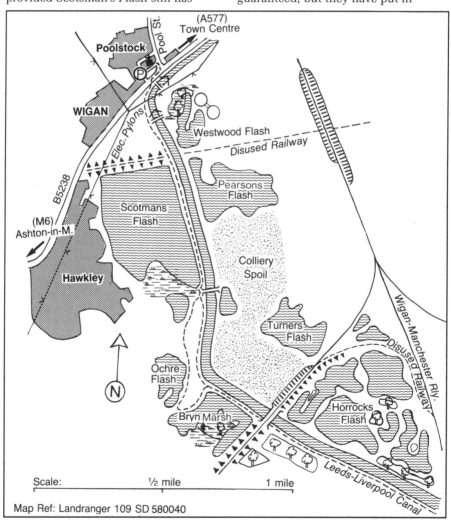

Scale: ½ mile   1 mile

Map Ref: Landranger 109 SD 580040

sporadic appearances here over the years.

Glancing left over Pearson's Flash, while making your way along the canal path, often reveals Goldeneye and Cormorant diving for food. I presume the water is quite deep in this flash, for 'dabbling duck' (compared with 'diving duck') seem instead to prefer the larger Scotsman's with its shallow, sloping edges. The cormorants sit in the dead trees above Pearson's Flash, with wings outstretched, reminiscent of a cross between a vulture and the bat-like creatures from a Hammer horror film! These same dead trees, when not tennanted by cormorants, sometimes host passage Osprey, resting from their migration routes. So far, my walks here have not coincided with a visiting Osprey, though friends report excellent views of these beautiful birds from time to time; usually during the months of April or May. Nevertheless, I always scan the dead branches with care, no matter what the time of year, in the faint hope that one of those cormorants might turn out to be something larger and altogether more impressive, with a hooked raptor beak and pale flinty eyes, grasping a fish with massive grey scaley claws, ending in wickedly pointed huge black talons!

However, I digress. Back at Scotman's Flash, you may enjoy views of species such as a single female Smew, a drake Ferruginous Duck, or occasionally a Long-tailed Duck bobbing among the great rafts of commoner species — mallard, Tufed Duck, Shovelar, Canada Geese, Coot, the increasing numbers of Ruddy Duck and the diminishing Mute Swan. By the way, high winds at this venue can make your eyes watery and the binoculars difficult to focus — but that is all part of the appeal of bird watching.

Personally I derive little pleasure from seeing rare sea-birds inland that the weather has forcibly driven from their normal environment. I prefer to see the unusual species which, although not regularly encountered, do migrate through Lancashire quite normally in small numbers and without too much obvious mishap. The eager anticipation of seeing rare visitors following gales seems more than a little morbid and I fail to find any cause for celebration, having cared for a variety of distressed and injured species over the years. For example, a gale-blown Manx Shearwater recovered in our bath on a diet of tinned pilchards . . . there was also a young House Martin, a victim of September gales, which slept to recovery on the clothes-horse beside the ironing. A migration Wheatear, newly arrived, rested wearily in my cat's basket (but not at the same time as the cat!) and on another occasion a poisoned Dunlin died slowly in one living room chair, while a female Kestrel recovered in the opposite chair, taking a few days to get over her wind-blown tangle with overhead wires. The sight of rare diving birds inland causes me the most distress, for all-too-frequently they prove to be sickly and sooner or later are found dead, their once powerful frames pathetically wasted. The post-mortem examination often reveals this to be the result of starvation or internal damage sustained during severe weather. For most of the time birds are indeed 'lords of the air' but at the same time, our feathered friends suffer appallingly when the weather is rough and I feel we 'birders' ought to bear this in mind when getting excited about seeing a bird which is really outside its normal environment.

Incidentally, in view of my disclosure regarding sick and injured birds, perhaps I should mention that taking these birds home and caring for them is a mammoth task, requiring hours and sometimes weeks of nursing and should not be undertaken lightly. And of course, young birds should *always* be left in their parents care and not taken away, for they are seldom lost. They might look anxious and afraid, but more often than not this is simply because you are too close.

However, returning to our winter walk along the canal, a surprise was awaiting on the small water near the railway known as Bryn Marsh. A small open patch, near the reeds, was not stilled with ice, and three wild and wary Whooper Swans were "hooting" softly with alarm at the sight of two humans, emerging from the snowstorm, where ten minutes before there had been nothing but a few stray flakes . . . the snow was wet and sticky and we were so coated as to look more like a pair of 'Yeti'.

Our last visit at the end of September revealed a Kingfisher flying along the canal near Bryn Marsh. It veered sharply away, shouting with alarm on seeing us, dropping down below the far banking to continue flying, out of sight, only to reappear still flying and shouting further along the canal. We thought that there may be a late brood of recently fledged young nearby. The adult in beautiful plumage, its colouring accentuated by the overcast autumn weather and grey water, flew on, passing through the railway arch, its sharp call bouncing off the walls as it continued its flightpath, following the canal.

Wigan's waters are also a fascinating place to visit during the summer months, when a search for interesting flora frequently results in the discovery of a variety of resident nesting birds. Perhaps the adage should not be 'killing two birds with one stone' but 'finding two birds with one flower . . .?' The area around Westwood Power Station and its two gigantic cooling towers, has

been famous for its orchids and helleborines over a number of years and was also private at one time, though it is under discussion by the authorities concerned (at the time of going to press), to be included within the park scheme. Perhaps controlled entry by way of guided walks, led by the future wardens will allow those interested to view this area, which is rather dangerous because of its swampy nature. Marsh and Common Spotted orchids flourish, along with all manner of hybrids resulting from these two species growing in such close proximity. In one spot, the tiny blooms of Smooth Tare were found, an obvious member of the vetches (*Vicia*) family which is in turn a member of the *Leguminosae* (pea) family. It closely resembles its near relative, Hairy Tare, though the pods are smooth, not downy, the flowers are a deeper shade of lilac and at aproximately 6mm in size, are a touch larger than their hairy cousin. Yellow Birdsnest now grows here, in appearance resembling a brownish-yellow version of the parasitic Toothwort. The latter species colonises living tree roots, whereas the birdsnest is a saprophyte which lives on dead and decaying organic matter.

The most interesting area around the Flashes for wetland plants is Blackwater's or Turner's Flash, which boasts an amazing variety of species. Delights such as Skullcap and Purple Loosestrife, Water-cress, Water Forget-me-Not, Marsh Bedstraw, Marsh Pennywort, Marsh Woundwort, Water Mint and Gypsywort all thrive at Turner's. There is also a selection of pondweeds, including the commonly-found Broad-leaved Pondweed and the often-overlooked water starworts. The species list continues with Sweet Flag, Reed Sweetgrass, Reed Canary Grass, Reedmace and Cyperus Sedge with

REED WARBLER

its diagnostic hanging 'flowers', though these are not as droopy as Pendulous sedge. My own particular favourite is False Fox Sedge, which I first spotted through binoculars at Pennington and positively identified after wading through one of the duck ponds (wearing white plimsolls) during my 1983 flower survey for the park. The plimsolls were ruined — but I was delighted with my find of False Fox Sedge! Other rush-type species found here include Common Spiked Sedge and the most uncommon (inland that is) Glaucous Bullrush which is that peculiar bluish-green shade its name implies, originally from the Greek word *glaukos*, meaning greyish-blue. A casual and by no means encompassing list of plants for 1986 revealed 165 species without much exertion — a concentrated search would doubtless reveal many more.

Meanwhile, as you stroll around, many breeding birds will be giving throat in defence of chosen territories, building nests or even feeding their young around you. The rich tapestry of sound will include the trilling and wheezing of Yellowhammer, the metallic notes of the Reed Bunting, and the rattling, non-musical warbles of Reed and Sedge Warbler, while Grasshopper Warblers sound like freewheeling runaway bicycles. Whitethroat and Lesser Whitethroats also chatter discordantly. Many of the duck will be shepherding broods of young, some even on the canal itself and at times they seem in imminent danger of being 'run down' (at 4mph, that is!) by the procession of pleasure boats, for this is a busy waterway at the best of times, especially in summer, when beautifully decorated longboats are a common sight.

However, in addition to these winter and summer walks, you should consider another two visits at the twice-yearly migration times of Spring and Autumn when other 'birding' species, such as passage waders, lure and beckon. When the proposed wader scrapes (areas of insect-laden mud cleared of Common Reed and grasses and left bare for waders to feed upon), have been completed, there will probably be more frequent occurences of species such as godwits, Curlew, Whimbrel, Greenshank, Sanderling, Dunlin and Oystercatcher. Added for good measure to the new park as a whole may be other birding delights, such as Little Gull, Redstart, Whinchat, Black Tern and White-winged Black Tern, whilst not forgetting the appearance of the now locally famous — due to its rarity — Pratincole (pronounced prat-in-coal). A friend once dubbed it 'prat-inckle' . . . which I think I prefer!

All in all, this makes Wigan's waters like household bills — needing immediate attention four times a year! Visiting any less frequently could be construed as unwise at the very least, hence the answer to that original question posed at the start of the chapter: 'Going anywhere good?'

'Anywhere good? You can say that again!'

QUICK GUIDE: This walk involves roughly three miles of reasonable level tow-path walking following one side of the canal until you can overlook Horrock's Flash, then return either by the same route or along the opposite bank for a very slight variation! Can be muddy at times, and is often bitterly exposed in winter. The area is due for Country Park status in the near future. BIRDS: Wildfowl, waders, Heron, Cormorant, grebes, divers, raptors, terns, gulls, swamp, scrub and tree warblers, chats and Wheatear, buntings, finches and a variety of migrant visitors. FLORAL HABITAT: Rich wetland, reed-beds and scrub ranging from alkaline to acidic. Open water (seven main subsidence flashes).

Pennington Flash Country Park Leigh

THE country park which now surrounds the water at Pennington was not in existence 15 years ago when I first moved to Leigh from Lytham. The mining subsidence lake of Pennington Flash however was hemmed-in at that time by coal spoil tips, corporation refuse dumps and a variety of disused railway debris. Not the place for watching wildlife you might have thought? But you would have been wrong — the whole derelict area overflowed with natural history. I had been depressed at the thought of leaving Lytham's fresh air, waders and wildfowl, but my delight knew no bounds on discovering this

marvellous place, during that very first week of push-bike 'sorties.'

Perhaps this is the point at which to mention that my account of Pennington differs from all the others in this book, for as might be expected, it is the place I visit most

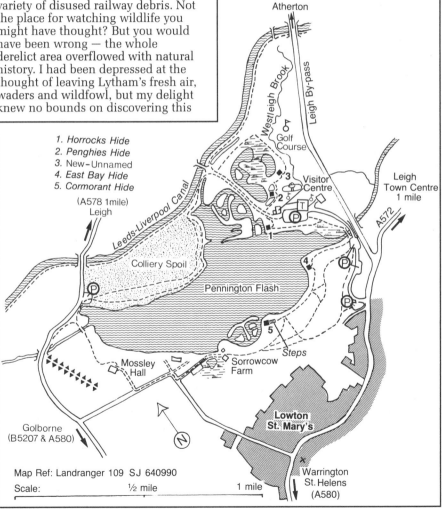

1. Horrocks Hide
2. Penghies Hide
3. New–Unnamed
4. East Bay Hide
5. Cormorant Hide

(A578 1mile)
Leigh

Atherton

Westleigh Brook

Leigh By-pass

Golf Course

Visitor Centre

Leigh Town Centre
1 mile

A572

Leeds–Liverpool Canal

Colliery Spoil

Pennington Flash

Steps

Mossley Hall

Sorrowcow Farm

Lowton St. Mary's

Golborne
(B5207 & A580)

N

Map Ref: Landranger 109 SJ 640990

Scale: ½ mile   1 mile

Warrington
St. Helens
(A580)

143

and in this particular instance familiarity breeds only contentment. But I should warn that this chapter is slightly sentimental for I have a different, very special and on-going relationship with Pennington. Perhaps many of you will recognise yourselves in my sentiments, and know that you too have this sort of association with some favoured haunt, which is physically both near your home and emotionally close to your heart.

The area of the 'Flash' has changed considerably during 1 years and reclamation has resulted in the refuse dumps being grassed-over and planted with trees. A golf course replaces the railway dereliction and most importantly, the remaining features suitable for wildlife have been preserved and protected by fenced-in nature reserves, and are to be found in several localities within the country park. Yet as near as it is to my home, I rarely walk to reach it. Habits change little over the years and I have simply progressed from those first pedal-powered two wheels, to the petrol driven variety!

AMENITIES: Public toilets are in the golf course club house, incorporating disabled cubicles, although these are only available when the golf course is in use. Opening times vary from Summer to Winter depending on the hours of daylight. Winter: 0800 — 1600 /dusk; Summer: 0800 — 2100 /dusk. An information centre is provided and there are several free car parks scattered in the area of the park. A programme of the guided walks, lead by wardens, is available from the centre. (For further information telephone Leigh 605253). Picnic benches are located near the car parks. Dogs are allowed. There is no entry for the public to certain sensitive parts of the reserve. A variety of hides for birdwatching are available — the one nearest the car

park and information centre is suitable for disabled people and wheelchairs, with ramp access and lower viewing slits. Likewise, the path through the middle of the reserve is particularly suitable for chair-bound persons. Make and take your own food if planning a whole day visit — soup or stew in a flask is probably best, plus a coffee flask for winter wildfowl visits. Pennington can be exposed to high winds and bitterly cold during Winter and, conversely, hot and humid in Summer.

MAP REF: SJ 640990. Following the A572 through Leigh, and travelling in a south-westerly direction towards Lowton, you will find the entrance road on the right after passing the traffic lights for the new by-pass, and immediately before the telephone kiosk. The Railway public house is directly opposite the opening. Once into entrance road, beware of speed ramps and pass over small bridge close to the by-pass, bending round to reach major parking spaces on the left, at the end of the road. Park and set off to the first hide, calling in or by-passing the information centre on the right just as you wish.

The newest hide — your first stop if you follow my recommended route — should bring some rather choice waders into view, especially if your visit coincides with the Spring or Autumn passage times. Redshank, Ringed and Little Ringed Plover, plus Common Sandpiper are frequent visitors, with an occasional Little Stint, often feeding along the edge of the first inlet/moat which separates the shingle spit from human access. These waders have at times been so close to this hide that the binoculars would not focus on them! Over the years, the spit has seen much bird activity; wildfowl and gulls rest and preen, and Heron and Oystercatcher stand silhouetted during bright evenings. Terns have displayed pair-bonding behaviour (passing small fish delicately to one another) and eventual nesting is eagerly anticipated. Dunlin, Turnstone and Sanderling have provided many a half-hour of contented 'birding' as they run and feed among the small stones, jumping back from the waves during squally weather, when the Flash becomes decidedly choppy and rough. I did hear tell some years ago, when human access was allowed onto the shingle spit, the tale of a 'birder' dropping his binoculars and they bounced and plopped, never to be seen again, into the 20ft deep water on the right of the shingle bar . . . an unfortunate accident which lead no doubt to one or two volatile comments. The binoculars, by the way, are still at the bottom!

Great Crested Grebe nested during 1986 in the vicinity of this new hide and the 'peeping' call of the single remaining chick permeated the hide constantly, during both daylight and darkness. The cheeping increased in tone and volume each time the chick saw the parent come to the surface with food and they both swam toward one another, necks outstretched, as though to make the 'hand-over' of the tasty morsel less of a struggle, for young Great Crested Grebe are extremely demanding of their parents attention.

Seeing this species at close quarters was my very first 'birding' experience at Pennington and I was delighted, having previously only seen them at long distance in the river at Lytham. My 16×50 binoculars were suddenly much too high-powered for Pennington and their days were numbered, for I soon adopted a pair of 7×50s, which in those early years barely moved from round my neck — friends suspected I even slept in them and certainly the 8×30s I now treasure 'live' beside my typewriter, in readiness for making certain the identities of anything

ususual passing by or through the local park that my worktable overlooks. Tree Creeper, Greater Spotted Woodpecker, Wood Warbler, Siskin, Peregrine Falcon and Pink Footed Geese have all been noted from this vantage point over the years, and many have departed in the direction of Pennington Flash.

However, I digress, let's return to Pennington. Before the picnic and parking area was created, the waters edge here sported Sweet Flag and Reed Sweet Grass, among others, and I found a hidden perch for myself — a discarded wooden reel from the local cable works. This giant 'bobbin' was lodged in the waterside plants and from this 'private hide' I watched enthralled as pairs of Great Crested Grebe waved their chestnut head-dresses at each other, while indulging in their courtship rituals . . . marvellous. As I sit here writing, 97 great crested are present on Pennington's several waters.

When I wasn't in the reeds at Pennington I was up a tree — a tree with a view like no other, for a Barn Owl passed by at regular intervals, carrying food (mainly voles and mice) for his mate and young family. Their nest was in the disused outbuildings of Penghies farm, not 150ft from my perch. The ruins of this farm, and the barn owls home, were bulldozed away to make room for the new golf course and as a breeding species the barn owl was lost to Pennington. Sadly, this fate is overtaking many barn owls at an alarming rate countrywide, as buildings are repaired or demolished.

On leaving the first hide, turn left and head toward the middle path that separates Penghies pond on the right from the pools on the left. Since gaining country park status all these small waters have enjoyed a steady increase in a variety of less wary wildfowl. Shooting was freely indulged in here before the creation of the park made the discharge of firearms illegal within its boundaries, as in all country parks. Now, you can lean on the fence overlooking Penghies at your leisure and watch reasonably unconcerned wild duck going about their business. During Winter and especially Spring the immaculate drakes of Shovelar, Pochard, Tufted Duck, Teal, Goldeneye and that 'toy-looking' species the Ruddy Duck can all be seen in courtship display before their respective females. The pools on the left of the path have, on occasion, held a few surprises too. For example, there was the Water Rail — that normally shy member of the crake and rail family, which appeared day in, day out for weeks, feeding openly round the muddy edges, its behaviour not in the least secretive. Ambling past these pools one evening, deep in conversation with friends, I realised with a jolt that we were walking by a handful of very select waders, which were instantly recognised as Black-tailed Godwits! There were four of them — barely 170ft away from where we were standing. It was dusk so our view was not as clear as it might have been, but this did little to lessen our collective fascination.

Follow the middle path almost to the canal, then divert via a right turn into the track running parallel with the canal, which takes you round the boggy pool (shaded and protected by *Phragmites*) and known to locals as the 'swamp.' The only way to have a clear view of this peice of water, is from the canal bank, where an overall scan becomes possible. Short-eared Owls are frequently observed from this point too as they overfly the surrounding fields and small islands.

Please do not be tempted to climb over any of the fences marked 'nature reserve.' Frightening birds into flight in winter causes them to needlessly waste valuable energy which is necessary for their survival, whilst frightening duck in the breeding season results in the ducklings being scattered while flightless, and separated from 'mum' which frequently brings death to these 'abandoned' young, for predators find them easy pickings without their mother's protection.

Drop back to the path if you have been observing the pond from the canal bank, and continue as it gradually bends round to the right on its way back to the car park, by-passing as it does so, Pennington's newest wader scrapes, carefully hidden and protected by another moat outside a circle of piled-up earth. A new hide overlooking this promising lagoon and its marshy hinterland was built and sited in late 1986. Lapwing and, perhaps more excitingly for the birder, species such as Green and Wood Sandpiper, plus Whimbrel took an interest in these scrapes almost as soon as the machines and spade-toting wardens had departed. Winter, I predict, will see this area regularly covered with wildfowl, for it floods at times in severe weather and yachting on the main flash will persuade duck to take refuge on this most recent and promising section of the reserve.

Pass through the line of poplars that once housed Penghies farm and the owl family, and head slightly to the right, towards Penghies hide — hidden in the willows! The hide overlooks Penghies pond and rewards with a different viewpoint to that seen from the central pathway. The shallow 'scrape' at the rear of the water is only visible from this hide, and has hosted a variety of wildfowl over the years from Mallard and Teal to Gadwell. Kingfisher sometimes perch on the pole protruding from the reeds — thus causing the hide and its contents to 'quiver' a little with excitement, while one severe winter saw a Wren

KINGFISHER and SWEET FLAG.

trying to roost in the warmth of the hide. Perhaps this bird could read and was apparently taking the sign 'bird hide' at face value.

Leaving Penghies hide, head back toward the car park. Fit and energetic folk may now wish to explore on the opposite, southern side of the Flash. If so leave your vehicle where it stands and set off along the waters edge, this time in the opposite direction, by-passing the fenced-off reserve area that borders the main waters' outlet stream. Cross the wooden bridge, turning right and then right again to follow the stream round to the next hide. The view of Rivington and its television mast, crouching over Horwich, now slowly unfolds on your distant right. In front are the distinctive head-gear of Bickershaw Colliery overtopping the coal spoil heaps. Like Farnworth's Nob End, I fel Pennington's skyline would be bereft if these winding gear towers were to be removed.

Black Horehound provides boanical interest beside this path, before the hide, but it is unfortunately losing the battle to the more vigorous species of bindweed, nettle and Japanese Knotweed or 'Rollicking Molly' as it is known locally! Pennington fares well for plants and is as rewarding for the botanist as it is for the bird watcher. Species range from such delights as Foxglove, Red Bartsia and the uncommon Ternate-leaved Potentilla, to Small Toadflax, Small Flowered Evening Primrose and the unusual Fine-leaved Water Dropwort. Wood Sage is common, as are Hedge and Marsh Woundwort and their hybrid, *Stachys ambigua*. Added to this are the delights of Century, Teasel, Lucerne, Cornflower, Kidney Vetch and Cowslip, the Common Bullrush, Lesser Reedmace and False Fox Sedge, which all contribute their special individual appeal to Pennington. In the summer of 1984

the rare Bristly Hawksbeard (*Crepis setosa*) flowered just once, then vanished. The botanical list is almost endless and the Flash is worth a visit in summer for its flora alone.

Following your scan of the water from this first hide on the souhern side, leave by turning right and continuing along the shoreline toward the second hide. This is built on stilts, so unfortunatley this hide is inaccessible to the disabled by reason of its steep steps. The high vantage point offered in this hide is most useful, particularly for sorting out the identities of the numerous gulls coming to roost on the water in Winter's dusky afternoon twilight. Roosting gull numbers are regrettably declining perhaps due to the closure of Slag Lane refuse tip, where they once fed in thousands. The chap driving the bulldozer, flattening the waste, must have frequently worked in a flapping, white storm of birds, for both the air and the ground were full of screaming, scrapping gulls, fighting for possession of our kitchen waste! 'Birders' came from far and wide to witness this spectacle and hopefully locate the few Iceland and Glaucous Gulls which were usually present. Arguments gently raged between 'birders' regarding the identities of these two species, for frequently we all saw extra large Iceland birds which could have been Glaucous, together with small Glaucous which were thus mistaken for the Icelandic species. Beak and head size, and slimness (or otherwise) of neck are perhaps the best guides to recognition, though these are by no means infallible, hence the confusion.

According to the time of year other 'birding goodies' have also been recorded from this hide, for to the left it overlooks yet more wader scrapes. Greenshank, Spotted Redshank, Ruff, Ringed and Little Ringed Plover, Teal, Heron, Kestrel and Wheatear — have all given satisfaction to keen-eyed birdwatchers. From this hide, retrace your steps to your vehicle if your intention is not to complete the circular walk, otherwise continue ahead from the bottom of the steps, turning right as soon as the path allows and continue your circuit of the main water. Ascend the short rise, cross the small bridge at the bottom of the following slope and round a ditch stuffed-full with Reedmace, Water Plantain and in hot, still weather, dragonflies. If you have pets with you, now is the time to put them on their leads as you reach the private land of Sorrowcow farm. The footpath passes through the farmyard and the farm's several guard dogs are chained outside their kennels. Having crossed the yard and closed the gate behind you, you will be back beside the main water and this viewpoint has on more than one occasion been the best place for seeing rare divers and grebes, Cormorant and Red Breasted Mergansers.

Continue up the road, past the houses, and turn right on joining the main road at the T-junction. Keep to the footpath across the road, re-crossing when you see the name board for Mossley Hall Farm. Please keep pets under control again, as this is also private land. Skirt the house entrance and follow the path through a leafy bower into the fields, — a lovely place on a fine day for viewing the Flash and the surrounding area stretching from Rivington to the Derbyshire hills. Continue down the hedgerow, toward the small concrete bridge over the inlet stream.

Head for the main road and turn right, making for Slag Lane car park. Pass through the car park and set off on your return journey. One recent late evening 'breather' at this car park found us watching the mating dance of male Ghost Swift Moths, with the aid of car headlights. Their

display, so well-likened to a swinging pendulum, soon attracted the larger tan-coloured females, whereupon the mating business was speedily instigated without delay or finesse, as the nearest male seized the first available female and down they plummeted, into the grass to secure their embrace and procreate future generations of Ghost Swift Moths.

Another insect is frequently found at this end of the Flash when the brambles in Autumn are swathed with its web. The orb weaving spider (Araneus quadratus) is a larger relative of the commonly found Garden or White Cross Spider, (A. diadematus). I discovered a large female quadratus slowly ascending my trouser leg, whilst I was lazing in warm Autumn sunshine, allegedly 'birding'. The large size of roughly 20mm indicated a female and she was most attractive in appearance, conveying none of the unpleasant impressions frequently associated with this species. Far from being an ugly, black, long-legged 'creepy crawly', in colour at least she was the glowing chestnut-auburn of a healthy bay horse. On her back were four large white spots set in a square, and surrounded by other white marks and 'squiggles', while her legs

ARANEUS QUADRATUS

149

were alternately banded black and cream. In subsequent years I have found many more *quadratus* of all shades from yellow, through red to silver grey, though none have been quite as impressive or weighty in the hand as this first magnificent lady, as I discovered when I gently replaced her on the brambles.

Follow the path along the edge of the coal spoil, rounding the corner into the panorama of Ramsdales Flash, partly dissected by the shingle spit. By ascending a short distance up the spoil here you can, with the aid of binoculars or telescope, check the shingle for any small waders which may have arrived during your stroll. In the afternoon, the sun will be over your shoulder to throw a little light on the matter. When the main water is busy with yachts, the wildfowl move onto Ramsdales Flash and this elevated viewpoint is excellent, but make sure your silhouette does not stand out on the skyline, as this will make the wildfowl uneasy and wary.

After exploring the water here, continue round the edge of the pool, turning right into the main pathway once again to take you back to the car park and a well-deserved 'cuppa' from your flask. The original Grebe Lodge, since removed, stood, at the time of the incident I am about to recall, overlooking 'Ramies' and the ponds which held the godwits. It was the location for my most treasured recollection in more than 20 years of nature watching. Whilst peering through the cracks in the side wall of Grebe Lodge at a Heron, I spotted a rabbit swimming, or rather struggling, across the pond through a blanket of weed. It appeared to me that the rabbit was losing the battle so I rushed outside to help, casting off shoes, socks and trousers whilst wading into the water, at which point the rabbit keeled-over and rapidly started sinking. As I reached down to gently lift it clear, my 'drowning rabbit' took off as though jet-propelled, cleaving water and weed like a sharp knife . . . it reached the far bank in record time, hauled out and shook itself whilst casting a bemused glance at this foolish-looking human, stood thigh deep in water and whose underwear bore the slogan 'Marvellous on Mondays!' The resulting loud curses would have made a pitman blush and my companion subsided to the floor, weak and weeping with laughter. I still prefer to think that a Pike had it by the back leg . . .

Pennington really deserves a book all to itself and the definitive 'birding' guide is already in print, written by David Wilson and entitled 'Birds and Birdwatching at Pennington Flash' — it is an excellent record of the diversity of species seen at Pennington, and a pointer to what may continue to arrive here in future. Meanwhile, I hope to continue taking speedy breaks from working and 'nipping down the road' to Pennington Flash County Park — it is truly a park *par excellence!*

QUICK GUIDE: The full circuit at Pennington involves up to five miles of good, resonably level, stone-surfaced footpaths. Almost $\frac{1}{4}$ mile is on pavement beside a minor, but well-used road. Paths in the park can be muddy at times in certain spots. Choice of five hides, (four with level or ramp access, the fifth is on stilts, with steep steps.) BIRDS: Very similar to the preceeding chapter: Wildfowl, waders, Heron, Cormorant, terns gulls (plus Winter gull roost). swamp, scrub and tree warblers, chats and Wheatear, bunting, finches, wagtails, grebes, raptors. Occasional divers and other migrant visitors. FLORAL HABITAT: Wetland, reed-beds, wader scrapes, shingle spit, meadow and scrubland. Open water (1 main flash and a variety of ponds and pools).

Risley Moss Nature Park, Warrington

THIS park is packed with all kinds of natural history interest. For a fungal foray I can think of nowhere easier; the fungi seem to line the paths, and are almost impossible to miss. These paths provide good, easy walking and are often sheltered and warm, allowing time to be spent poring over their often bewildering array of fungal species. Or you can leave your mushroom guide book at home and take one of the park's organised walks, led by an expert who will make identification easy. In the depths of Winter, after donning plenty of protective warm clothing, a spell sat in the woodland hide birdwatching can be a very rewarding experience — and don't forget to take a hot drink! Equally rewarding on occasion is the observation tower, though prolonged lingering in this all too often draughty and desperately cold niche is usually only indulged in by stalwart, determined 'birders,' who appear impervious to all weather conditions!

Spring and Summer bring a wealth of flora and birdsong and is pleasant in itself, without any ulterior wildlife-watching motive. A proportion of the park is not open to public access, being resrved for the wildlife to live in, undisturbed by people. However, I can recommend the programme of guided walks which covers the natural history spectrum throughout the year, and allows a closer look into these normally closed areas. I will not forget my view of their solitary Royal Fern or the exquisite Fritilliary plant with its gorgeous checkered bloom. Any of these arranged walks are worthwhile, requiring only booking in advance and payment of a small charge — 50p per adult and 25p for a child. Tel. Warrington 824339 for details. Risley Moss is owned and administered by the Warrington New Town Development Corporation.

AMENITIES: Opening hours are as follows: Monday — Thursday 0830-1700. Saturday and Sunday 0830-1800. Closed all day Friday. Bank holiday openings are as weekends. The Information centre is open Monday — Thursday 0900-1630. Saturday and Sunday, 0900-1700. Car parking and toilet facilities are provided though there are no special disabled facilities. Hot drinks and snack machines are available. An exhibition showing aspects of peat-cutting and past mossland life, is of interest, together with information about the munitions depot that covered a sizeable part of the nearby mossland during the last war. There is a lecture room and educational facilities. Ramps up to the Information Centre make access with a wheelchair possible, and two wheelchairs are available at the centre for people temporarily unable to move around the park easily. Unfortunately, neither of the two hides are suitable for chairbound persons, which is sad, for the woodland paths are particularly suitable for wheelchairs and prams. Dogs are allowed — but on leads at all times please. A programme of the special events is available from the centre, and this includes sketching, childrens crafts and fungal forays. You would be well advised to make and take your own hot food and drinks if a prolonged visit is planned.

MAP REF: SJ 669921. The entrance to the park is sited on Ordnance Avenue, in the Birchwood district of Warrington. Travelling south on the

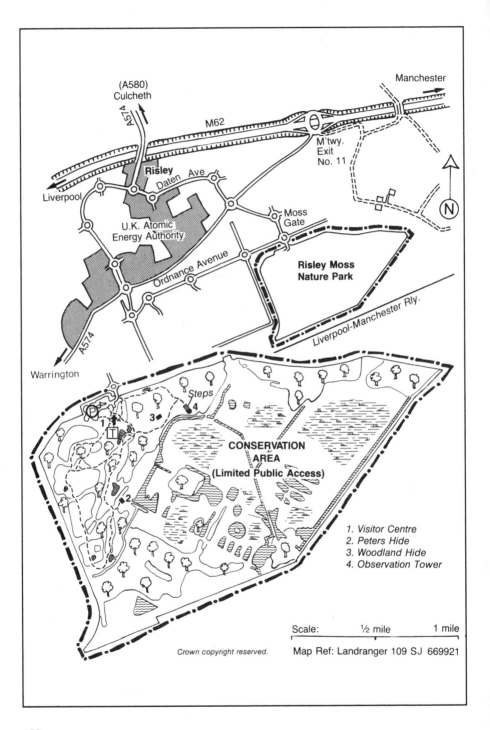

Scale: ½ mile · 1 mile

Crown copyright reserved.

Map Ref: Landranger 109 SJ 669921

152

A574 from Culcheth towards Warrington, pass over the M62 and take the first left turn at the next roundabout, into Daten Avenue. Continue, following signposts for the park around the numerous traffic islands, which all look very similar to each other until the last one at Moss Gate leads directly to the park entrance.

On leaving the visitor centre through either of the front entrances, facing the car park, turn left for the relaxing and easy circular ramble round the woodland. This is a delightful circuit with good paths, opening at intervals into lovely grassy areas, warm and protected from the wind and delightful for idling, especially in Autumn when the perimeters of these lawn-quality havens are bursting with fungi. Amateur mycologists, and I place myself firmly in this class, can often be seen kneeling over some small fungal 'umbrella', feverishly searching through a tattered and invaluable mushroom field guide frequently whilst looking perplexed and muttering incoherently!

The most noticable fungi here is the Common Inkcap. It seems to sprout every few yards and some were fresh specimens, their caps oval, pale and clean looking with white gills showing where some had been broken. These caps expand into maturity, very often splitting in the process, and the gills blacken while producing quantities of date-brown spore dust, before finally digesting themselves and breaking down (deliquescing) into a black liquid. Drawing ink was produced at one time from these fungi, hence their common name. It must have been difficult in times past for the town-planners and architects if their supply of ink ran out before autumn came round again!

Common Inkcaps are edible when young, though accompanying these mushrooms with your favourite alcoholic 'tipple' will result in some highly unpleasant side effects, such as nausea and heart palpitations — not that I speak from experience! Analysis of this species has isolated a chemical similar in make-up and action to one manufactured in the drug 'Antabuse', given to chronic alcoholics . . . it sounds to me like another case of the cure being worse than the ailment?

Moving on, I noticed that Red Campion was still flowering though the blooms were pale and wan and well past their best. Hogweed had seeded and the now-empty umbel-heads looked like a graveyard of stranded cartwheels, forlorn and broken on the end of their axels. One or two signs placed in strategic positions proclaimed that 'Berries are for the birds' hinting that the blackberry pie lovers are encouraged to do their picking elsewhere. The birds need this rich boost of vitamin-filled food to build them up before winter.

A surfeit of Jays, many of them young birds, judging by their extra shrill voices and paler colours, were screeching and chasing one another, whilst the Robins melancholy winter song rained down at noticeably frequent intervals. I concluded there was either a plethora of robins, or one bird in particular was trailing in my wake doing his or her best to depress me with repeated forebodings of the dying year. Both male and female robins stake out a piece of land as their territory in Winter and they sing both to proclaim ownership and to warn other robins to stay away. That wonderful Robin melody is nothing but a war cry!

Rounding a 'kink' in the path, a pond came into view on the right and I peered for a few minutes into its weedy waters. Pond Skaters, (the insect *Gerris laccustris*) or 'water boatmen' as they are often called, were 'rowing' across the waters surface and sudden movements below took my eye down to — a tadpole? In October? Several more appeared, dark coloured, with four legs and a long tail and I tentatively identified them as young newts, but was undecided as to which precise species, and leaning any further over would have seen me disappearing head first into the water! Nearby, on a dead and blackened tree stump, was a gorgeous show of fresh Candlesnuff fungi, soon followed by the 'fumes' of a Common Stinkhorn emanating from a patch of Bramble.

A variety of russulas populate the woodland edges and one lone specimen I identified as *Russula aeruginea*, its cap a uniform clay to greyish-olive shade. Across the way, in another grassy sward, were three tall spindly fungi of the genus *Paneolus*, their caps a rich, deep brown with a dark margin round the bottom and a tan centre raised in an umbo, or boss. When fully ripe, both the gills and spore dust are black, while the stem is a descending and deepening tan shade. A great Spotted Woodpecker 'jik-jikked' somewhere closeby, and I noticed a dead birch stump in the next woodland patch contained three neatly bored-out woodpecker nest holes in the softly decaying wood. A Willow Tit suddenly warned of my presence with his loudly uttered 'zee-zee' call and this also prompted a Wren and a Dunnock into giving warning notes.

My walk finally came full circle, by-passing in the last grassy plot a lone Shaggy Inkcap, which was tall, well proportioned and newly-sprung from the ground, its cap not yet open to reveal white gills which on opening will quickly turn pink. They subsequently deliquesce into a black, dripping liquid, releasing the spores and ensuring the propagation of further generations of Lawyers Wigs as they are more commonly known.

Instead of returning to the Information Centre and car park, which the post indicates are now on your left, keep straight ahead for the two hides, where a spell of intensive 'birding' will complement your fungal foray. Many common species of birds appear in front of the baited woodland hide, particularly during severe weather, although summer will find this area deserted, with not a bird to be seen! Winter will find a profusion of Great, Blue and Coal tits, Blackbird, Robin, Chaffinch, Greenfinch and quite often a smattering of the less common or more shy species. Nuthatch, Willow Tit, Long-tailed Tit, Corn Bunting, Siskin, Redpoll, Woodpecker, Jay and Wood Pigeon, all visit this tiny area, which the wardens keep supplied with food most necessary to the birds survival — peanuts, fat, cheese and seeds. I say 'intensive birding' because the activity in front of the woodland hide is spectacular, as these feathered dynamos flit rapidly from one source of food to the next. Until the local Sparrowhawk puts in an appearance, that is, his presence causing a volley of shrieked alarm notes, from a variety of birds who are diving for cover. A few crouch down where they are, moving their heads slowly from side to side, trying to catch sight of the grey-backed death with sulphur yellow eyes hunched over the lifeless form of a Greenfinch, which minutes before had been disputing with another finch as to who was 'king of the nutbag' . . . Not surprisingly, the exclamations reverberating from the walls inside the hide prompted the sparrowhawk to leave, in search of a more secluded spot in which to pluck and enjoy his warm meal in solitude.

The opportunities for Winter bird watching and photography from this hide are tremendous, the only drawback being that your feet will have apparently turned into blocks of

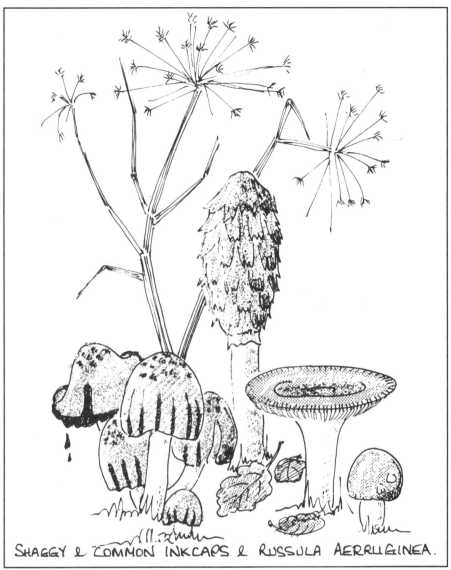

SHAGGY & COMMON INKCAPS & RUSSULA AERRUGINEA.

ice long before your eyes have tired of observing! Perhaps the really organised person would pack a hot water bottle as well as a flask of coffee? And so, when numbness in the legs can no longer be ignored, make a short 'hobble', going left from the woodland hide, to follow the path marked 'observation tower.'

From here you may be rewarded with views of hunting Hen Harrier and Short-eared Owls, especially later in the day towards dusk, when these owls seem even more active than usual. Views of these two birds of prey are becoming increasingly common at Risley and particularly likely during bad weather.

However, my last visit on a warm October day found the tower hide a pleasant place to linger, though there was a marked paucity of birdlife. Two jays and a Moorhen were the sum total of 20 minutes careful observation. A dragonfly 'whirring' and landing on the sunward side caused me to peer out for a closer look and I found myself staring straight into its face. The light shimmered in the brilliant iridescence flickering through the hundreds of facets in those incredible eyes like some tiny laser show. A pulse throbbed under its 'chin' and rythmically vibrated the length of the dark, rather thick-set body with its red markings. These markings together with the smallness of size and pale 'face' led me to identify this insect as a male White-faced Darter, *Leucorrhinia dubia*. You may have noticed on your way into the park that a dragonfly is the logo of Risley Moss Nature Park, and at the last count it boasted 12 different species, some of which are rare for this part of the country. In the summer of 1986 a Hobby Falcon was reported spending some time helping himself to Risley's supply of dragonflies. Both the common and the rarer species of these insects were seen disappearing down this rare raptor's throat. An exciting spectable for bird watchers, though I can understand why people who find dragonflies an exciting subject would regard this insect-devouring exhibition as a disturbing prospect. Thankfully, dragonflies generally have few predators, the Hobby Falcon being one of only two birds in this country to regularly hunt these insects with proficiency, the other being the Spotted Flycatcher. Abroad, the dragonfly fares less well, falling prey to predators including bee eaters, rollers, flycatchers and shrikes.

On a clear day, with no hunting raptors capturing your attention, you will find that the tower boasts a far-reaching view for a place, which at best, including the tower's own elevation, is less that 100ft above sea level. To the far left is the bulk of Edale Moor, advancing up to that pinnacle of the High Peak, Kinder Scout, a rather amazing 27 miles distant. The Pennine panorama slides into the Goyt Valley to rise again over Sponds Hill sitting watchfully over Lyme Park. The range curls on round beyond Macclesfield before climbing over Croker Hill, topped by a telecommunications mast, then dipping and rising to the Cloud — not the fluffy sky variety — but a sizeable hill near Congleton. Much closer, on the right, is the sandstone ridge on which the village of Stretton sits, blocking your view of the southern end of England's backbone, (the Pennines) while separating the Mersey Valley from the south Cheshire plain. All this and wildlife too in an area of human surburbia makes Risley a gem and a place to be proud of.

QUICK GUIDE: A visit to Risley Moss Nature Park comprises a gentle stroll of no more than $1\frac{1}{2}$ miles on good, stoned or ash paths, through mainly birch woodland and open glades. Choice of two hides and one observation tower high on stilts and approached by two flights of steep steps. Sheltered for the most part, except in the observation tower — which can be bitterly exposed in Winter! *BIRDS:* Common woodland species. Swamp, scrub and tree warblers, flycatchers, raptors, woodpeckers, Nuthatch, wildfowl, waders, finches, buntings and occasional migrant species. *FLORAL HABITAT:* Birch woodland, remnent raised peat bog — acidic conditions. Open water (woodland ponds and boggy pools in the open mossland area). *FAUNA:* 12 species of dragonfly, foxes.

Red Rocks, Hoylake

RED ROCKS is the last of my high-tide wader roost venues, and is sited at the mouth of the River Dee. Unfortunately the viewing of fewer and fewer waders is becoming an increasingly common occurance here and it is difficult to pinpoint the reason for this paucity. Pollution of their food perhaps? This is difficult to accept, for Lancashire's rivers in general — and the Dee and Mersey in particular — are cleaner now than at any time in the past 50 years: unless, of course, the clean-up campaign arrived too late and irreversible damage has already been done to marine life? Or is it human pressure? Maybe my forebodings for Hest Bank (see page 45) have already come true for Red Rocks, where horse riders are seen to urge their mounts at flocks of roosting birds — why I cannot imagine, for there is plenty of empty beach available to avoid causing this kind of disturbance. Perhaps they think it is romantic to gallop through thousands of airborne birds. Young people, from very small children to teenagers, ride a variety of motorbikes along the sands; ordinary outdoor-loving folk exercise their dogs regularly and birdwatchers arrive in dozens at the merest hind of some vagrant oddity. This all combines to produce a high degree of disturbance and if the birds can

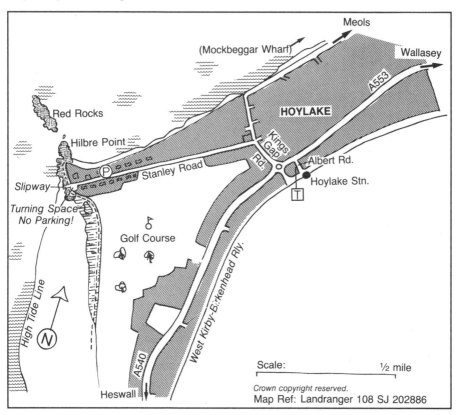

Scale: ½ mile

Map Ref: Landranger 108 SJ 202886

avoid it, they will. However, the underlying explanation for the decline in Dee wader flocks — most notably Knots — may be due entirely to some other influence of which we know nothing yet.

AMENITIES: Pub meals, shops, fish and chips are all available locally. Taking your own hot food and drink, especially in winter, is an advantage for you can then eat and bird-watch simultaneously. Toilets are in Albert Road — return to the traffic island (see 'Map Ref.' section), turn left onto the A553 and take the first right turn into Albert Road. The toilet block is on the right, and car parking is allowed on the left of street. No disabled facilities are provided. Although Red Rocks is not a place for pushing wheelchairs, if you are determined, it is possible to carry the chair and person (particularly a child) for 100 yards or so, and place them, well wrapped-up for warmth and securely positioned, for the duration of the tide, perhaps in Autumn when the weather is warm.

MAP REF: SJ 202886. Travelling in a westerly direction towards Hoylake on the A553 from Wallasey, at the traffic island opposite Hoylake Railway Station turn right into King's Gap Road and then left into Stanley Road at the Green Lodge Hotel. Continue to the end of the road, and please do not park your car in front of the gated slip-way or in the turning space, but turn around and park on the left-hand side of the road, being careful not to obscure any of the residents driveways.

The best times to visit Red Rocks are during the Spring and Autumn migration times, April/May and September/October. Choose a medium high-tide of approximately 30ft or so and plan to arrive and be ready $1\frac{1}{2}$ hours before the tide reaches its zenith.

Set off on foot towards the slip-way, pass through the gate and turn right, walking the 100 yards along the top of the sandstone rocks to the end of the wall, to find a comfortable place and settle down. As the high tide approaches there should be a steady stream of species flying past, especially during the Autumn passage. The birds follow the coastline as they travel south, cutting diagonally across the mouth of the Mersey, along Mockbeggar Wharf and Last Hoyle Bank, passing your waiting binoculars, before crossing to Hilbre and on to the Welsh coast at the Point of Ayr. Using a telescope I have noticed that some species, notably terns, skuas, Kittiwake and gulls take a direct line, leaving the coastline at Formby Point and fly in an almost straight line to the Point of Ayr, missing the Wirral altogether. However, Red Rocks does on occasion receive a small share of these lovely birds also.

If luck is with you, the advancing tide should be pushing before it flocks of Oystercatcher, a few godwits and Knot, Dunlin and Redshank and perhaps even a small number of Turnstone, to gather on the exposed rocks just off the mainland. Smaller waders, Ringed Plover and Sanderling can be seen running about on the still-uncovered sand on your right towards Hoylake, as this is high ground and the last place to disappear under water. If the tide is not very high, this area will remain uncovered and provided no-one walks across it, the smaller waders will continue feeding throughout the tide.

A visit here in early December, on our way home, with the tide still some way distant but rising nonetheless was extremely unproductive of birds here in any form; a rather disappointing end to a somewhat 'bird-less' day. Half-a-dozen Redshank were feeding and bathing in the pools at the sea-ward

GULLS, KITTIWAKE & RED THROATED DIVER.

side of Red Rocks, but otherwise the mudflats were completely empty of birdlife as far as the eye could see, giving the impression that the world had ended and no-one had thought to tell us! I suspect the Dee wader flocks have found quieter feeding grounds, Gayton Sands perhaps, or hidden beyond the marsh at Parkgate or private areas nearer to the Welsh side. They have maybe even chosen a complete change — the Ribble estuary for example. On our last visit, fresh but dried droppings and feathers on the dry top of Red Rocks however, indicated that some birds had been roosting and preening here recently.

Once the high-tide wader roost activity is receeding with the tide, you can go on to discover the tiny reserve of Red Rocks Marsh, by retracing your steps to the slip-way and continuing for 100 yards or so, in a southerly direction. Unfortunately, I was able to visit this fascinating reserve only once in 1986 — during the middle of August. The reserve comprises a reedmarsh slack, surrounded by lime-rich damp grassland growing on sandy ground, enriched with calcium from the many thousands of broken shells, and the whole is sandwiched between two rows of dunes. It is yet another fine example of duneland and my notebook informs that a rich variety of plant species were discovered. Soapwort was one of the first to catch my eye — and rubbing the leaves in water does, as its name suggests, produce a soapy lather!

The white globe-shaped heads of the umbellifer Angelica soon followed, while the inconspicuous 'flowering spikes' of Sea Arrow-Grass and Sea Beet were noted nearby. Rather more obvious were the blazing reds, purples and pinks of Marsh and Common Spotted Orchid and their hybrid progeny — as these two species cross-pollinate quite willingly to produce an amazing number of varied blooms. In direct contrast with the reds, was the unbelieveable powder-blue colour found in several patches of Sea Holly — the whole plant is 'bluish' in hue, yet the umbel-type flower heads are a particularly vibrant shade when viewed at their best; it positively glows in the dusk! And then it was back to the 'hot colours' with the brilliant flowering spikes of Purple Loosestrife, followed

SEA HOLLY.

rapidly by the rich gold of Yellow Iris or Flag as it is sometimes known.

The pale and delicate lilac shade of Sea Rocket — a fleshy, succulent member of the *Cruciferae* (cabbage) family next caught my eye, as did the slightly darker tiny lilac flowers of the foetid-smelling Black Horehound. The grassland contained swathes of Yellow Rattle and the yellowy-orange shades of Kidney Vetch. In my opinion even a cultivated garden cannot outshine the myriad concoction of colour provided by duneland habitat in a seemingly endless magic carpet of shades. Nevertheless, I must not forget the humble green plants which lack showy flowers and were represented by such species as Common Club Rush, together with Sand and Slender Sedge among others, even a hybrid and unusual horsetail flourishes. It is also the only place on the Wirral peninsula where

Natterjack Toads have a breeding colony, as the Information Board in the reserve will tell you. All in all, an amazing number of interesting species grow in this tiny area and it is certainly worthy of a look in passing. I anticipate renewing my acquaintance with this lovely place and look forward with pleasure to finding even more floral delights to improve and set-the-seal on a day spent 'birding' on the Wirral. Red Rocks Marsh Reserve is owned and administered by the Chesire Conservation Trust.

During September, in a near-by derelict space left for house building, I glimpsed the tall spikes of Great Mullein, growing enthusiastically from the rubble with the yellow umbellifer Wild Parsnip and swathes of the sickly-scented Sweet Alison. This latter plant is a cultivated garden variety and it is a prolific grower in coastal habitats, once it is 'on the loose.' Sea Beet and Common Storksbill were plentiful, all clamouring to efficiently cover and conceal the landscapes scars. The Sweet Alison, unbelievably, was still in flower at my most recent visit (in December) though the two small clumps were admitedly a little care-worn and haggard, with not a whiff of scent remaining!

The other end of Hoylake, at Meols, is worthy of interest, car parking is allowed on the promenade and there is a handy toilet block near the end of the road. Sea-watching here can be attractive, although if unable to leave your car you will be hampered by the high sea wall. The tide reaches this wall and washes over it when conditions are only moderately rough — you would be well advised to remember this fact before placing your telescope on the top! Also, please do not consider sitting on this wall before an incoming tide (especially children) — it only takes one freak wave for disaster to follow, as there are no steps or way out, should you fall in the water. I have observed Kittiwake, Great and Arctic Skua, Red-throated Diver and several species of sea duck mixed in and around the many small craft anchored off-shore here. Gannet and Cormorant fly past nearer to the skyline and on one occasion a Bar-tailed Godwit, fearfully beaten by bad weather, was found walking down the middle of the road, tired, bedraggled and confused.

Leaving your car and taking a walk along the concrete raised promenade towards New Brighton brings lovely views of birds flying past, frequently at a very low height and close-in. This is an unusual viewpoint, for waders especially are more often seen in silhouette against the sky.

QUICK GUIDE: This chapter describes what must be the shortest outing in the whole book — measuring one mile at the very most — including the walk to the vantage point opposite the 'rocks', plus a circuit of the Red Rocks Marsh Reserve; although bear in mind that these two sites may need separate visits to obtain the very best results: Autumn/Winter for wader-watching and Summer/early Autumn for botany in the reserve. Can be bitterly exposed in Winter, wrap up warmly. Track to the 'birding' viewpoint follows the reasonably level sandstone cliff-top (5ft high at the most) and flat boardwalks and sandy turf wind around the reserve — yet beware, it is wet and marshy here if you leave the path! *BIRDS:* Waders, wildfowl, sea-duck, sea-going species, grebes, divers, gulls, terns, Cormorant, Gannet, auks, skuas and shearwaters. Plus breeding species on and near the reserve, warblers, finches etc. *FLORAL HABITAT:* Sandstone. Nearby reserve is coastal, lime-rich grassland, willow scrub, dunes, reed-bed, marsh and slack. Open water (slack, freshwater to brackish and sea). *FAUNA:* Frogs, toads and varied insect life.

Hilbre Islands and Reserve

I have come to the conclusion that the main attraction at Hilbre for me is not any single bird species particularly associated with this venue such as skuas or petrels, for example but the excitement and anticipation beforehand. Planning the proposed visit days in advance, watching the weather forecasts, looking speculatively at the weather when the morning arrives — will it stay fine? By the time I actually arrive, I am bubbling with expectation! I must be a frustrated expeditionist!

Having beaten the tide to the main island and become cut-off there by the sea you are commited to the outing, no matter what the weather now decides to throw at you, and this only increases the excitement for me. You then settle down to 'sea watch'; hoping to observe the species which pass the Lancashire coastline

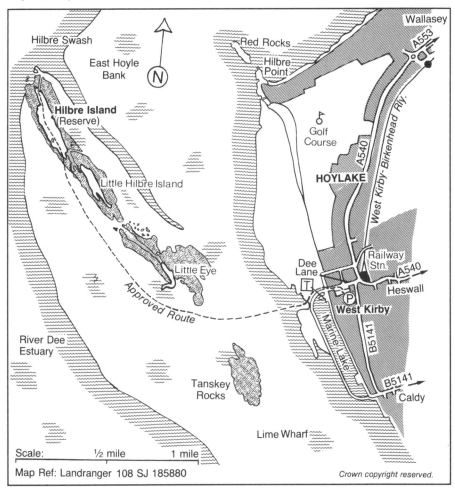

Scale: ½ mile 1 mile

Map Ref: Landranger 108 SJ 185880

only twice during the bird watching year, as part of the Spring and Autumn migrations. The Hilbre chain of islands are owned and administered by the Wirral Borough Council.

AMENITIES: There are no special facilities on any of the islands — you must strictly make and take your own food and refreshments. Toilets are on the promenade at the end of Dee Lane, next to the Chandlery, please remember there are no toilet facilities on any of the islands. Various shops, pubs and fish and chip shops are located in West Kirby centre. A permit is required in advance to visit the Hilbre chain of islands. Permits can be obtained free of charge by writing to (or visiting) the Wirral Country Park Information Centre, Station Road, Thurstaston, Wirral, Merseyside. Unfortunately, this venue is not suitable for wheelchairs due to the dangers of being cut-off by the tide before reaching the safety of the islands. Dogs must be kept on a lead on the islands.

MAP REF: SJ 185880. If arriving by car, parking is free in Dee Lane at West Kirby, or there is a pay and display area to the rear of the free spaces. The crossing from the end of Dee Lane to **any** of the Hilbre island chain is the **only** safe route across the sands — **under no circumstances attempt to cross from any other point on the Wirral Coast.** A notice giving details of weekly tide times is posted on a board near the Chandlery and slip-way, but once again I recommend the purchase of the Liverpool Tide Table booklet, as detailed in the Authors Note.

This is a pleasant walk, especially on warm sumer evenings; peaceful, quiet dreamy and, separated from mainland pressures. This results from the simple fact that you can only arrive at Hilbre by your own efforts, not by 'wheels', and you get the impression that life is conducted by the few inhabitants of this isle in a more natural and harmonious manner than on the neighbouring mainland. If your plan is simply to walk out to Hilbre and back at low tide you *must* allow yourself fully 3 hours *before* the next high tide, to make your return from the main island to the mainland. The numerous channels fill before the water covers the whole of the sands, and leaving departure till the last minute means you risk wet feet at the very least. However if you wish to spend the duration of the tide cut-off from the mainland as I describe, then you must leave West Kirby front $3\frac{1}{2}$ hours *before* high tide and be suitably dressed in warm clothing — you are going to be outside for 5-7 hours with no shelter whatsoever. The other birdwatchers, who will undoubtedly be present (it is extremely difficult to have Hilbre all to yourself!) will not appreciate your running around and leaping about in an effort to keep warm! Wellington boots are preferable and will keep your legs warmer, as well as allowing you to leave more quickly after the tide. Also, carry waterproofs if you do not possess one of those marvellous waxed jacket-and-trouser sets; an extra woolly pullover, hat and gloves in your pack can be useful, together with flasks of soup and coffee. Sea watching is a very cold business and really only profitable in Autumn, Winter and early Spring and the bird watching is enhanced by windy weather. A compass, map and the knowledge of how to use them can be an advantage, even so I have heard anecdotes of experienced people leaving the islands in fog, bound for West Kirby on compass readings, only to arrive back at Hilbre an hour or so later! The moral of this story is simple: do not attempt this outing if

LEACHS PETREL & GREY SEAL.

there is any prospect of fog or very severe weather.

Having taken careful heed of these warnings, do visit Hilbre and thoroughly enjoy another north-western bird bonanza, with a charm (albeit cold!) all its own. During your walk across the sands prior to high water, waders will already be 'buzzing' around the estuary, the earliest movers being the Oystercatchers flying overhead in pied chequered skeins uttering nervous piping calls from bright orange dagger-shaped beaks. Curlew are also quick to move from the tideline, and apparently anxious to go to roost; small parties of these species can be seen heading-off in the direction of Wales, to the Point of Ayr roost, where quite a few Oystercatcher and Curlew also gather whilst others head up the river towards Heswall and Parkgate. Small mixed groups of wading birds gather round the edges of Middle and Little Eye, assuming there are no people to

scare them away.

Little Eye has been made famous over the years, by visiting bird photographers settin up 'hides' (green canvas structures) and Eric Hosking and the Duke of Edinburgh have both successfully captured waders on film in this manner. We noted a photographer assembling his hide on the Little Eye as we passed on our way to the main island, and during our stay I glanced back through binoculars and could see he was experiencing some luck, as several species of waders were obligingly posing in front of his lens.

On arrival at the main island, we found the tide was already lapping round the lower rocks and prompted a last minute 'dash,' even though we had set off from West Kirby in plenty of time. A strong west wind will, as I have already warned for the other venues, make the tide higher and earlier than predicted in the tide tables and this should be taken into account with great care. As we climbed the track to the top of the island my companion suddenly realised he had changed jackets — and our permit was in the other jacket, safely locked in the car at West Kirby! Fortunately, the warden had been spotted some 20 minutes earlier heading for the shore in his Landrover, and so we were not approached during the day for our permit!

We followed the path over the top to the northern end of the island, to the old sandstone life-boat station and were rewarded immediately by a deliciously close view of a Leach's Petrel — a Hilbre speciality — a small dark tube-nosed seagoing bird. This can be distinguished from its near relatives (Storm and Wilson's petrels) by its strong bouyant flight and forked tail which is only easily seen from close quarters.

The hours passed happily and easily in the company of other bird watchers (six in number) who had arrived earlier. Once the tide was in and we were cut off, birds flew past in fits and starts: Artic Skuas, those piratical gulls of the sea, were much in evidence and we eventually became quite blase about their presence . . ."Oh yes — another skua to the left . . . yes, and two more just out there . . .!" Terns moved by in small, yet regular groups, including Common and Arctic species, both close enough to distinguish the black-tipped bill of the Common and blood-red bill of the Arctic. These birds are aptly named sea swallows because of their graceful flight. The heavier and more raucous Sandwich Terns passed by at intervals, their squeaky-sounding young hatched this spring and migrating for the very first time. Cormorants flew by occasionally, quite close at first and then veering away when they spotted us watching them. Telescopes were trained on distant Manx Shearwater and dark juvenile Gannet; the shearwaters are easily recognisable even at great distances by the dark upper parts and brilliant white undercarriage. It did not take long for seals to appear, their lovely dog-like heads poking out of the water, filled with curiosity at what these odd humans get up to in their spare time! These were female Grey or Atlantic Seal, having flatter heads and a smaller, more delicate build than the male or bull seal. They played and porpoised in the water with accustomed ease and finally slept, noses pointing skywards and eyes tight-shut, bobbing like empty bottles as the tide lost its impetus and entered the becalmed spell before beginning to recede.

A Great Crested Grebe, looking oddly out of place somehow on the sea, being more normally associated with inland waters, fished round the island. During winter and severe weather, when many inland waters freeze over, rafts containing many hundreds of Great Crested Grebe can be seen together on the sea. More natural looking were the small numbers of young Guillemot and Razorbill which are difficult to distinguish at this age, fishing around the island and further out in the estuary. One bird looked quite sickly, listless, with tail up and wings drooping and an hour or so later a freshly-dead young 'razormot' floated past — perhaps the same sickly bird.

During a lull in the bird passage a variety of food appeared from bags and back-packs, a mouth-watering array of sandwiches, barm cakes, soup in flasks, cold pasties and even a box of home-made cake provided by one of the gentlemans' wives! All was heartily consumed, with appetites spurred-on by the fresh air! An hour or so later, during another lull in birds, all our mouths were set watering again, when one of the chaps from the early party produced a methylated spirit-fuelled primus stove, and a large bottle of water to brew a billy-can of delicious fresh tea. The rest of us had to be content with the cold dregs in our flasks!

As the tide dropped, waders took wing and skeins flew past as areas of mud were gradually exposed again and feeding could be resumed. Flocks of Turnstone, some still in smart breeding plumage, landed below us and began probing and turning small pebbles, searching for fresh tide leavings. One or two Purple Sandpiper were also seen, another Hilbre speciality which increases in numbers as the autumn and winter progress.

The few small stunted trees on the main island are coverd by Heligoland Traps - netted aviary-type constructions for catching passerine (perching) birds such as warblers, wagtails and the like for the purposes of ringing. By 1983 a total of 17,600 birds were ringed here from 82 species, thereby adding to our knowledge of migration patterns. If you ever find a dead bird anywhere and it has a leg ring containing details and numbers, please remove the ring and post it to the address shown, or post copied details if it is not possible to remove the ring.

Hilbre's position just off the coast means that some of the passage migrants are rarities; foreign warblers, pipits, buntings and larks have all made landfall on the island, as well as the rare sea-going birds which pass by. Three species of divers have been recorded just off-shore, most frequetly in December and January, of which Red Throated Diver are the ost commonly seen.

For botanists, Hilbre does boast some interesting plants and during this visit we found the fern Sea Spleenwort— a lovely leafy, shiny and healthy-looking specimen tucked into the cliffs. However, I must admit to never having visited Hilbre during spring and summer but I will do so soon. A plant survey in 1978 recorded 146 species,

according to the official guide book, among them Parsley Water Dropwort, Sheepsbit and Rock Sea Spurry and I look forward to my botanical incentive for visiting this marvellous wildlife sanctuary.

Our day ended in a blaze of glory, a Manx Shearwater setting-the-seal on a great days sea watching, by flying past obligingly close on the landward side causing much excitement among our small band. Together with the early view of the Leach's Petrel, this visit leaves a lasting impression on my memory. We headed back towards West Kirby, a happy party whose thoughts and appetites were already turning towards the prospect of fresh, hot, large fish with an ample portion of chips . . . and what better note on which to end? I wish you much naturalistic rambling pleasure in the future!

QUICK GUIDE: The circular walk across the estuary to Hilbre and back measures approximately 4-5 miles of level hard-sand walking. Wellington boots are compulsory if you wish to avoid wet feet ! A pleasant outing in summer, a cold expedition for 'birders' in winter. No shelter or facilities on any of the islands, and it is EXTREMELY cold at times — wrap up warmly ! I would class this winter bird-watching trip as suitable for the enthusiast only; it is a long walk and it means a long stay (5-7 hours) in the open air until the tide receeds. BIRDS: Similar to preceeding chapter. Waders, wildfowl, sea-duck, divers, grebes, auks, terns, gulls, skuas, and shearwaters. Breeding birds on the island: larks, buntings, wagtails, finches, plus twice yearly migrant species: chats, shrikes, redstarts, warblers etc. FLORAL HABITAT: Estuarine sandstone islands. Heathland, grassland, cliffs and muddy foreshores. Open water (1 freshwater pond and sea.) FAUNA: Seals, varied insect and shorelife.

MANX SHEARWATER.

Further useful reading

Birds of Britain and Europe, a field guide by Roger Peterson, Guy Mountfort and P. A. D. Hollom. (Collins, Third Edition 1974).

British Mosses and Liverworts by E. Vernon Watson, B.sc., Ph.D. (Cambridge University Press 1955).

Caterpillars of Britain and Europe, a field guide by D. J. Carter and B. Hargreaves. (Collins 1986).

Excursion Flora of the British Isles, by Clapham, Tutin & Warburg. (Cambridge University Press, Third Edition 1981).

Ferns, Mosses and Lichens of Britain by Hans Martin Jahns. (Collins, 1980).

Flora of the British Isles by Claphan, Tutin & Warburg. (Cambridge University Press, Second Edition 1962).

Grasses, Ferns, Mosses and Lichens of Great Britain and Ireland by Roger Phillips. (Pan Books, 1980).

Insects of Britain and Northern Europe, a field guide by Michael Chinery. (Collins 1985).

Macmillan Guide to Britain's Nature Reserves, by Jeremy Hywel-Davies & Valerie Thom. (Macmillan, 1984).

Moths of the British Isles, a colour identification guide by Bernard Skinner. (Viking, 1984).

Moss Flora of Britain and Ireland, by A. J. E. Smith (Cambridge University Press, 1980).

Mushrooms and other Fungi of Great Britain and Europe, by Roger Phillips. (Pan Books, 1981).

Mushrooms and Toadstools, a field guide by Morten Lange & F. Bayard Hora. (Collins, 1981).

New Concise British Flora, by W. Keble Martin, MA. DSc. FLS. (Edbury Press and Michael Joseph, Third Edition 1978).

The Oxford Book of Flowerless Plants, by B. E. Nicholson & F. H. Brightman. (Peerage Books, 1985).

The Reader's Digest Nature Lover's Library series, (Field Guides): Animals of Britain. (1984) Birds of Britain. (1981) Butterflies and other insects of Britain. (1984) Trees and Shrubs of Britain. (1981) Water Life of Britain. (1984).

Shorebirds, an Identification guide to the waders of the world, by Peter Hayman, John Marchant & Tony Prater. (Croom Helm Ltd, 1986).

Spiders of Britain and Northern Europe, the Country Life guide by Dick Jones. (Country Life, 1983).

Wild Flowers of Britain and Northern Europe, by Richard Fitter, Alastair Fitter & Marjorie Blamey. (Collins, 1974).

Wild Flowers of the British Isles, by Ian Gerrard & David Streeter. (Macmillan 1983).

Acknowledgements

MY acknowledgements and heartfelt thanks go to the following people for the wide-ranging variety of help, advice and support they have unstintingly supplied during my labours: Tony Aldridge, Lorna Bamford, Tim Dean, Ian Harper, Howard May, Judith Moore, Charlie Owen, Roy Rhodes, Dr. Barry Rose, Mavis Smith, Roy and Rene Titterington, and John Wilson. A special thankyou goes to the many authorities, committees and societies who also gave helpful advice in the latter stages; the North West Water Authority, The Nature Conservancy Council, The National Trust and several County Conservation Trusts, to name but a few. Another special thankyou goes to my father for invaluable help with the maps. Last, but not least, thanks are due to my publishers who have patiently endured my artistic neuroses at every stage of the production   . . .